D0846818

OUR ENDURING VALUES
REVISITED

ALA Editions purchases fund advocacy, awareness, and accreditation programs for library professionals worldwide.

OUR ENDURING
VALUES
REVISITED

LIBRARIANSHIP IN AN EVER-CHANGING WORLD

MICHAEL GORMAN

AN IMPRINT OF THE AMERICAN LIBRARY ASSOCIATION
CHICAGO 2015

MICHAEL GORMAN, the former dean of library services at the Henry Madden Library, California State University, Fresno, served as president of the American Library Association in 2005–2006. He was the first editor of the *Anglo-American cataloging rules*, second edition (1978), and of the 1988 revision of that work. He is the author of numerous books, including *Our enduring values* (2000), the winner of ALA's Highsmith Award in 2001 for the best book on librarianship. Gorman has been the recipient of numerous awards, including the Margaret Mann Citation in 1979 and the Melvil Dewey Medal in 1992.

© 2015 by Michael Gorman

Extensive effort has gone into ensuring the reliability of the information in this book; however, the publisher makes no warranty, express or implied, with respect to the material contained herein.

ISBNs
978-0-8389-1300-0 (paper)
978-0-8389-1305-5 (PDF)
978-0-8389-1306-2 (ePub)
978-0-8389-1307-9 (Kindle)

Library of Congress Cataloging-in-Publication Data
Gorman, Michael, 1941-
    Our enduring values revisited : librarianship in an ever-changing world / Michael Gorman.
        pages   cm
    Includes bibliographical references and index.
    ISBN 978-0-8389-1300-0 (print : alk. paper)—ISBN 978-0-8389-1306-2 (epub)—
ISBN 978-0-8389-1305-5 (pdf)—ISBN 978-0-8389-1307-9 (kindle) 1. Libraries—Aims
and objectives—United States. 2. Library science—Moral and ethical aspects—United States.
3. Librarians—Professional ethics—United States. 4. Librarians—Effect of technological
innovations on—United States. I. Title.
    Z716.4.G673 2015
    027.073—dc23   2014040989

About the cover: Presiding over the Library of Congress from a central position is Minerva, the Roman Goddess of learning and wisdom. In this mosaic by Elihu Vedder, she is portrayed as the Minerva of Peace and appears as the guardian of civilization with her armor partly laid aside. Image and description courtesy of the Library of Congress; photograph by Carol M. Highsmith. Cover design by Kimberly Thornton.

Text design by Alejandra Diaz in Adobe Garamond Pro and Brandon Grotesque typefaces.

♾ This paper meets the requirements of ANSI/NISO Z39.48–1992 (Permanence of Paper).

Printed in the United States of America
19 18 17 16 15   5 4 3 2 1

This book is dedicated to the memory

of my brother
DAVID GORMAN
1946–2005

and my friends
COLIN ANDREW
1933–2013

JOHN GARFORTH
1934–2014

BRYAN McENROE
1941–2011

Let their memory be a blessing.

CONTENTS

ACKNOWLEDGMENTS

I thank Tony Molaro, LIS educator, for suggesting this book; Rachel Chance, acquisitions editor at ALA Editions, for her encouragement at each stage of this project; my skillful copy editor Johanna Rosenbohm; Kim Thornton, designer of the cover; Alejandra Diaz, designer of the book; and Don Chatham, ALA Associate Executive Director for Publishing.

Most of all, I thank my wife, Anne Reuland, for too many things to list.

THE WORLD TURNED RIGHT SIDE UP?

There is no shortage of people prophesying the "death of libraries," some with glee, some with sadness, and some just consumed by techno-lust and laissez-faire economics. One such is someone called Tim Worstall, who called, in *Forbes,* the magazine for greed-heads, for the closing of public libraries; those libraries to be replaced by free subscriptions to "Kindle Unlimited"—an Amazon.com product giving access to more than 600,000 e-texts.[1] A more serious person, Dr. Mark Miodownik, a British materials scientist and broadcaster, stated in an interview broadcast on the BBC World Service,[2] that hackerspaces (communal workshops also known as "makerspaces") are "more important than public libraries" and that cities should convert their public libraries to hackerspaces. He argued that everyone had "access to more books than they could ever want" and could download them and read them on their smartphones in their homes at any time. Also, that there is universal access to "information" but not to the skills, tools, and materials needed to make useful objects in order to transform citizens from consumers to makers and society from a culture of waste and landfills to a culture of recycling and conservation.

I wrote *Our enduring values* in the late 1990s. It was published by ALA in 2000, the last year of the twentieth century and of the second millennium of the Common Era. In the decade and a half since, the world has endured the savagery of September 11, 2001; the deaths of millions in wars and other conflicts, many waged in and over the cobbled-together countries that are the poisonous legacy of colonialism and imperialism; the almost complete collapse of the post–World War II financial architecture and the Great Recession that cupidity-fueled collapse caused; the ideologically and economically driven sustained attack on the public services of which libraries are such an ornament; the economic rise of China, run by communists who are much better at capitalism than the capitalists of the West; the looming and multifaceted environmental challenges of anthropomorphic climate change; the promise of the Arab Spring and its repression; and a variety of other unsettling global and national societal happenings and trends. Since I wrote that book, we have been blessed (or otherwise?) with iPod and iTunes (2001); Facebook (2004); YouTube (2005); Twitter (2006); the mass adoption of smartphones and streaming video (2003–); devices for downloading and reading e-books, such as the Amazon Kindle (2007) and Barnes & Noble Nook (2009); the enormous economic reach of the advertising-company-with-a-search-engine Google, which has contrived to hit brand gold by becoming a verb that is the near-universal substitute for "use a search engine"; Wikipedia (2001) and the whole social media, hivemind, crowd-sourcing, "wisdom of the crowds" thing, felicitously summed up as "digital Maoism" by Jaron Lanier;[3] a huge and lucrative videogame industry; giant flat-screen digital televisions foreshadowed by Ray Bradbury (and the Jetsons) decades before; three-dimensional "printing" (relatively inexpensive consumer devices available since 2010)—all these, variations on them, and many more digital innovations great and small adding up to a complex world with endless opportunities for infotainment, commercial exploitation on a massive scale, and—to put the case for positive results— the creation of giant, ever-connected "communities" and new dimensions of education and creativity.

No library is an island, and libraries and the practice of librarianship have been rocked, socked, shaken, and stirred by all these societal, economic, and technological changes. Very few libraries can say that they are better off than they were before the Great Recession eight years ago, and many—or even most—will tell you they are much worse off. Many of our colleagues have lost their jobs; many have had to take jobs that pay substantially less than they and their contributions are worth; and many graduates of LIS programs cannot find jobs, have had to take part-time positions, or have had to move to places far from where they really want to live. For the first time in my more than fifty library years, I have hesitated when asked if I would recommend someone to enter an LIS master's program. All this when public libraries are increasingly society's only serious attempt to bridge the digital divide that threatens to deny the advantages of the brave new technological world to the poor, the rural, the armies of the unemployed, and all the others whose noses are pressed up against the windows of the glittering salons of the digerati. All this when academic libraries are under the unprecedented strain of trying to do more with shrunken budgets, aggravated by the pressure of managements and IT departments obsessed with shiny and new tools and lacking any idea of the ends to which their digital means are to be applied. All this when cuts in government spending and savage corporate retrenchments have attenuated or abolished many special libraries. So it goes, but libraries battle on, boats against the current, continuing to do good work and serve individuals and communities.

In the preface to *Our enduring values*, I wrote of the defeated British and German troops marching away after the surrender of Cornwallis in Yorktown in October 1781. They played an old British march called "The world turned upside down." Fifteen years ago, I wondered if the world of libraries had been turned upside down and if the time had come for librarians to beat a retreat. I did not believe that then, and I do not believe that now. The ideas that the digital revolution has made libraries irrelevant, that libraries can no longer be afforded, or that libraries are no longer needed seem, at best, based on ignorance and the willful avoidance of realities and, at worst, the malign triumph of ignorance, materialism, and philistinism. I believe that librarians have a duty, now more than ever, to organize convincing rebuttals to those arguments and to revisit the values that inform our profession. That is why I have revisited and updated a book from the last years of the twentieth century.

The magnitude of the task ahead can be seen in the remarks of Dr. Miodownik, the respected and influential scholar referred to in the first paragraph of this preface. He is neither an ignoramus nor a vandal. Quite the reverse: he is an advocate of an enlightened turn away from consumerism and waste in favor of communitarian effort to restore the dignity of labor that would have been familiar to, and welcomed by, the likes of William Morris.[4] Why would such a man call for his workshops to take over public library buildings? (Rather than taking over, say, dollar stores, payday loan shops, off-track betting centers, or any of the many other institutions that prey upon the poor?) The simple answer is that he has bought into a number of cybermyths (in this case, that "everything" is available, free and freely, on the Internet; that "everybody" can find what she wants with ease; and that "everyone" can apply the critical thinking necessary for the productive use of "everything") and that he, as with the majority of even highly educated people, has only the sketchiest idea of what libraries are and what they do, and of the role of librarians.

The following examination of our professional values is intended to illuminate the present and likely future state of libraries as we adjust to a world that seems to be turned upside down with some regularity without ever being quite the right side up.

NOTES

1. Worstall, Tim. "Close the libraries and buy everyone an Amazon Kindle unlimited subscription." Forbes.com. www.forbes.com/sites/timworstall/2014/07/18/close-the-libraries-and-buy-everyone-an-amazon-kindle-unlimited-subscription/ (July 14, 2014; consulted August 21, 2014).
2. On "The life scientific" program. March 11, 2014.
3. Lanier, Jaron. "Editing digital Maoism: the hazards of the new online collectivism." *Edge: the third culture* (May 29, 2006). http://edge.org/conversation/digital-maoism-the-hazards-of-the-new-online-collectivism.
4. See, for example: Morris, William. "The development of modern society." *Commonweal,* volume. 6, numbers. 236–240 (July–August 1890); and Wilde, Oscar. "The soul of man under socialism" (1891). http://libcom.org/library/soul-of-man-under-socialism-oscar-wilde (consulted July 14, 2014).

CHAPTER 1

VALUES

Let us begin with some definitions:

- *Values* are beliefs and ideals that are major, significant, lasting, and shared by the members of a group. Values define what is good or bad and desirable or undesirable for that group. They are the foundation of thoughts, feelings, attitudes and policies within that group and act as commonly held bases for those attitudes and policies.
- In psychological terms, values represent the way that members of the group define themselves both within the group and within the wider society.
- *A value system* is a set of those beliefs and ideals that has been adopted and/or has evolved within a group as a system to guide actions, behaviors, and preferences in all situations.
- *Ethics* are moral beliefs held by a group or community (what is good and bad or right or wrong) and a definition of the moral duties (to do or not do certain actions) that stem from those beliefs.
- *Principles* are starting points for reasoning or guides for thinking and action.

Values, ethics, principles, and morality are related, overlapping, and intertwined concepts. They are often circular in that they define each in terms of the others. For example, *Webster's Third* defines "ethics" as "the discipline that deals with what is good and bad or right and wrong or with moral duty . . . a set of values . . ."[1] I, in common with most of the rest of humanity, am not qualified to pronounce on morality and have no intention of doing so here. That reluctance to deal with moral questions is one of reasons why I am more concerned here with values than with ethics, principles, or morality. In my opinion, the study of values is concentrated on what is valuable and desirable to do and to avoid more than it is with matters of morality and other abstractions. In other words, defining, agreeing on, and acting on values can be of practical utility rather than dealing with what are ultimately abstract matters that belong in the realms of philosophy, theology, and aesthetics.

THE WIDER WORLD

Libraries, library services of all kinds, and librarianship are inextricably of the world and cannot exist without context. They are part of, and affected for good and ill, by the societies they serve, the communities in which they live, the countries in which they exist, and the wider world. Though libraries have undergone dramatic change (heavily influenced by technological change) in the last decades, those changes must be seen as influenced by wider changes in society, politics, lifestyles, and every other aspect of human life. In 1999, I listed trends and changes that had made an impact on humanity in the previous quarter of a century. The following updated list contains many of those changes (the originals listed in italics):

- the globalization of trade
- the consequent flight of manufacturing to low-paid developing countries
- the change from industrialized to service economies in the developed world
- the economic, political, and military rise of China
- *the creation of an interdependent world economy*
- the explosive growth of social media

- the economic centrality of the online world
- the rise of global terrorism
- dramatic increases in cybercrime
- the "War on Terror" and its subsequent actual wars
- *the transformation, for good and ill, of societies (politically and economically) in Eastern Europe and Asia*
- advances in medicine that have increased life spans and led to the aging of populations
- the success of the women's movement in developed countries
- *the advent and sweeping power of global information-technology-based companies*
- the shape-shifting of higher education
- the "death of privacy"
- the financial collapse that led to the Great Recession
- *the rise of fundamentalism across the world*
- the current and future impact of anthropogenic climate change
- the Arab Spring

It is remarkable how many of those trends have endured and developed since 2000 (including a number of the trends given in roman above that are extensions or rewordings of those listed fifteen years ago). It is also obvious that many of these changes are driven—or, at least, influenced by—technological innovation and that many of them are entwined with others. Globalization depends on communication technologies. The change from manufacturing to service industries in the developed world is technology driven. Terrorists have websites that appeal to and develop would-be terrorists. Cybercrime, cyberbullying, and the assault on privacy are some of the other monsters that result from technological change. We live, ineluctably, in a world in which the blessings and afflictions of technology pervade our lives. It is important to maintain perspective and remember that crime, bullying, intrusions into private lives, terrorism, transnational companies, booms and busts and the other contradictions of capitalism, transnational communications, and all the rest existed long before computer networks were ever dreamed of. Closer to our concerns, the recurrent rows about "filtering" and other forms of preventing access are peculiar to the online environment, but the desire to censor for religious, political, and moral reasons has been with us for centuries.

WHY VALUES?

Fifteen years ago, I wrote that we live in a time of change, and it is obvious that the times have been a-changing ever since—and show no sign of ceasing to do so. That churning has meant that things and ideas that used to be certain are no longer. People now in middle age can remember a time when printed newspapers, IBM, Dodge cars, South American dictators, cameras with film in them, the big TV networks, cursive writing, VHS tapes, the solidity of banks, and public libraries were central and seemingly immutable parts of everyday life. I can still remember the shock I experienced two years ago when my then seven-year-old grandson, on seeing a bottle of Parker Washable Blue ink on my desk next to my fountain pen, asked me "What's that blue stuff?" Given uncertainty and the indefinite prospect of more in the totality of our lives and in the world of libraries, it is important to find at least a few truly unchanging underpinnings for our profession to be an agreed framework for discussion and, I would hope, a pathway on which to proceed with hope and confidence.

Humankind intensifies the search for meaning when it is prosperous. That search intensifies in societies in which the basic physical needs—food, housing, education, health care—are widely available. Religion may be the opium of the poor, but it seems to offer, even in the vaguest terms (e.g., "spirituality"), not an escape from the rigors of life for the prosperous but an enhancement when one is well-off enough to come to the idea that material things are not enough. It can also be a consolation for those who fear change. Outside and beyond religion, individuals and groups seek principles, ethics, values, and determining beliefs. The results of that search not only define individuals and groups and give their various lives meaning, once they are beyond the struggle for survival; but also give them the means of overcoming the fear of change or even for preparing for the unknown changes to come. In libraries, a microcosm of the wider world, we are buoyed and even enhanced by technology while being challenged and threatened by it simultaneously. We are experiencing changes that most of us understand partially, if at all. This is a fertile environment for snake-oil sales pitchers of various kinds—library conferences these days feature a gallery of hucksters and Gladwellian one-trick ponies awash in tipping points, ten roads to success, and all the rest of the jargon-ridden eyewash. We have undergone a series of seismically negative economic events; and we are buffeted and worn down by in-group verbiage, new demands for new services, febrile searches for the next shiny new technological innovation (the one that replaces the one we were so excited about six months ago), and, above all, that queasy, omnipresent, indefinable sense of the ground shifting under our feet in the world of libraries and in our whole lives. I do not claim that a clear grasp of our fundamental and enduring values is a panacea for our ills, but I do believe they provide a foundation upon which productive and satisfying library lives can be built.

WHEN VALUES ARE DANGEROUS

Values are, as I have stated, lasting and fundamental beliefs and ideals that can be the basis for positive action and for making work more fulfilling. In thinking about values and taking action based on values, however, we walk an intellectual tightrope that stretches between lives made dreary and unfulfilling by the absence of beliefs and ideals and the lives of those to whom values have become absolutes and ideals and beliefs have curdled into fanaticism. We must, in my view, have beliefs and ideals, but we should never seek to impose those beliefs and ideals on the unwilling. There is a vast difference between defending one's values and making others conform to those values. Take, for example, the question of intellectual freedom— the belief that all people should be free to read what they wish, write what they wish, and think what they wish. Librarians, of all people, should be unyielding defenders of that value against those who wish to restrict reading, expression, and thought. What of people who sincerely believe—for religious, political, or other reasons—that some texts and some expressions of thought should be censored? In defending intellectual freedom, are we imposing our beliefs and stifling theirs? No, because no librarian would insist on someone reading a text that she found offensive. It is the censors who insist on imposing their values, not the believers in intellectual freedom. The distinction lies right there—the point at which beliefs become rancid is when they are imposed on others, something common to fundamentalists of all stripes. Librarians should always seek to open avenues of thought and research and stand against those who wish to close them. In other words, values that open avenues and broaden enquiry should always have preference over beliefs that seek to shut off avenues and narrow enquiry.

LE PLUS ÇA CHANGE . . .

The clichéd Chinese curse concerning "interesting times" appears to be always in effect. Reading the literature of any place at any time will tell you that people in each of those places and each of those times believed they were living in an era of unprecedented change. It may have been ever so, but the change we experience today is always more fraught than past change, for the simple reason that we know the results of past change but have no way of telling the outcomes of the changes we are experiencing, still less the changes that are forecast. However you look at it, change happens and more change is coming. There are two ways of dealing with these inevitabilities. The first is to be passive and reflexive, allowing what happens to happen. The other is to plan for and, where possible, to control and guide change. This is not a book on planning—there are far too many of them already— but a book that urges consideration of the values that underlie our work as librarians and library workers, because planning can never be effective in the absence of intellectual and principled underpinning. Without that, planning dissolves into the kind of jargon-infested Kabuki that darkens the soul. Human beings need a rationale for their activities because that rationale can raise work above drudgery and wage slavery and lift human lives to a higher level. This is by no means to advocate the veiling of burdensome toil or the sanctification of unnecessary labor, but to advance the idea that service and other values have a power to validate useful work. I imagine that, in our hearts, we librarians and library workers know that the results of what we do are useful and good and that the cumulation of our good and useful working lives is far greater than the sum of its parts. Despite this, in my experience of fifty and more years in libraries, there are now more of us who question what we do—the bases of our working lives—than ever before. Two words account for this phenomenon: change and uncertainty.

VALUES AND VALUE

In every aspect of our lives, we live in an age of uncertainty. The prosperity of the 1990s and the end of the Cold War were succeeded by the low dishonest decade of the September 2001 attacks, hot wars, the "war on terror," global financial chicanery that combined with debt bubbles to bring the post–World War II global financial system to its knees, the resulting Great Recession and its sour legacies (economic, political, and social), the uneasy feeling that the government knows more about you than you like but not as much as Google and Amazon, and other ills too depressing to contemplate. Despite some significant social changes for the good, small wonder that many people are sick of change, yearn for certainties and imaginary past golden ages, and fear the changes yet to come.

The wider fears of society pervade our working lives. For at least three decades now, controversy has swirled around our profession, and it is difficult for working librarians, library workers, and LIS students to deal with the realities of budget cuts and doing more with less and with the unrealities of gaseous futurology. How are they to assess those various predictions, particularly those that say that libraries are obsolescent and librarianship is doomed to die? There has been, in those two decades and more, an ever-growing gap between nonlibrarian academic theorists, "information scientists," many LIS educators, and even some library leaders, on the one hand, and those working in, and served by libraries, on the other.

A LIBRARY?

In a discussion of the "right to forget" (the harebrained idea that individuals might be able, and can be empowered, to scrub the Internet of images, etc., that now embarrass them) in "Morning edition" on National Public Radio on May 23, 2014, one of the contributors likened it to "going into a library and telling them to pulp books." Whatever one thinks of the practicality and morality of individuals whitewashing their digital history, the analogy with library bibliocide is both inaccurate and misleading. It is, alas, a manifestation of a widespread misunderstanding of the nature of libraries. Ellyssa Kroski has listed "7 things librarians are tired of hearing," which sum up the misunderstandings that will cause all of us to veer between rueful smiles and tears of frustrated rage. They are:

- "Do people still even go to the library now that there's Google?"
- "So, are you like, a volunteer?" Usually followed up with "What? You need to have a master's degree to be a librarian?!!"
- "But isn't print dead at this point?"

- "You're a librarian? That's so hot!"
- "That must be great to just be able to read all day."
- "So you, like, get to shush people all day?"
- "Well what do you think the future is for libraries? I have a theory . . ."[2]

(My smile is all the more rueful because I heard at least two or three of those things fifty years ago.)

I wish I had a dollar for every time I have heard or read a lazy-minded commentator likening the Internet to having "the content of many libraries at your fingertips." Let us leave aside the demonstrable nonsense of "at your fingertips." It is vital to remember that the library is not just its collections, important though they are. Those collections would be useless without two other essential components: a trained and value-imbued staff and a bibliographic architecture. The staff create and maintain the collections (tangible and virtual) and make those collections usable in the construction and maintenance of the bibliographic architecture and by providing help and instruction in their use. One has only to contemplate how children are being failed by the far too numerous school "libraries" with no librarian to realize the importance of having all three components—collections, librarians, and an organization and retrieval system.

THE HUMAN RECORD

At the moment, the most powerful marker, the feature that distinguishes our species most decisively from closely related species, appears to be symbolic language. . . . Humans are the only creatures who can communicate using symbolic language: a system of arbitrary symbols that can be linked by formal grammars to create a nearly limitless variety of precise utterances. Symbolic language greatly enhanced the precision of human communication and the range of ideas that humans can exchange. Symbolic language allowed people for the first time to talk about entities that were not immediately present (including experiences and events in the past and future) as well as entities whose existence was not certain (such as souls, demons, and dreams). The result of this sudden increase in the precision, efficiency, and range of human communication systems was that people could share much more of what they learned with others; thus, knowledge began to accumulate more rapidly than it was lost. Instead of dying with each person or generation, the insights of individuals could be preserved for future generations. As a result, each generation inherited the accumulated knowledge of previous generations, and, as this store of knowledge grew, later generations could use it to adapt to their environment in new ways. Unlike all other living species on Earth, whose behaviors change in significant ways only when the genetic makeup of the entire species changes, humans can change their behaviors significantly without waiting for their genes to change. This cumulative process of "collective learning" explains the exceptional ability of humans to adapt to changing environments and changing circumstances. It also explains the unique dynamism of human history. In human history culture has overtaken natural selection as the primary motor of change.[3]

The process of "collective learning," described above by Dr. David Christian, depends on the existence of symbolic language. That symbolic language is the necessary prerequisite of the human record. The human record is the vast assemblage of textual, visual, and symbolic creations in all languages, from all periods of history, and found in all communication formats—from clay tablets to digital assemblages of binary code. Interaction with the human record is how ideas and literary works conquer space and time; how we know what unknown ancestors and persons in far distant places knew and thought; and how we can exercise our ability to learn and to create new knowledge, new ideas, and new literature for our unknown descendants. Though many people now think that digital technology has created an entirely new way of learning, the fact is that there are only three ways in which human beings learn and that digital technology is but the latest manifestation of the third and most recent of those ways.

Humans learn:

- from experience (physical interaction with, and observation of, the world) and have done ever since the first humans learned that one red berry may be tasty and healthful and another might kill you;
- from communicating with people who know more than they do (speech and hearing) and have done so since the first wise woman taught the first band of early humans huddled in the safety of a cave; and

- from interaction with the human record (written, symbolic, and visual records) and have done so since the age of miracles began with the invention of writing many millennia ago.

The third way of learning permits the first two ways to extend across space and time—the records of experience and knowledge allow those remote in time and distance to learn from the experience and knowledge of others.

The human record is central to learning, and its preservation and onward transmission are crucial to civilization and the perpetuation of culture. Thus, facilitating learning by fruitful and wide-ranging interaction with the human record is crucial and should be understood as the ultimate mission of all librarians.

THE HUMAN RECORD AND CULTURAL HERITAGE

The human record (all those texts, symbolic representations, and images in all formats that have accumulated over the millennia) is best understood when viewed in the larger context of cultural heritage. In 1972, the Unesco Convention on cultural heritage defined its subject in terms only of tangible human-made and natural objects:

Article 1
For the purposes of this Convention, the following shall be considered as "cultural heritage": monuments: architectural works, works of monumental sculpture and painting, elements or structures of an archaeological nature, inscriptions, cave dwellings and combinations of features, which are of outstanding universal value from the point of view of history, art or science; groups of buildings: groups of separate or connected buildings which, because of their architecture, their homogeneity or their place in the landscape, are of outstanding universal value from the point of view of history, art or science ; sites: works of man or the combined works of nature and of man, and areas including archaeological sites which are of outstanding universal value from the historical, aesthetic, ethnological or anthropological points of view.

Article 2

For the purposes of this Convention, the following shall be considered as "natural heritage": natural features consisting of physical and biological formations or groups of such formations, which are of outstanding universal value from the aesthetic or scientific point of view; geological and physiographical formations and precisely delineated areas which constitute the habitat of threatened species of animals and plants of outstanding universal value from the point of view of science or conservation; natural sites or precisely delineated natural areas of outstanding universal value from the point of view of science, conservation or natural beauty.[4]

Thirty-one years later, Unesco broadened the definition and agreed to a Convention on what it called "intangible cultural heritage." That Convention recognized "the deep-seated interdependence between the intangible cultural heritage and the tangible cultural and natural heritage." The Convention defined intangible cultural heritage thus:

1. The "intangible cultural heritage" means the practices, representations, expressions, knowledge, skills—as well as the instruments, objects, artefacts and cultural spaces associated therewith—that communities, groups and, in some cases, individuals recognize as part of their cultural heritage. This intangible cultural heritage, transmitted from generation to generation, is constantly recreated by communities and groups in response to their environment, their interaction with nature and their history, and provides them with a sense of identity and continuity, thus promoting respect for cultural diversity and human creativity. For the purposes of this Convention, consideration will be given solely to such intangible cultural heritage as is compatible with existing international human rights instruments, as well as with the requirements of mutual respect among communities, groups and individuals, and of sustainable development.

2. The "intangible cultural heritage," as defined in paragraph 1 above, is manifested inter alia in the following domains:
    a. oral traditions and expressions, including language as a vehicle of the intangible cultural heritage;

b. performing arts;

c. social practices, rituals and festive events;

d. knowledge and practices concerning nature and the universe;

e. traditional craftsmanship.

3. "Safeguarding" means measures aimed at ensuring the viability of the intangible cultural heritage, including the identification, documentation, research, preservation, protection, promotion, enhancement, transmission, particularly through formal and non-formal education, as well as the revitalization of the various aspects of such heritage.[5]

Intangible cultural heritage includes all aspects of culture that can be recorded but cannot be touched and cannot be interacted with without vehicles for those aspects of culture. (These cultural vehicles are called "Human Treasures" by the UN and include Living Human Treasures—"persons who possess to a high degree the knowledge and skills required for performing or re-creating specific elements of the intangible cultural heritage."[6]) The centrality of intangible cultural heritage is expressed by Unesco as:

> The importance of intangible cultural heritage is not the cultural manifestation itself but rather the wealth of knowledge and skills that is transmitted through it from one generation to the next. The social and economic value of this transmission of knowledge is relevant for minority groups and for mainstream social groups within a State, and is as important for developing States as for developed ones.[7]

A crucial point of these definitions of cultural heritage is that knowledge of them and their preservation is dependent upon them being recorded (textually and/or visually). The range of such recordings is almost limitless—they can include videorecordings of performances; sound recordings of music; texts of recipes; dictionaries of endangered languages; video and sound recordings of Living Human Treasures; photographs of costumes, buildings, artefacts, etc.; records of anthropological and sociological research; and on and on. The essential point of all recording and documentation is that, once made, they form part of the human record. As with all the human record, those records must be organized for retrieval, made widely available, and preserved for posterity. The aims of Unesco's Conventions cannot be met without such recording, organization, dissemination, and preservation. The human record and the tangible and intangible cultural heritage of humankind overlap and interact dynamically. This process is easy to see when dealing with intangible cultural heritage but operates even in the case of monuments and buildings. For example, historical photographs of architectural sites contribute greatly to the understanding of the cultural heritage of those sites and are an invaluable part of the transmission of that heritage.

I stress the importance of the human record and its interrelationship with the question of cultural heritage because it seems to me that librarians, libraries, and archives have a major role in the dissemination and preservation of both the human record and the cultural heritage of which it is a part. That also leads me to the belief that librarianship is properly seen as a part of an intellectual, cultural community centered on cultural heritage that includes archival work, museum and art curation, and all the other disciplines that contribute to learning and the use and preservation of the records of human culture in all its manifestations.

THE CULT OF INFORMATION

Individual parts of the human record have been referred to as "information" for decades now. The same word is what drives "information science" and, of course and ubiquitously, "information technology." "Information" so used is all-embracing to the point at which it verges on the meaningless. The word "information" applied to statistics on peanut cultivation in the United States; Canova's *Venus Italica*; Eliot's *The waste land*; a cute cat video; and, the score of Beethoven's *Fifth symphony* is incoherent and, to put it mildly, unhelpful. If a normal understanding of the word is applied to the first of these and not the others, where does that leave the cult of information? I believe that this (mis)use of the word "information" points to a problem that goes far beyond the semantic—it points to muddled thinking and results in the fact that libraries and librarians have been seduced into accepting value systems that are antithetical to the true mission of our profession.

Let me try to clear the ground by reiterating three definitions proposed twenty years ago in a book cowritten with Walt Crawford,[8] and adding a fourth to define the content of the various types of resource that constitute the human record as it is encountered and experienced in libraries:

Data: Facts and other raw material that can be processed into useful information.

Information: Data processed and rendered useful.

Knowledge: Information transformed into meaning and made manifest in texts, cartographic, and other visual or audiovisual materials.

Imaginative/aesthetic creations: Literary texts, graphic/visual/audiovisual creations, and the like, in which the aesthetic transcends the utilitarian.

The first three are, in ascending order, the first steps on Mortimer Adler's "ladder of learning," which leads, again ascending, to understanding and wisdom.[9] The fourth may or may not draw on one or more of the preceding three. To illustrate, *data* on temperatures and other climatic phenomena can be aggregated and synthesized into *information* that, when collated, suggests the existence of significant climate change; and that and other information can be combined with learning and experience to generate scholarship resulting in recorded *knowledge* in the form of, say, a scholarly text on anthropogenic climate change. It should be noted that the degree and depth of human intervention and shaping increases steeply when moving from data (which can be gathered with little or no human intervention) to information (which increasingly can be generated by computers using programs created by humans) to recorded knowledge (a product of the human mind). The latter is obviously also true of imaginative/aesthetic creations.

In all the current chatter and unthinking acceptance of statements about "information," "the information age," "postmodern societies," and even the idiotic slogan "information wants to be free," and so on, we can see important fissures in modern thought. This clash of culture and values shows up in the contrast between:

- commoditized information on one side and recorded knowledge and imaginative/aesthetic creations on the other;
- the consumer and infotainment culture on one side and the culture of learning and reflection on the other;
- mind control, censorship, and conformity on the one hand and freedom of thought and enquiry on the other;
- profit-driven information technology and scientific management on the one side and humanism, unfettered creativity, and spirituality on the other.

In many ways, one side of the culture and values chasm is dominated by individualistic materialism, in which the driving forces are possessions, access to "information" and entertainment to make the individual physically comfortable in a society that, while preaching individualism, exacts the price of conformity for these desired things. The other side (the true domain of libraries) is dominated by self-realization through learning—a true individualism that, again paradoxically, is often expressed in service to society and a belief in the greater good.

The eminent library historian and educator Wayne Weigand has pointed out that the common misconception that libraries are part of the world of information is an inversion of reality. In particular, Professor Weigand argues the importance of the library as an institution and physical place central to the promotion of culture (in particular, through reading), social interaction, and for the building and exchange of social capital.[10] The truth is that information is part—and not the most significant part—of the world of libraries. Further, libraries have and should have concerns that are far more complex and important than the storing and imparting of information. Once this idea of the library and its role is assimilated, one can see that library work and services go beyond any particular communication technology, though technology is clearly a central tool in achieving some of the library's objectives. To put it simply, libraries are concerned primarily with the resources that constitute the human record and only secondarily with the medium by means of which messages are transmitted. Then we can see the library clearly as part of the general context of the history of human cultural evolution and learning and in the context of the societal institutions that promote education, learning, social cohesion, and the higher aspirations of humankind.

Libraries and librarians took a wrong path in the period between the late 1960s and the late 1980s. The consequences for libraries, library education, and the future of librarianship have been both profound and malign. That wrong path taken was the embrace of, and domination by, two systems—scientific management and information technology—that are, ultimately, antithetical to the enduring values and mission of libraries. They are antithetical because the things their proponents and adherents value—speed, efficiency, the bottom line, information rather than knowledge—are not the *primary* aims of libraries and librarians, any more than they are the primary aims of a vast range of cultural institutions with which libraries should be aligned and whose values we share. There is an alternative to the wrong path; it lies with those cultural institutions and in seeing information technology and management as what they are: tools that can, if they are put in their place, be useful in furthering the aims of libraries. They can assume that useful role, but their values should have never been allowed to be the main drivers of librarianship.

Much library literature today is concerned with the applications to library service of various technological innovations and services—social media (e.g., Facebook, tweeting), videogaming, streaming media, 3-D printers, and so on. Since there is an abundance of information and discussion on this topic elsewhere, the reader should not be too sorry to read that those concern me, as far as the scope of this book, only when they affect the use and onward transmission of the human record and, in a wider context, only insofar as they improve library service. To illustrate: online, chat, and IM reference services may or may not represent an improvement in library service—the use of the human record—but do not affect its content or onward transmission. Also, Twitter, Facebook, Instagram, and videogames may enrich and enliven the lives of many (including many library workers and users), but they scarcely add to the store of knowledge through which understanding and wisdom are gained. This is not to say that libraries are wrong in using social media, encouraging videogaming, installing 3-D printers, or engaging with their communities in any way, technological or otherwise; just that they should not confuse these activities with the task of facilitating human interaction with the human record. Our central concerns are with *content*, not the *means of communicating that content*, and certainly not with modes of communication that are peripheral to the human record.

THE IMPORTANCE OF READING

One important feature of this contest of values is the devaluation of reading and of the print culture of which it is a part. Though almost everyone agrees that literacy is important to children, the subtext of discussions about communications technology and the future of libraries is that sustained reading of complex texts is not a necessary part of mature life in an "information age." The topic of sustained reading, inevitably, brings up the question of the best format for reading and the often absurd arguments about the benefits or otherwise of reading print on paper or words on a screen. A *Scientific American* article gives the edge to print on paper, citing its "unique advantages."[11] Another writer has no doubt. Peter Herman, a professor of English at San Diego State, writes:

> First, reading an e-book is a different, and lesser, experience than [sic] reading a paper book, just as *watching a movie at home differs from watching one in a theatre*. There's a huge difference between casual and college reading, and recent studies prove beyond doubt that while e-books are perfectly fine for the latest John Grisham or *Fifty Shades of Grey*, they actively discourage intense reading and deep learning. For example, a 2007 study concluded that *"screen-based reading can dull comprehension because it is more mentally taxing and even physically tiring than reading on paper."* And a 2005 study[12] by a professor at San Jose State University proved that online reading encourages skimming while discouraging in-depth or concentrated reading.[13]

I am wedded to "the book" only because it is demonstrably the best format for both sustained reading and for the authenticity and preservation of the textual part of the scholarly human record. If another format were to be shown to be superior on both counts, I would embrace it. After all, it is the fixed, authentic text as created by its author that is of central importance, not the carrier of that text. My devotion to the text is transcendent, my devotion to the book utilitarian.

Though the human record includes many visual and symbolic records of art and civilization, its key element is the vast store of texts that have accumulated since the invention of writing some eight millennia ago. That store of texts has increased exponentially since the introduction of printing to the Western world five centuries ago. The Western printed codex ("the book") is important not primarily because of its intrinsic value but because it has proven to be, at least up to now, the most effective means of both disseminating and preserving the textual content of the human record. Texts have always been contained in other formats (e.g., handwritten on paper, vellum, or scrolls, scratched on papyrus and palm leaves, incised in stone or on clay, stamped on metal, as microform images, created digitally) but none of these methods can compare to the book in both dissemination and preservation—particularly when we are thinking about long complex texts.

The longevity and potential for transmission to posterity of digital texts are both problematic and unproven for a variety of economic, technical, and social reasons. Despite the superiority of "the book" up to now, it must be emphasized that, ultimately, it is texts that are important, not the carrier in which they are contained. In English, believers in the great monotheistic religions are often called "people of the book," but they would be more accurately called "people of the text," since it is the words in them that are held sacred by the faithful, not the pages on which those words are printed.

The existence of texts and, increasingly, other manifestations of the human record, led to a community of learning that transcended national boundaries centuries before the much-vaunted commercial globalization of the late twentieth and early twenty-first centuries. Long before we lived under the shadow of postmoral, transnational companies and before people all over the world felt the positive and negative effects of modern globalization; there was a global community of scholars and learners united in their search for truth and wisdom in the human record, to which the great libraries of the world gave access. The chief allegiance of that community of learning was to the search for truth, not the narrowness of feudal or national entities. In many ways, that community of learning and research is still with us—aided, in many cases, by modern technological innovations that, paradoxically, are seen by some as threatening the culture of learning in which that community is rooted.

LIBRARIES AND THEIR WIDER CULTURAL CONTEXT

Libraries and librarians should form alliances with institutions and professionals that share our values and work with them in various ways that will enable libraries and those institutions to flourish and prosper. Our values are not those of the culture of materialism; of "information" and the technological cult of information, or of the doctrines of cost-efficiency espoused by theorists of scientific management. I strongly believe that our future lies in working with the great range of cultural institutions that are concerned with the organization, preservation, and onward transmission of the human record—that vast manifestation of cultural heritage in all its many recorded forms. The policies and procedures of all these bodies and institutions are similar to the policies and procedures of libraries in that they play a part in:

- working with elements of the human record and of our common cultural heritage;
- furthering the use of the human record by fostering culture and learning and the creation of new contributions to the human record; and
- the preservation of all aspects of cultural heritage and the onward transmission of the human record.

The institutions, bodies, and groups with which libraries should ally themselves and form structures based on communities of interest include the following:

Archives. These important institutions contain manuscript and printed texts, sound recordings, films and videorecordings, still images, artifacts, and realia. They can relate to events, persons, institutions, places, and any other subject, and can consist of one form of communication or of many forms of material. In either event, many archival procedures and policies—though they may differ in detail from those of libraries—are based on the same general approach to such matters as selection, cataloguing, access, and preservation. Therefore, archives are a fruitful area, already characterized by cooperation with libraries, for the new orientation I propose.

Museums. Museums are institutions "devoted to the procurement, care, and display of objects of lasting interest or value."[14] Those "objects" can be man-made (artefacts of all kinds), documents, or found objects such as stones, gems, and fossils. Museums can be general (testifying to the history of entire civilizations), national, regional, or local; and/or they can be devoted to a particular topic or person. The chief overlap, in a practical sense, between museums and libraries is that the collections each have of textual material. More broadly, each is concerned with selection, cataloguing, access, and preservation of the documents and objects with which they are concerned and with the interaction of their collections in presenting and preserving the cultural heritage of humankind.

Art galleries and institutes. These institutions are, in a sense, specialized museums that concentrate on works of art (products of the fine arts—paintings, prints, sculptures, ceramics, etc.—in which the primary meaning is aesthetic rather than the conveying of knowledge) from all ages and all cultures. The overlap with museums and libraries/archives in the broad context of cultural heritage is obvious. Again, we can see the common activities of selection, cataloguing, access, and preservation, this time applied to art works, but existing on the same moral plane as other cultural institutions and with the same impulses and mission.

The mutuality of tasks for alliances devoted to the preservation of the human record and advancing cultural heritage issues center on selection, cataloguing, access, and preservation—all undertaken by libraries, archives, museums, and art galleries. However, other institutions, though less directly concerned, may have a role to play.

Learned societies and research institutes. Though these associations and institutions are not primarily concerned with collecting documents and objects that contain or convey knowledge or aesthetic pleasure, they are concerned with studying aspects of the arts and sciences and, in many cases, with creating new knowledge that, when documented, becomes part of the human record and our common cultural heritage. Because of these activities and preoccupations, such groups are natural allies in seeking a unified approach to cultural heritage, as are the many research institutes.

Performing groups. Some aspects of cultural heritage are only fully realized through performance—dance, music, drama, and the like. In order to be added to the human record, such performances must be recorded in some way, but performance is a necessary precondition of such recording. For that reason, performing groups and the institutions that make their work possible are important factors in the advancement of cultural heritage. These groups and bodies include opera houses, dance companies, orchestras, bands, performing arts centers, and their allied associations.

I repeat that, in rejecting the dominance of the values of information technology and scientific management, I am not saying that libraries and the networks of cultural institutions of which I wish them to be a part should eschew taking advantage of information technology as a tool and digitization as a strategy, nor am I saying that good management practices should be rejected—as long as all are seen and employed in a humanistic context and a culture of learning. What I am saying is that the complex of cultural institutions should embrace a mission that concentrates on ensuring the survival of the human record and of the testaments to the past that make up our common cultural heritage.

I call for cooperative bilateral and multilateral structures and agreements (including the framing and adoption of shared standards, policies, and procedures) between libraries and the cultural institutions listed above.

These structures and agreements would be aimed at pooling resources and harnessing energy and expertise to achieve common goals, especially the overarching goal of the organization, preservation, and onward transmission of the human record and the cultural heritage that it embodies. They would exist at all levels: international, regional (geographic and linguistic), national, province/state, and local.

No less than the future of a civilization based on learning is at stake. Libraries have a choice. We can continue to be inward-looking and decline into insignificance by following the materialistic, mechanistic, and—ultimately—trivial paths of "information" and management, or we can work with the cultural institutions that are our natural allies to create expansive structures in which knowledge and learning can flourish and the preservation and onward transmission of cultural heritage are assured.

NOTES

1. *Webster's Third new international dictionary.*
2. Kroski, Ellyssa. "7 things librarians are tired of hearing." August 2014. http://oedb.org/ilibrarian/7-things-librarians-tired-hearing/ (consulted September 2, 2014).
3. Christian, David. *This fleeting world: a short history of humanity.* Great Barrington, Mass.: Berkshire, 2008. page 8.
4. Unesco. "Convention concerning the Protection of the World Cultural and Natural Heritage, Paris 1972." http://portal.unesco.org/en/ev.php-URL_ID=13055&URL_DO=DO_TOPIC&URL_SECTION=201.html (consulted July 22, 2014).
5. Unesco. "Convention for the safeguarding of intangible cultural heritage, Paris, 2003." www.unesco.org/culture/ich/index.php?lg=en&pg=00006 (consulted July 22, 2014).
6. Unesco. "Encouraging transmission of ICH: Living Human Treasures." www.unesco.org/culture/ich/index.php?pg=00061&lg=EN (consulted July 22, 2014).
7. Unesco. "What is intangible cultural heritage?" www.unesco.org/culture/ich/index.php?lg=en&pg=00003 (consulted July 23, 2014).
8. Crawford, Walt and Gorman, Michael. *Future libraries.* Chicago: ALA, 1965. page 5.
9. Adler, Mortimer. *A guidebook to learning.* New York: Macmillan, 1986.
10. Weigand, Wayne. "Out of sight out of mind: why don't we have any schools of library and reading studies?" *Journal of education for library & information science*, volume 38, issue 4; (Fall 1997) page 314–326; and Weigand, Wayne. "The library as place." *North Carolina libraries* (online), volume 63, issue 3/4 (Fall/Winter 2005) pages. 76–81.
11. Jabr, Ferris. "Why the brain prefers paper." *Scientific American*, volume 309, issue 5 (November 20, 2013) pages 48–53.

12. Liu, Ziming. "Reading behavior in the digital environment: changes in reading behavior over the past ten years" *Journal of documentation*, volume 61, issue 6 (2005) pages 700–712.

13. Herman, Peter C. "The hidden costs of e-books at university libraries." *Times of San Diego*. September 29, 2014. http://timesofsandiego.com/opinion/2014/09/29/hidden -costs-e-books-university-libraries/ (consulted October 6, 2014).

14. *Webster's Third*. S. v. "museum," definition 2.

CHAPTER 2

HISTORY AND PHILOSOPHY

Do you want your philosophy straight, or with a dash of legerdemain?

—William J. Richardson, SJ

A DISTRUST OF PHILOSOPHY?

Throughout library history, from the Sumerians of the third millennium before the Common Era to today's many faces of libraries, librarianship has been seen as intensely practical. As late as 1933, Pierce Butler wrote:

> Unlike his colleagues in other fields of social activity, the librarian is strangely uninterested in the theoretical aspects of his profession. . . . The librarian apparently stands alone in the simplicity of his pragmatism; a rationalization of each immediate process by itself seems to satisfy his intellectual interest. Indeed, any endeavor to generalize these rationalizations into a professional philosophy appears to him not merely futile but positively dangerous.[1]

Butler was making a plea for the scientific method in librarianship and here, in the manner of writers at all times, overstates the opposite position. However, it is no coincidence that many of the towering figures of the founding years of modern librarianship were, essentially, doers rather than thinkers. For all of Melvil Dewey's philosophical underpinnings for his *Decimal Classification* (Aristotle and all that), he was primarily concerned with arranging books on shelves. Antonio Panizzi's whole career was one of overachievement and bustle—the typical Victorian man of action seeking problems and fixing them. Notwithstanding, there is a literature of the philosophy of librarianship, and there are some important library thinkers (notably Jesse Shera and S. R. Ranganathan); but most achievements in librarianship are the result of problem solving and the pragmatic approach. Even the more cerebral areas of librarianship—cataloguing and classification—turn out, on examination, to be based on theories that almost always have been developed after the event or by accretion of cases. (Ranganathan and Seymour Lubetzky are shining exceptions to this rule.)

We are, then, dealing with a profession whose practices and methods have evolved over many centuries without too much regard to philosophy, overarching principles, and values, but with great respect for the practical, the useful, and the utilitarian. One could almost say that we have evolved a kind of anti-philosophy of practicality—one that values what works and discards what does not. I hardly need to point out that utilitarianism is itself a philosophy—one that finds morality in the greatest good of the greatest number. One can be a perfectly good librarian if one acts on utilitarian principles. For example, constructing a catalogue that is usable by most library users and delivers relevant materials in the great majority of cases is utilitarian. Library instruction that reaches most library users and can be assessed as improving the skills of most students is utilitarian. A modern catchphrase tells us not to let the perfect be the enemy of the good, and that, too, is a utilitarian approach. To many of us, however, such intense practicality leaves a void, a sense of longing for more meaning and richer philosophical underpinning.

In her subtle analysis of Andrew Osborn's pivotal article "The Crisis in Cataloging" (1941), H. M. Gallagher remarks that Dr. Osborn (himself trained as a philosopher) distinguished between "pragmatism" in its common meaning and the "American Pragmatism" of William James, John Dewey, and others.[2] The latter was concerned not just with "what works" but with the broader question of what it is we are trying to work toward or to achieve in the most efficient manner possible. She makes a very persuasive case that Osborn's article (which did change the face of cataloguing completely) was based on the attributes of American Pragmatism. This is significant, not least because the two strains of practicality and philosophy were united in Osborn's approach.[3]

If librarians do exalt practicality over philosophy, it will be in the face of the similarities between librarians and philosophers pointed out by philosophy professor Abraham Kaplan:

> Like your profession, mine also has thrust upon it, as its appropriate domain, the whole of knowledge, the whole of culture; nothing is supposed to be foreign to us, and we ought to be prepared under suitable circumstances to be helpful with regard to any and every area of human concern. Like you, we cannot even begin to occupy ourselves with the substance and content of this endless domain, but only with its form, with its structure, with its order, with the inter-relations of the various parts.[4]

Pragmatism and Idealism

Jesse Shera echoed Pierce Butler in stating, "Librarians have seldom asked themselves about the philosophy of librarianship."[5] However, he went on to attempt a delineation of such a philosophy in the series of lectures from which that quotation comes. His idea of the profession of librarianship was of one rooted in two great ideas: *service* and a core of *intellectual theory*. The service rendered by librarians is performed, in Shera's words, "for the benefit of humanity and with a high sense of purpose and dedication."[6] That idea, expressed in that language, echoes a thought of Butler—"the librarian has come to conceive his office as a secular priesthood, administering a sacrament of cultural communion to individual souls."[7] This is high-flown to the modern taste but touches on the real feeling that there is something intangible and important behind the work we do—a feeling that is at war with our predominant mode of practicality and prizing what works best. Archibald MacLeish, poet and Librarian of Congress, was of the same opinion and spoke of the "true library," asserting that "there is, indeed, a mystery of things" and, later in the same speech, of "the library's implicit assertion of the immanence of meaning."[8]

The conflict between pragmatism and idealism is inherent in our work, and is always with us whether we think about it or not. Lee Finks, in an accessible and brief but nonetheless important article, distinguishes between the need for library service and the urge that impels librarians to fulfill that need.[9] In his words, "It is . . . a noble urge, this altruism of ours, one that seems both morally and psychologically good." However, he also notes that libraries owe their existence to the fact that society needs us for practical reasons, and we must fulfill those practical needs or perish. Perhaps pragmatism and altruism/idealism are not in conflict but are two sides of the coin of what we do—complementary impulses and ways of thinking? We would do well to accept these competing impulses and simply let our idealism inform our pragmatism while remembering that an impractical idealist is as much a menace to a library as is a practical librarian without visions and dreams.

To analyze the complex dualism of pragmatism and idealism in thinking about modern libraries, I will discuss the ideas on the topic of four twentieth-century librarians: S. R. Ranganathan, Jesse Shera, Samuel Rothstein, and Lee Finks.

Ranganathan's Five Laws

Shiyali Ramamrita Ranganathan (1892–1972) is, by common consent, the greatest figure of librarianship in the twentieth century. A mathematician by training, he brought to the study of "library science" (an unfortunate term—one of his few mistakes) a belief in the scientific method and rational examination of social phenomena. Though best known for his considerable contributions to the theory of classification and subject retrieval, he studied all aspects of librarianship and, based on that study, formulated his famous Five Laws of Library Science. It would be more accurate to call them precepts rather than laws, but they are based on his scientific training, his training as a librarian (at University College, London), and his rigorous, objective analysis. The five laws are:

- Books are for use.
- Every book its reader.
- Every reader his book.
- Save the time of the reader.
- The library is a growing organism.[10]

Though these laws are based on a scientific not philosophical approach, they do imply a context of values. If we examine them carefully, looking beyond the vocabulary of more than seventy years ago, we can see the values upon which they depend. The first law operates on a basis of *rationalism* and *utilitarianism*. It tells us that collections are useful or they are nothing. Treating the word "books" as a surrogate for all library resources in all formats, we understand that all collection-development policies must be based on the application of reason and the touchstone of utility. The rational approach is necessary if we are to answer the intensely practical question of which materials are useful—now and in the future—to the members of the community that the library serves. The second and third laws are expressions of both *democracy* and *service*. It is democratic to say that all library users are entitled to the materials they need, and that materials should be selected with an eye to meeting those needs. Without the ethic of service in action, it would be difficult if not impossible for all library users to find the materials they need or for all materials to reach the users for whom they are intended. The fourth law is also rooted in *service* and is strikingly modern in that every modern work on service (in both the private and public sectors) stresses the importance of time saving. The fifth law is another product of *rationality*, but it is also related to *stewardship* in that libraries must allow for growth in their collections and services if they are to be good stewards for the indefinite future.

It was an audacious thing to propose laws that define a whole profession in just twenty-four words, but Ranganathan had an unshakable belief in his scientific approach. The fact that we can still find meaning across the decades in those twenty-four words is a justification of his audacity.

Shera's Social Epistemology

Jesse Hauk Shera came to call his redefinition of librarianship "social epistemology" and discussed it in many of his writings.[11] "Epistemology" is defined as: "The study of the methods and the grounds of knowledge, esp. with reference to its limits and validity; broadly the theory of knowledge."[12] Shera's idea, therefore, was to broaden librarianship to comprehend everything about the nature of knowledge and how it is recorded, preserved, transmitted, and so forth, in society. This is an expansive and scholarly view that goes beyond the narrow pragmatism that characterizes some library methods and policies, and, though Shera is famous as a "bookman," it transcends any particular medium by which knowledge is recorded and transmitted. He envisaged his epistemology—"a body of knowledge about knowledge itself"—as serving the individual but also as working toward our ultimate objective, the betterment of society.[13] He implies that betterment is the ultimate value that underlies all our work. The components of "social epistemology" as proposed by Shera are:

- the problem of how humans know
- the problem of how society knows and how the knowledge of an individual becomes part of the knowledge possessed by society as a whole
- the history of knowledge and the philosophy of knowledge as it has evolved through time and across cultures
- existing library systems and how effective they are in meeting the communication needs of individuals and societies

This is far from a description of the curricula of today's successors to library schools and, alas, far from the American Library Association's standards for accrediting master's programs in "library and information science,"[14] but it would be hard to imagine a better basis for a would-be librarian's course of study.

Shera's concerns, in all his writings, are for knowledge, learning, scholarship, the transmission of the human record, and the role of the library in the improvement of society. He believed in the value of reading and learning and, though not opposed to technology per se, was skeptical about the transformational power of technology. In referring to the "information explosion" (a much-touted threat or promise of the 1960s), he quoted Archibald MacLeish with approval:

It is not additional "messages" we need, and least of all additional "messages" that merely tell us that the medium that communicates the message has changed the world. We know the world has changed. . . . What we do not know is how, precisely, it is changing and in what direction and with which consequences to ourselves.[15]

The values that we can derive by inference from Shera's social epistemology are *scholarship, stewardship, literacy and learning, service,* and *the greater good of society.*

Rothstein's Ethos

In 1967, Samuel Rothstein, then director of the library school at the University of British Columbia, gave a speech at the Canadian Library Association annual conference criticizing the ALA *Code of ethics for librarians* for its "generality and banality."[16] He described that *Code,* in a magnificent phrase, as "fatuous adjurations." His criticisms went beyond the deficiencies of that particular code of ethics to an attack on the very idea of a code of ethics with any relevance to work in libraries in the late 1960s. What we needed, in his opinion, was not such a code but a declaration of principles. The declaration would have three components:

- a statement of values, beliefs, and goals;
- a description of the abilities and knowledge that are special to librarians; and
- a list of the dilemmas, problems, and issues that face librarians in particular.

Rothstein's brief attempt to sketch such a statement of principles is of enduring interest, as is his linking of values, special abilities, and special issues that define librarianship. Rothstein listed four values:

- a special commitment to reading;
- enlarging the horizons and elevating the taste of the community, using the discriminating selection of materials as a tool;
- intellectual freedom; and
- helping people to secure the information they need.

Have the passage of time and the advancement and depredations of technology rendered Rothstein's values outmoded? Before answering that question, it is interesting to note that his appraisal of the needs of library users of all those years bears great similarity, rhetorically and substantially, to the common wisdom today. Before the smartphones, social media, digital networks, the Internet and the Web, and interactive digital streaming, before downsizing and job mobility, Rothstein wrote:

> In an age of mass media, which so often distort and debase communication, the library has a particularly important role to play in the fullest provision of impartial, many-sided information. In an age when information explodes and people must go on learning all their lives, librarians have a particularly important role to play in helping people secure the information they need.[17]

The world Rothstein saw was different in degree rather than kind from the world we see today. Though couched in terms that are different from those with which we feel at ease today, his proposed values should speak to us. Do we not believe that reading is "good and important" and that the understanding reading of complex texts is an essential component of scholarship? Do we no longer believe that we should do all we can to foster reading? The belief that reading lessens in importance because of technology is a common delusion of technophiles. The simple fact is that the ability to read and understand complex texts is central to the life of the mind. It is impossible to be educated and illiterate or aliterate at the same time. The first of Rothstein's values still stands.

It is possible that some will wince at the idea of librarians seeking to raise taste and encourage discrimination in the communities they serve. This is a noble goal but one that no longer has the foundation of belief that supported what was once a widely accepted view of the role of the librarian. In the 1880s, Melvil Dewey wrote:

> The new library is active; an aggressive, educating force in the community; a living fountain of good influences; an army in the field, with all guns limbered; and librarians occupy a field of active usefulness second to none.[18]

Whether this type of muscular librarianship is relevant today depends, to some extent, on the kind of library. It is easier for a school librarian and a children's librarian to seek to raise the cultural level of students and children in general, but, even in that milieu, charges of elitism are easy to level. The ethos of the modern public library seems to be in direct conflict with the ideas of discriminating selection and elevating taste. Society no longer has a generally agreed definition of taste or culture, and even in the academy, "great books" programs are seen by many as a form of elitism. The growing trend of universities being run on "business lines" and being rated on the amounts earned by their graduates certainly rejects such a view of academic librarianship, and even of education itself. If Rothstein's second value survives at all today, it survives in individual acts of selection and recommendation and in the missions and beliefs of individual librarians—a kind of cultural guerrilla movement rather than a generally accepted belief in action.

Intellectual freedom is, broadly speaking, accepted as a key value of the profession of librarianship today as then. It is up against different challenges because of societal changes, "the war on terror," and technology; but the old challenges remain, and the defense of intellectual freedom is no easier now than then. We should note that Rothstein's touchstone for the provision of library materials was legality. He wrote of the only acceptable censorship being that imposed by law and, even then, said that librarians should "hold themselves obliged to seek appropriate liberalizations in the law."[19] Even in many democratic countries, the twin threats of an empowered surveillance state and a Big Technology assault on privacy make the defense of intellectual freedom harder than it was in previous generations. National and local laws concerned with intellectual freedom are, in some ways, more liberal now than they were decades ago, but the application of "community standards" in small communities provides a persistent threat to the intellectual freedom of those communities.

Rothstein's final value—helping people to secure the resources they need—is surely unchallengeable today as it was then. When it comes down to it, libraries exist to make the connection between their users and the recorded knowledge and information in the human record that they need and want. Everything that we do—building collections, giving access to digital resources, performing reference work, providing a bibliographic architecture, and on and on—is dedicated to that connection. The disputes are not about that value or the ends to which we are dedicated, but about how to realize them and which means should have higher priority than others.

It is interesting to note the abilities that Rothstein deemed necessary to realize his values and the problems and issues that stand in the way of that realization. (One can only admire the way in which he described the three parts of his statement of principles in what amounts to a one-page manifesto. Concision and clarity are not always found in library literature.) He thought a professional librarian should possess ability and skill in the following areas:

- collection development
- bibliographic control
- reference and information services
- reader's advisory work
- a specialized field, where appropriate
- administration

The issues and dilemmas he outlined also have a familiar ring:

- Is librarianship one profession or are we a loose confederation of related groups?
- "Do books and libraries and librarians have a future, or is librarianship as we know it to be phased out in favor of 'bits' and 'data banks' and documentalists?"[20]
- Are librarians educators or just technicians and managers?
- Do we try to reach everybody or just the small percentage that appreciates our services?
- Do librarians set policy or execute policy set by others?
- What is the relationship of the chief librarian to the professional staff—a first among equals or a general giving orders to subordinates?

It is not easy to believe that any of these questions has been answered satisfactorily or that any one of them has no resonance today. All go to the heart of the professional nature of librarianship—indeed, the very existence of that profession.

Rothstein believed that his delineation of our values, abilities, and dilemmas, considered together, constituted an "ethos"—the distinguishing characteristics that define librarians and librarianship. One might argue with some of the specifics, but it is difficult to argue that his concept is irrelevant or his conclusions outdated.

Finks's Taxonomy of Values

Library educator Lee W. Finks wrote the most important article on values in librarianship of the past few decades.[21] In it, he described his "personal taxonomy of values," divided into three broad categories accompanied by a category of "rival values." Finks's categories are:

- professional values
- general values
- personal values

Finks defined professional values as those that arise out of the nature of librarianship and the functioning of libraries in society. The first of these is *service*. As with the other values adduced by Finks that are the subject of other chapters, I will not dwell on this value here but use Finks's description in the appropriate chapter. His second professional value is *stewardship*. By this he means not only our responsibility for passing the records of humanity intact to future generations, but also our duty to be good stewards in our everyday work. We must ensure that we are seen to be, in his words, "honest, industrious men and women who know our jobs and do them well." His next subcategory of professional values is itself a group that he calls *philosophical values*. They are a belief in reason and learning, a respect for scholarship, neutrality in the "battle of competing ideas"; and prizing the good over the trivial and vulgar. Then come *democratic values*—an attachment to democracy as a societal ideal and openness to all kinds and conditions of people. His last professional value is an attachment to *reading and books*. Even in 1989, his blunt statement that "we are bookish" may have been less debatable then than it is now. One would like to hope that most librarians are indeed women and men who love books and reading and find the latter "a superior way to pass the time," but it may not be so. It is certainly a love that I share and value and believe is essential to the survival of libraries, but it is not something that all librarians *must* adhere to in order to do their work. In my sunset years, I would guess that this is an issue that breaks largely on generational grounds. I suspect, without empirical proof, that a reverence for books and reading is all but universal in librarians over the age of fifty and less commonly found in those below middle age.

Finks defined general values as those that are shared by "normal, healthy people, whatever their field." (One of the many engaging things about this seminal article is the robust directness of Finks's views and worldview.) He calls the first group of general values *work values*. This term encompasses *competence, professional autonomy,* and *the search for excellence.* He quite correctly points out that the realization of these values depends greatly on the environment within which the individual librarian works. It should be sobering for all library administrators to realize that even the most gifted and dedicated librarians cannot reach their goals and fulfill their aspirations unless the library in which they work has an atmosphere and actuality that allows the fullest flowering of abilities and ideals. Values work only in places in which they are allowed and encouraged to work. Finks's next grouping is *social values.* These include *tolerance* and *respect for others* and all the other things that we are supposed to learn in kindergarten and carry throughout our lives. The reader will realize that she is reading someone from the idealistic end of the pragmatism-idealism scale when Finks mentions *optimism* and comes up with the sentence that summarizes what all his values are about: "Being happy librarians in happy libraries; it is not an impossible dream." His last general values group is *satisfaction values.* These might be summed up as the fact that it is impossible for us to serve individuals and society unless we have self-respect and self-esteem.

Finks's personal values are those that apply particularly to librarians as a class. Without falling into stereotyping or rejecting the diversity of our profession, it is possible to agree with Finks that most librarians share or aspire to certain characteristics. He defines them as *humanistic values, idealistic values, conservative values,* and *aesthetic values.* I share Finks's view that most librarians are humanists and idealists believing, in his words, "that the human spirit can flourish" and hoping for "inspiration, self-realization, and the growth of wisdom in all people." I also agree that most librarians are (very small "c") conservative in that we tend to prefer steady evolutionary change, order over disorder, and standardization. (Many years ago, I was told that hard-core cataloguers always vote for the party in power because, if it wins, there will be far fewer government headings to change in the catalogue. The precipitous decline in the number of cataloguers means that this phenomenon is of decreasing psephological importance.) Finks points out that our innate conservatism is a necessary curb on our idealism—the yin and yang of a librarian's soul. Last, I agree that aesthetics are important to librarians. We seek to satisfy our aesthetic sense through harmony in the architecture of library buildings; beauty in literature, music, and the arts; and even elegance in library systems.

An idealistic and optimistic picture of librarians and their values is constantly threatened, in Finks's view, by what he calls rival values— *bureaucracy, anti-intellectualism,* and *nihilism.* Bureaucracy can sometimes be found in small libraries and is endemic in large libraries. It is, in one sense, the natural product of our desire for order and regular procedure. There is an anti-intellectual tinge to much of the discourse about technology that can be found in statements that equate cyberspace and a research library; "research" using search engines and serious reading; any of a number of "literacies" with true literacy; and playing videogames with learning. We stand for excellence and the intellect, for scholarship and culture, or we stand for nothing. Nihilism is the philosophy of the despairing, and a librarian who loses faith in the future of libraries or the value of librarianship is succumbing to that despair.

Finks's values and taxonomy of values are the most important accessible statements on the topic. If every librarian were to absorb them into her working life, the future of libraries would be both guaranteed and bright.

CENTRAL OR "CORE" VALUES

My reading and distillation of the four authors discussed here and other writings on librarianship have led me to formulate the following central values of librarianship. I am sure that the list of values that I offer is different from those that others might advance, but it is difficult to believe that these values (possibly with different wording) would not show up on any composite list.

Stewardship

- preserving the human record to ensure that future generations know what we know
- caring for and nurturing education for librarianship so that we pass on our best values and practices
- being professional, good stewards of our libraries so that we earn the respect of our communities

Service

- ensuring that all our policies and procedures are animated by the ethic of service to individuals, communities, society, and posterity
- evaluating all our policies and procedures, using service as a criterion

Intellectual Freedom

- maintaining a commitment to the idea that all people in a free society should be able to read and view whatever they wish to read and view
- defending the intellectual freedom of all members of our communities
- defending the free expression of minority opinion
- making the library's facilities and programs accessible to all

Rationalism

- organizing and managing library services in a rational manner, applying rationalism and the scientific method to all library procedures and programs

Literacy and Learning

- encouraging literacy and the love of learning
- encouraging lifelong sustained reading
- making the library a focus of literacy teaching

Equity of Access to Recorded Knowledge and Information

- ensuring that all library resources and programs are accessible to all
- overcoming technological and monetary barriers to access

Privacy

- ensuring the confidentiality of records of library use
- overcoming technological invasions of library use

Democracy

- playing our part in maintaining the values of a democratic society
- participating in the educational process to ensure the educated citizenry that is vital to democracy
- employing democracy in library management

The Greater Good

- seeking through all our policies and practices to work for the good of all library users and the communities and societies in which they live

I examine each of these values in individual chapters of this book, with an eye to describing the present state of libraries and the likely future of libraries and librarianship.

Having listed the core values of librarianship, let us consider the value of libraries . . .

NOTES

1. Butler, Pierce. *An introduction to library science.* Chicago: University of Chicago Press, 1993; Phoenix Books, 1961. page xi.

2. H. M. Gallagher, "Dr. Osborn's 1941 'The crisis in cataloging': a shift in thought toward American Pragmatism." *Cataloging and classification quarterly,* volume 12, numbers 3/4 (1991) pages 3–33.

3. For a further discussion of "The crisis in cataloging," see: Gorman, Michael. "1941: an analysis and appreciation of Andrew Osborn's 'The crisis in cataloging.'" *Serials librarian,* volume 6, numbers 2–3 (Winter 1981/Spring 1982) pages 127–131.

4. Kaplan, Abraham. "The age of the symbol." In *The intellectual foundations of library education;* edited by Don R. Swanson. Chicago: University of Chicago Press, 1965. pages 7–16.

5. Shera, J. H. *Sociological foundations of librarianship.* Bombay: Asia Publishing House, 1970. page 29.

6. Ibid.

7. Butler, *An introduction to library science.* page xiii.

8. MacLeish, Archibald. "The premise of meaning." *American scholar* 41 (Summer 1972) pages 357–362 (adapted from an address delivered at the opening of the library of York University, Toronto).

9. Finks, Lee W. "Values without shame." *American libraries* (April 1989) pages 352–356.

10. Ranganathan, S. R. *The five laws of library science,* second edition. Bombay; reprint, New York: Asia Publishing House, 1963.

11. See, for example: Shera, Jesse H. "Toward a theory of librarianship and information science." In Shera's *Knowing books and men: knowing computers too.* Littleton, Colo.: Libraries Unlimited, 1973. pages 93–110.

12. *Webster's Third new international dictionary.* Springfield, Mass.: Merriam-Webster.

13. Shera, "Toward a Theory of Librarianship." pages 95–96.

14. *Standards for accreditation of master's programs in library & information studies* (2008). www.ala.org/accreditedprograms/standards (consulted July 16, 2014). These standards are, as I write, undergoing revision, but the draft revisions show little, if any, improvement.

15. MacLeish, Archibald. *Champion of a cause.* Chicago: ALA, 1971. page 246.

16. Rothstein, Samuel. "In search of ourselves." *Library journal* (January 15, 1968) pages 156–157. See also: ALA *Code of ethics,* promulgated in 1938 and reprinted in the *American library annual, 1958.* New York: Bowker, 1958. pages 111–112.

17. Rothstein, "In search of ourselves."

18. Quoted in: *Noted living Albanians and state officials: a series of biographical sketches.* 1891. AccessGenealogy.com. www.accessgenealogy.com/new-york/biography-of -melvil-dewey.htm (consulted July 16, 2014). Please note that an "Albanian" in this context is an inhabitant of Albany, New York, not Albania.

19. Rothstein, "In search of ourselves."

20. Ibid. Note that "documentalists" were earlier, more benign, versions of those who now call themselves "information scientists."

21. Finks, Lee W. "Values without shame." *American libraries* (April 1989) pages 352–356.

CHAPTER 3

THE VALUE OF LIBRARIES

Technological devices come and go, empires rise and fall, but libraries persist.

—Dennis Dillon[1]

WHEN THE GOOD TIMES ENDED

The idea of the public library is, on the face of it, improbable. Only recently in human history has there been widespread agreement that people have human rights deserving of universal respect. (Remember that the United States enforced chattel slavery until 1865.) The idea that every person should be educated is an even more recent and radical one. The idea that society should provide its members with the means to continue their education independently was more radical still.[2]

The radical notion in the last sentence of this quotation encapsulates the true value of libraries—simply that libraries allow every person in the communities served by those libraries to continue his education, to become more knowledgeable, and to live the life of the mind in the way in which he chooses. This essence of the value of all libraries is sometimes obscured by the day-to-day minutiae of library use. A person asking a question in a corporate library, a child listening to a story in a children's library, a person consulting an academic library's online databases—none of these may be thinking of himself or herself as being engaged in lifelong learning, but each of them is.

WHAT IS THE VALUE OF LIBRARIES?

Through lifelong learning, libraries can and do change lives, a point that cannot be overstated. Within that overarching value—and depending on the community it serves—a library is one or more of the following:

- a focal point of a community
- the heart of the university
- the one good place in a city
- the collective memory of a research institution
- the place remembered fondly by children when grown
- the solace of the lonely and the lost
- the place in which all are welcome
- a source of power through knowledge

When looking at the image of libraries over the years, it is easy to see that the public perception has varied and, though libraries are almost always viewed positively, they are not always understood and prized for what they are. The phase we are going through now illustrates that well. Public misunderstanding of information technology and its potential has led to misunderstanding of the reality of libraries and of their present state and possible futures. Let us look at the development of libraries and at the threats and alternatives with which we are faced.

LIBRARIES OVER THE YEARS

An unprecedented growth in libraries and the development of the profession of librarianship took place in the United States, the United Kingdom, and Canada from the latter half of the nineteenth century to the end of the 1920s. Thousands of libraries of all kinds were built (many with the conscience money of Andrew Carnegie). The great public and private university libraries of the United States came to flower. Public library service was extended to almost every citizen. The profession of librarianship saw the establishment of national library associations; the creation of a system of library education; the beginning of scientific study of libraries and their users; and the intellectual innovations of cataloguing codes, classification schemes, professional journals, and collaborative systems of all kinds. In less than a century, modern libraries and librarianship were born and came to maturity and self-confidence. It was an age of great achievements and of library heroes and heroines—the first if not the last Golden Age of Libraries. The interwar years of prosperity and depression followed those years of the founding of the modern library. Libraries grew in number and size in the 1920s and were an incalculable public good in the hard years of the 1930s. Libraries survived the Second World War, as did many social entities, with a feeling that, with fascism defeated, we were in for progress as far as the eye could see.

In those years following World War II, many librarians assumed that libraries were so patently, palpably good that they needed no justification. They had a basis for that opinion. Communities took their libraries for granted; academic institutions competed with each other about their libraries and boasted of the size of the collections and the excellence of their staff; schools gave pride of place to their libraries and librarians; and companies, governments, and other entities developed libraries and library services at a great pace. This largely happy state of affairs came to a screeching halt sometime between the first Carter energy crisis in the 1970s and the first Reagan recession in the 1980s. Decline and decay became the order of the day, and most libraries hit rock bottom in the early 1990s. From the mid-1990s to the waning years of the George W. Bush presidency, libraries bounced back. Then the greed-is-good Gordon Gekkos scuppered the global financial system and gave us the long dark years of the Great Recession. They have been years characterized by the collapse of the housing industry and local taxes, by massive unemployment, and by misguided slashing of public services (the ideology-fed punishment of the victims while the perpetrators wallowed in their sublime One Percent-ness). Funding (or rather, the lack of it) was the main proximate cause of the travails of libraries in this and previous dark ages. It would be a grave mistake to blame funding alone. The fact is that precipitous declines in funding have occurred at almost the same time as the steep increase in the cost of library materials and the rise of information technology (hardware, software, infrastructure, and staff) as ever-hungry consumers of more of library budgets. The combination of these factors has been almost a deathblow for some and a grievous problem for all.

In the early days of the automation of library processes, many administrators (and even some librarians who should have known better) really believed that it would save money. Similarly, the extraordinarily rapid growth in the number of digital resources available to libraries and their users caused some to believe that those resources would supplant expensive collections and services. In both cases, the opposite has proven to be true. Digitized library processes may be more cost efficient than manual processes, but that is because they increase efficiency, not because they lower costs. The "inevitable" coming of the all-digital library has been just around the corner for more than two decades, and the corner is as near and far away as ever at the time of writing. Economics, practicality, and human preferences are the intertwined strands of the problem.

Let us suppose that the all-digital library is a desirable aim and all that remains is how to get there. One important component would be that all the texts now available in printed form would be available in digital form. It would require total digitization of the contents of the libraries of the world resulting in readily accessible, readable versions accompanied by high-level, usable catalogues. Any user of the results of the Google digitization project and other smaller similar endeavors knows that they do not, in reality, come anywhere near to meeting the specifications of that requirement. They are, in reality, text atomization projects that deliver snippets of text out of context, yielded by free-text searching of the kind that is useless for most scholarly research. Even if the digitization requirement were to be met, what is the economic infrastructure that will make available in perpetuity, say, minor nineteenth-century novels or eighteenth century plays or seventeenth-century religious treatises? The millions of poorly printed books from previous centuries are further degraded by digital scanning. Are we to rely on what is, essentially, a digital advertising broker to maintain the human record for twenty-second-century, twenty-third-century, twenty-fourth-century . . . humans? The great libraries of the world exist, in one sense, to preserve the little-used and the forgotten parts of the human record for posterity. Is that a function likely to be carried out by a rapacious commercial concern that kowtows to repressive dictators in search of the almighty dollar? Who is to say that commercial concern may not, when in decline financially, jettison huge databases that make them very little money? It would fly in the face of history if they did not.

Scholarly journals pose other conundrums. Much as iTunes has changed the unit of musical sales from the expensive album to the inexpensive song, users of scholarly journals have made it evident that it is the article to which they wish to have access, not the journal or even the issue of the journal. An ideal system would be one in which all individual articles were assessed, rated, added to databases, and made available inexpensively. Unfortunately, there is no economic or scholarly architecture to provide such a system in sight; hence the chaotic state of journal publishing. (A separate but germane question is, why do we need the "journal" anyway in a world in which the article is the desired object?) Though there are many more purely digital journals than before, the lack of a satisfactory economic model has impeded an orderly transition. In particular, if print journal publishers cannot make money publishing digital-only journals and go out of business, what will happen to scholarly journal publishing?

Music and film publishing are similarly in a state of flux, to put it kindly. The future of newspapers is cloudy, but none of the forecasts are encouraging. It is said that we all want the instantaneous gratification of everything online everywhere *as long as it is free*, but I see paper everywhere I look, and those who are online or on smartphones all the time are reported to be up to their ears in Kardashians, cute cats, and K-pop. Is that how the human record will end—in a swamp of trivia? I would like to think not and, even more, that libraries embracing all forms of communication are what can save us from that fate.

GOING ALL-DIGITAL?

Before discussing alternatives to the "traditional" library, it would be well to describe that library. I use the word "traditional" with great reluctance and simply for want of anything better—its pejorative overtones of clinging to the past, of being place-centered and exclusively book-centered, bear no relationship to the experience of modern libraries. The only other available term—"real library"—implies that there is something illusory about the terms "virtual library" and "all-digital library." Though tempting at times, it is a serious mistake to treat the all-digital library as merely high-tech smoke and mirrors, though most writings in favor of virtual libraries have a decidedly glassy and cloudy aspect, smacking more of conjuration than reality.

The "Traditional" Library

My idea of a "traditional" library is of one that selects, collects, and gives access to all the forms of recorded knowledge and information that are relevant to its mission and to the needs of the community it serves, and assists and instructs in the use of those resources. More than that, the "traditional" library welcomes, as it always has, new forms of communicating knowledge and information—including digital resources.[3] The "traditional" library is not one that rejects change and innovation; it is a library that welcomes all means of serving its community better. The conflict between "traditional" libraries and all-digital libraries turns out, under examination, to be an elaborate shadow dance choreographed carefully by those who think that real libraries are obsolescent. The true choice is between real libraries with a substantial component of digital services and collections, on the one hand, and a replacement that has only digital services and collections, on the other. We have to think about building and maintaining a global network that collectively constitutes a vast repository of recorded knowledge and information (the human record) organized for ready access (the library) as compared to the strikingly disorganized wilderness of cyberspace. Proponents of the all-digital library will, of course, say that we are on the low beginners' slope of the mighty mountain yet to be scaled, but we seem to have spent a long time there; and, in any event, one cannot analyze predictions and promises unsupported by evidence and adding up to little more than virtual sleight of hand—still less refute them.

The All-Digital Library

The alternative to real libraries is sometimes called "the library without walls"—a silly term that implies current library service is contained entirely within the walls of library buildings. It is sometimes called "the digital library" and, other times, "the virtual library." In a remarkable paper, Jean-Claude Guédon demonstrates that the two latter terms are not synonymous.[4] "Digital" refers to the practice of recording information in terms of zeros and ones—that is, a means of recording and storing that is different in kind but not in degree from other means. One might as well refer to a nineteenth-century library as a "letters-on-paper library." In Guédon's thinking, the term "virtual library" refers to something a good deal more ambitious—one in which all the library's functions, processes, staffing, mission, and purpose are reconsidered, reorganized, and shaped around digital documents. Whether such a transformation is practical, possible, or even desirable is the central question of the future of libraries. There are, when it comes down to it, only the two mutually exclusive alternatives. One, which has the weight of history behind it, is the library of the past and today incorporating *digital* resources into its programs, collections, and services, and making the necessary changes to allow that incorporation. This is what libraries have done over the centuries as new means of communication (successively manuscripts, printed texts, printed music, cartographic materials, sound recordings, films of all kinds, digital resources of all kinds stored and delivered in a variety of ways) have arisen; and, because of that process, libraries have been changed and enriched while preserving a tradition that spanned the centuries. The alternative— the all-digital library—calls for a break with that tradition: the complete replacement of all other forms of communication in favor of digital documents. We should note that the balance of "traditional" resources and services will vary greatly from library to library, depending on the type of library and the clientele served. The range will have medical, law, and science and technical (e.g., engineering) libraries (with a preponderant or even exclusive reliance on *digital* resources and services) at one end, and rare book and children's libraries at the other.

The all-digital library has been the subject of a tsunami of books and articles far too numerous to list here. (Only a mean-minded person would ask why so many prophets of the imminent all-digital future turn to print on paper to communicate their message.) All those books and articles concentrate on the how of creating all-digital libraries (if only rarely the financial "how" and its implications), base their writings on unquestioned assumptions, and never examine the why or especially the eternal skeptical question, who needs it? The all-digital library calls for the demolition of the traditional library (literally as well as figuratively) and new ways of looking at every aspect of the library. In fact, there is good reason to ask if the word "library" is applicable in any sense when talking about the all-digital library. Guédon is at pains to point out that there is a difference between "virtual" and "unreal" in this context, stating that "the virtual is nothing but potential and as such it is reality (possibly) in the making."[5] Charles Martell echoes Guédon in saying, "The creation of a readily identifiable 'intellectual and logical' cyberspace for libraries will be of the utmost importance . . . decades from now when the physical library will be less visible to the public than the virtual library in the new cyberspace environment."[6]

These are fascinating, if complicated, topics, and Guédon's and Martell's vision of the virtual library as a transformation in the act of becoming is a welcome change from the dreary mechanism and determinism of most writers on the topic. However, whether one approaches the virtual library as a vision or as a technical process, there still are some unavoidable questions to be asked and some hard answers to be sought. The first question, and the hardest to answer, is . . .

Why the Virtual Library?

It seems that proponents of the virtual library have only three possible answers to that short question. The first is practical and financial—the ease of online access, the increase in access for people distant from physical libraries, and the supposed financial savings are seen as outweighing any and all of the disadvantages of digital documents (e.g., being mutable, perishable, and unverifiable). The second is teleological—that there is a grand design and the virtual library represents an inevitable manifestation of progress toward the fulfillment of that design. To believers, there is an inevitability about each innovation in human communication, and each innovation is demonstrably superior to its predecessors.[7] The only other answer is "why not?"—one that is offered implicitly by those who take up each fad and accept without question banal phrases like "the age of information." I discuss rationalism and irrationalism elsewhere in this book, but pause here to suggest that answers to "Why the virtual library?" that are based on belief in a grand design or on unthinking acceptance are not intellectually coherent. The practical arguments are more easily quantified and can be used to justify a virtual component of library service but, by no means, the idea of an all-digital library. Moreover, even if you believe that digital communication is part of a great plan, it is difficult to argue that each form of communicating and recording knowledge is superior to its predecessors. What happens is that human beings concentrate on the positive aspects of all innovations and tend to underplay or stay willfully ignorant of the negative consequences and attributes until they are so manifest—often long after the bloom is off the rose—that they can no longer be ignored. Proponents of digital communication stress the ease and speed with which messages are created and disseminated, but rarely dwell on their lack of durability. Politicians and computer scientists have pressed successfully for schools to be enabled to give all schoolchildren online access, but ignore the underfunded or nonexistent libraries in those same schools and the negative effect of such neglect on reading and the literacy levels of those schoolchildren. Futurists predict that digital technology will supplant "the book" sooner rather than later, but ignore the fact that technology has made book production and high production values quicker, easier, cheaper, and more accessible to more publishers.

One librarian who has looked at the all-digital library—in this case, the "book-free" (revealing term) public library opened in 2013 in San Antonio, Texas—does not like what he sees. Among the very pertinent remarks made by Adam Feldman are:

> Digital evangelism has lulled many of us into what I think ought to be an embarrassingly anti-intellectual comfort zone. Some comfortable folks among us are coming to believe that everything we need to know about the world can be skimmed in a compulsively reloaded feed, algorithmed, and tailored to all our narrow biases. It is a mistake to assume that because of all of the reading on screens that we do these days that libraries are undergoing some sort of seismic shift.

He adds:

> Run by a fraction of the staff necessary for a brick-and-mortar library, our e-book collections of pulp genre fiction and best-sellers steadily rank among our busiest branches when you count "circulation" statistics. The popularity of pulp is nothing new—leisure reading has long been an important part of library land—yet the complex webs of intellectual property law and vendor contracts guarantee that this "e-branch" is a pale shadow of the spectrum of human publishing represented by a real-life library curated by librarians who know their communities. The digital revolution is changing us but not in the way people who don't use libraries think it is. The meaningful life-changing core of the neighborhood branch is and remains the radical, flexible, dynamic education model that librarians build using every digital, physical, and human resource at hand. We are a cradle-to-grave people's pre-school through Ph.D.[8]

Beyond the general arguments and the specific charges leveled by Feldman lies the Law of Unintended Consequences. The postwar history of California is the classic instance of that law. Did those who boosted the development of Southern California really intend to destroy an agrarian way of life, pollute the air and water, create a strip-mall automotive culture, destroy the river systems, and go far to injure the very characteristics that led millions to move to the Golden State? Similarly, will the ease of digital communication blind its advocates to the possibilities of the loss of substantial parts of the human record in an age of all-digital libraries, and the creation of a world that has abandoned learning and is pervaded by trivia, isolation, and anomie?

LIVING WITH VIRTUAL LIBRARIES

What would the world be like if all libraries as we know them now were to be replaced by all-digital libraries? It will be like this or may already have turned into this:

- The buildings we now call libraries will be demolished or turned into indoor markets, skateboarding rinks, homeless shelters, or any of the other purposes to which they could be adapted.

- Most of the books and other printed items in research libraries will be transferred to huge warehouses (one copy of each title only) scattered across the nation; will be handed over to giant commercial concerns with no interest in the perpetuation of the human record to be digitized and pulped; or will simply be discarded.
- The stocks of other libraries will be pulped or burned or given to Third World countries.
- Attempts to digitize a respectable percentage of the recorded knowledge and information found in print and to make the fruits of that digitization widely available will continue to run into copyright, technical, societal, educational, and funding problems that will prove to be insurmountable.
- Most publishers of books and magazines will go out of business. Those that remain will publish small runs of hand-printed items for a small population of hobbyist readers; or large runs of trashy magazines, pornography, and comic books for a dwindling, aging readership.
- Scholarly journals will be replaced by a clearinghouse system for articles, run by a consortium of universities.
- The growing number of commercial "virtual universities" and massive open online courses (MOOCs) and the end of the tenure system in real universities will mean that fewer articles are handled by the clearinghouse system each year but that there will be a greater traffic between (mostly elderly) scholars in invisible colleges, thus resembling scholarly communication in the eighteenth century (see below).
- Fewer and fewer people will engage in sustained reading of long, complex texts. Most people will content themselves with reading brief texts from smartphone screens.
- The vast majority of young people will be functionally literate, if they can read at all, and easy prey to the commercial, political, and societal manipulation that will sugar-bomb them constantly.

These predictions may seem unduly pessimistic. They are, however, merely the logical extensions of some of the facts and trends we see today projected into an all-digital future, and of the economic and social consequences of a massive move from a print culture to a digital culture.

What Happens to the Books?

In August 2014, Karen Calhoun, the author of a book on digital libraries[9] asked some colleagues to send her one sentence each on digital libraries.[10] Predictably, the results consist of bromides about "conscious coordination of strategic actions" and the like, and blithe generalizations about digital libraries being "built with the needs and practices of end users (rather than librarians) in mind."[11] However, one of the sentences (from R. David Lankes) was well worth pondering (ignore the curious syntax):

> You can see the development of digital libraries from collections of stuff to communities of interest.[12]

"Collections of stuff" is an odd way to refer to the human record. Also, without any "stuff," what exactly are the communities of interest supposed to be interested in? One assumes that Mr. Lankes is referring primarily to books and other tangible carriers of knowledge and information as "stuff." Is their despised "stuff-ness" transformed when the texts in the "stuff" exist in digital form? "Communities of interest" (stamp collectors? ornithologists? videogamers?) may or may not be good things, but unless they come together around interaction with the human record, they most certainly do not constitute a library. In this kind of vision, libraries are the Cheshire cats of the twenty-first century, slowly fading away until nothing is left but the regretful smile that acknowledges the loss of what was.

In the all-digital future, public and school libraries would cease to exist. In poor communities, they would, with luck, be replaced by communal online centers. University libraries as we know them would cease to exist. The world of academia will be one in which most students and faculty interact only with digital resources and with each other at a distance. Almost all teaching and learning will be reduced to online job-specific learning. The collections of all these libraries will have to be dispersed, resulting from lack of use and interest. The sight of universities and colleges ridding themselves of collections that took lifetimes of work and hundreds of millions of dollars to build might be distressing at first, but would become commonplace and easily ignored. Keeping even one copy of each title in a warehouse would be quite expensive, and the future of those warehouses would be problematic as the habit of sustained reading gradually dies. It is likely that major parts of the human record would be lost to posterity. If you think this is an extreme prediction, just consider that even librarians in major research libraries are in the habit of referring to "legacy collections." If a chilling phrase like that comes readily to the lips of a librarian, imagine how little others of power and influence think of book collections and how readily they will dispose of them.

Digital Journals

The future of scholarly communication in the form of articles is even cloudier than that of other library materials. The great majority of digital journals, newspapers, and so forth that exist today are by-products of the print publishing industry. They are available to us—and only available to us—because the companies and institutions that produce them make money by selling the print issues. There are many online-only journals and magazines, most of which are subsidized by not-for-profit bodies or run at a loss. It is hard to envision an economic model that would support a profitable digital journal publishing industry. Witness the frantic efforts of serial publishing companies to impose "firewalls" on a public that, increasingly, thinks that everything online should be "free" and turns its collective back on texts and "information" for which they have to pay.

The journal as a form of scholarly communication was born in eighteenth-century Britain as a means of disseminating interesting findings in many fields (natural history, philosophy, etc.) among a small group of wealthy polymaths. Its evolution into today's massive apparatus of micro-specializations is wearisomely familiar, as is the burden that apparatus has imposed on academic libraries. Many librarians are salivating at the prospect of seeing the back of the scholarly journal, but they may be rejoicing too soon. If the print journal were to die, there is no evidence whatever that it would be replaced by some orderly, economically feasible system of digital dissemination. I think it is quite plausible that the twenty-first century will see something like the eighteenth century, only viewed through a glass darkly. Economics are paramount, but possible changes in academia may have just as great an effect. If the print journal industry collapsed, many of today's digital journals would vanish (because they are by-products, not autonomous publications). The rise of proprietary "universities," the slow death of liberal education, and the erosion of the tenure system will probably cause the number of published articles to decline by more than 90 percent. What would remain? To begin with, remaining scholars in the "poor" disciplines will form digitally linked "invisible colleges," in which they will exchange articles, much as eighteenth-century scholars wrote for journals and exchanged lengthy learned letters with their peers. There might be some money to be made in the "rich" disciplines, in which case the monied scientific, medical, and technical communities will evolve a new type of exchange of research results based on fees and purchase. If you think that academia is isolated from society now, just wait until the time when a few scholars in the liberal arts and sciences communicate only with each other, and scientists, technologists, and medical people sell their research results to megacompanies in a system in which the sole and ultimate value is profit.

What Happens to Reading?

The online world is a world of graphics, short texts, videos, and sound recordings. Anyone whose intellectual life is predicated on online interaction will give up on the sustained reading of complex texts, because true literacy (as opposed to functional literacy) will be an unnecessary skill. Sustained reading will be a habit of a dwindling few and, eventually, a lost art. Is there anyone who thinks that the world will be better off when reading is infrequent and devoted only to short bites of microtexts?

What Happens to Librarians?

I suppose a few librarians might be gainfully employed in a world of all-digital libraries. It is difficult to see much more than that. After all, most of our skills and abilities either will not apply or will not be valued. When the libraries are closed and all their former users are existing online and settling for anything that a search engine can find for them, what could a librarian do to help? It is not just that our unique skills—bibliographic control, collection development, reference work, and so on—would not apply. Even our values—service, intellectual freedom, and the like—would not apply. It is tragic to think the great enterprises of learning, human progress, and the betterment of society would be irrelevant in a world of images and thought bites, a world in which human society regresses to the point at which it consists of isolated individuals living bemused, intellectually stunted lives in the digital equivalent of the caves of Lascaux.

The One Good Thing . . .

. . . is that it will not happen! It will not happen because humanity is, in the end, both practical and idealistic. We will keep and cherish all the forms of communication (including the book) that we have now because they are useful and because they work. Learning and scholarship and libraries will continue because human beings value them for their own sakes and because they make life and society better. We will continue to incorporate digital technology into our libraries and lives for practical reasons and because, rightly used, that technology can enhance real libraries and bring illumination and pleasure to individual lives and to society.

Why Libraries Will Survive

I believe libraries are valued by many different and influential sectors of society. That esteem and positive valuation may be more latent than overt, but it is there—and we need to capitalize on it. The positive result of the generally negative fact that libraries and other educational institutions are in a constant battle for funding is that it has forced those seeking to increase funding for public services (including librarians and friends of libraries) to work to obtain funding and to bring out the vote for bonds and the like. The votes and the people who value libraries are there—they just need to be informed, courted, and energized. The time has gone, if it ever was, when we could be confident that our libraries and their funding would be supported without question. The lesson is that we all have to work in formal and informal ways to increase and maintain support for libraries among as many people and groups as we can. We certainly should not shrink from modern persuasive techniques—advertising, public relations, and so on—or from locating and tapping alternative sources of funding. The truth about real and all-digital libraries is one of the vital things that we should explain to the wider world. We have a lot to combat. For example, it is astonishing to me that many educated people still swallow the virtual hype and, without any malice toward libraries and learning, assume that "the book" is dying or already dead.

We should begin with our natural supporters: the middle-aged and old people, parents, teachers and faculty, students, scholars and researchers, education- and literacy-minded politicians (not all of whom are progressive in other areas of public policy), and general users of libraries. Securing your base is a political axiom, but so is the idea that you cannot win with only the base on your side. That means that libraries, individually and collectively, need to identify other groups that might not be thought of as library supporters, especially those with money and influence. Though we may wish it were not, library funding is a political issue and one that needs to be addressed as such. That includes the dissemination and clarification of the positive image of the library and the countering and obliteration of any negative images. For example, how many people on a university campus realize that, 99 percent of the time, the library is the—or one of the—most technologically advanced units in the academy? Have people who still see libraries as hushed, repressive places even been in a children's or college library lately? Do most people realize the depth and breadth of the collections held by major city public libraries?

There has been a lot of discussion and writing about the importance of advocacy for libraries. In recent years, the American Library Association established an Office for Library Advocacy, which has accomplished much in this area.[13] Advocacy, in this context, means organized, continuing discussion of the value of libraries (particularly as a source of access to digital resources) and pressure on politicians to maintain and increase library funding. My belief is that this advocacy is best done by individuals and by local and regional library groupings, rather than by national associations of librarians, though the latter can greatly assist local efforts. However it is done, libraries have a compelling story, and librarians have a duty to tell that story. This is particularly true in this time, in which the implicitly antilibrary exaggerations of technophiles too often go unanswered. We must use all possible means of communication and all possible political strategies to tell our story and assert our value.

The public's perception of the value of libraries is tied, to a great extent, to their perception of the library as place . . .

NOTES

1. Dillon, Dennis. "Why libraries persist." *Journal of library administration*, volume 51 (2011) pages 18–36.

2. Lerner, Fred. *The story of libraries*. New York: Continuum, 1998. page 138.

3. See the idea of the "digital library" in: Buckland, Michael. *Redesigning library services: a manifesto*. Chicago: ALA, 1992.

4. Guédon, Jean-Claude. "The virtual library: an oxymoron?" (1998 Leiter Lecture, National Library of Medicine, Bethesda, MD, May 1998.) *Bulletin of the medical library association*, volume 81, number 1 (January 1999). http://blueline.mlanet.org/publications/old/leiter98.html (consulted August 13, 2015).

5. Ibid.

6. Martell, Charles. "Going, going, gone." *Journal of academic librarianship*, volume 25, number 3 (May 1999) pages 224–225.

7. See, for example: Odlyzko, Andrew. "Silicon dreams and silicon bricks." *Library trends*, volume 46, number 1 (Summer 1997) pages 152–167.

8. Feldman, Adam. "This librarian is not impressed by your digital, no books library." *Next city*, August 2014. http://nextcity.org/daily/entry/computers-libraries-no-book-libraries-ebooks (consulted August 14, 2014).

9. Calhoun, Karen. *Exploring digital libraries: foundations, practice, prospects*. Chicago: Neal-Schuman, 2014.

10. See "10 thoughts on digital libraries: where they're going." CILIP (Chartered Institute of Library and Information Professionals). www.cilip.org.uk/cilip/news/10-thoughts-digital-libraries-where-theyre-going (consulted August 16, 2014).

11. A nifty example of the kind of malignant use of straw men to attack real libraries. As if those librarians have not had the needs of users (end or otherwise) paramount in their planning and can only be rescued from their wicked ways by being abolished.

12. "10 thoughts on digital libraries."

13. ALA Office for Library Advocacy (OLA). www.ala.org/offices/ola (consulted August 14, 2014).

CHAPTER 4

THE LIBRARY
AS PLACE

*. . . the chill that runs up my spine when I hear library leaders ponder the viability
of saving librarianship by abandoning the library as a physical place and recasting
the librarian as a consultant who helps paying clients navigate a path through
on-line information services . . . my fear is that the virtual library will render the
philosophy of librarianship invisible and will insulate the library from impassioned
debate about who has access to its resources. That loss, I would argue, is more than
we should be willing to bear.*

—Abigail A. Van Slyke[1]

There was a time, a long time ago, when the idea of the library (an
abstraction made up of all library collections, staff, services, and
programs) and the place (a room or rooms, a building or buildings) called the library were coterminous. As library services were made
available—by a variety of means—away from the place called the library,
those places became less important in some people's minds. The idea of the
all-digital library is an implicit challenge to the idea of the library as place

and must be measured in that light. The notion is seductive on its face: all the citizens of a digital nation, each in the "communities" that cater to her tastes, finding all they need in the way of recorded knowledge and information without having to do more than tap or swipe their smartphones, tablets, or laptops. Such an idea depends, essentially, on three things:

- that all recorded knowledge and information (the human record) be available, and kept permanently available, in digital form;
- that all such digital and digitized recorded knowledge and information be organized and readily retrievable; and
- that all individuals be able to interact fruitfully and deeply with the universe of recorded knowledge and information without the assistance of any other humans.

It is almost impossible to overestimate how far we are from those three basic requirements. Let us take the recorded knowledge and information that is the traditional concern of libraries (as opposed to the oceans of mostly disorganized information found online by the random access bestowed by search engines). By this, I mean the organized, edited, filtered, and formally published recorded knowledge and information created over the centuries and found in books, printed serials, cartographic materials, and so on. Though increasing amounts of organized, edited, filtered, and formally published recorded knowledge and information are created digitally, that quantum is a tiny proportion of digital recorded knowledge and information and a minute part of the human record in total.

To take just serial literature, most *current* scholarly journals and other periodicals are available in digital form, and the efforts of JSTOR and other initiatives are pushing that availability back a few years for, as yet, a relatively small number of serials. Even so, the digital availability of serial recorded knowledge and information is a minority of the total produced now and in the past (higher for scholarly serials than for popular serial publications). It is well worth noting here that the availability of current journals in digital form (either for a price or as part of the "open access" movement) is, with some exceptions, a by-product of print journals. There is, at this time, no economic model of digital-only journal publishing that makes sense. We can see this both in the numbers of such publications and in their origins. The relatively small number of "born-digital" journals is less significant than the fact that those that do exist are either the product of the cash-strapped not-for-profit sector (universities, learned associations, etc.), ego-driven loss leaders, political interests, and the like. We also have no guarantee that serial literature available online now will continue to be available permanently.

Unfiltered, unedited, informal online information and data has been added to "traditional" recorded knowledge and information in incalculably vast quantities. It is unorganized and largely irretrievable according to the most minimal library standards. I know of no one who believes that the authority control and controlled vocabularies that are essential for good retrieval will ever be applied comprehensively to the digital swamp. Then there is the question of unmediated interaction with digital resources. If you doubt that there is a great need for assistance in the use of digital resources, just ask any reference librarian.

All this adds up to the fact that we need physical libraries—places called libraries—for the indefinite future for the following purposes:

- to house the print and other tangible collections—not only those from the past but also those that will be created in the future
- to provide spaces for the integration of technological resources and services and "traditional" resources and services
- to house spaces for people to study, to do research, and to read, view, and listen for pleasure
- to provide places in which any person (especially those on the wrong side of the digital divide) can obtain online access to the whole range of electronic resources, and can obtain assistance in their use
- to provide areas for specialized collections and associated library services (sound recording and video libraries, rare book rooms, manuscript collections and archives, etc.)
- to provide meeting places within the community served by the library
- to provide suitable spaces in which library users can be assisted by professionals
- to provide suitable spaces for instruction (library instruction, literacy teaching, information competence) leading to the empowerment of members of the library community
- to provide spaces for social interaction, both high-intensive (e.g., meetings) and low-intensive (e.g., conversations)

THE HUMAN DIMENSION

We also need the library as a place because we are human beings. "The library" (the building that houses both the physical library and its immanence) is always one of the focal points of its community. From the great national libraries to rooms called "the library" in high schools and corporations, there is tremendous force in the library idea made manifest in buildings and public spaces.

Let us consider another kind of public place. Religious people may, and do, pray in private, but most feel the need to assemble in churches, temples, synagogues, mosques, and other places dedicated to the idea of religion. Why do they do that? Certainly it is to get the assistance and mediation of people—priests, imams, rabbis, bonzes—more learned in their religion than they. Equally surely, it is because of the human need to gather with other humans and, in so doing, to sanctify that place of assembly so that even, say, a revival tent becomes a sacred place. It can scarcely be considered too far-fetched to suggest that there is a parallel with libraries. They are places that embody learning, culture, and other important secular values and manifestations of the common good, and there is a need arising from our common humanity to visit such places. People go to them for the assistance to be obtained from other people—librarians in this case—who are more knowledgeable than they about the human record. Also, just as individuals go to religious buildings to pray alone sometimes, individuals go to libraries sometimes to pursue their interests without assistance from librarians. Analogies are treacherous things, more often misleading than illuminating, but I think it is worth at least a passing thought that TV evangelism and online religious sites have not led to calls to replace religious buildings with "virtual houses of worship." There is a human need for human contact and appropriate buildings in which to gather, and the believers in all-digital libraries ignore that need at their peril. These observations on the correlation between libraries and "sacred buildings" (first published in 2000) have been raised by others. That correlation is, for instance, discussed and studied in a more extensive manner in a study by Jackson and Hahn.[2] The authors refer explicitly to the "sanctification" of public spaces and quote Freeman: "The academic library as place holds a unique position on campus. No other building can so symbolically and physically represent the academic heart of an institution."[3] Their study of student preferences at three universities shows that, while those students appreciate the added amenities (coffee shops and so forth) found in modern academic libraries, they also prefer those amenities to be in the context of the library as the special space on, and symbolic heart of, the university. That "sanctification" (the preservation and creation of distinctive spaces and buildings) and recognition of the need for the marriage of practicality and inspiration is not at variance with the optimal use of current and emerging technologies. In the words of Marshall Breeding, "Technology can supplement inspiring architecture as a contributing factor in the success of the physical spaces of the library."[4]

What is the alternative to the bleak vision of the all-digital library advocates? I believe the answer lies in exactly the opposite direction—in expanding the roles of the library as place, not in abolishing that public place. Robert McNulty says:

> A library can be "the great good place in the city"—a literacy, Internet, and film center, a place for lectures, concerts, and exhibitions. . . . A library can also host coffee houses and restaurants, serve as an information center for visiting tourists, be a safe place for kids and a meeting spot for civic groups.[5]

(Neal Pierce points out that Andrew Carnegie built a boxing gymnasium into one of his Pittsburgh libraries and a swimming pool into another, so the idea of the expansive library as place is hardly new.[6])

In their survey of public libraries in Scandinavia, Aabø and Audunson note:

> The dominant finding is that the library first and foremost stands out as a public place, in the sense that it is open to all, and that most of the visitors are strangers to each other. It serves as a private space, however, regarding the character of the activities the users perform. The users come to the library with their individual projects related to studies, work, or private life. At the tables in the study areas, in the newspaper room, at the computers, and in the sitting areas, they weave an individual net around themselves that does not invite communication with others. They are performing their activities in parallel.[7]

Academic libraries, too, can play that central role in their university and college communities and should look beyond their traditional roles and services to enhance those roles and services. In many cases, an all-digital "library" would be a cruel imposition on many of our students. Those who get all swivel-eyed about the prospects for cyberspace and the all-digital future seem to forget that many, many people live and work in circumstances that do not offer them a quiet place to study and think. For many such students, the library is one of the few places that is free from the distractions of everyday life, and in which assistance in their studies is freely available. Quiet space is as available as air to the affluent and the comfortable, and the concept of being connected everywhere and at any time to the world's "information" must seem affordable and attractive. To the poor and the struggling, such a setup would be unattainable, and replacing real libraries and real library service with an all-digital service is yet another fantasy, another cruel hoax. It seems to me that we need more walls, not fewer—more library buildings with more to offer, and not phantom libraries catering to alienated and isolated individuals bereft of human warmth and a human context.

INTEGRATED PLACE OR NO PLACE?

It is both easy and often done to accuse anyone who has doubts about an all-digital future of being anti-technology, as if the library as place were defensible only in nostalgic and romantic terms. There is, of course, something to be said for both nostalgia and romance, but the lack of universal availability of online access to digital resources is creating yet another practical reason for preserving the library as place. As long ago as the last century, the US Department of Commerce issued a report called *Falling through the Net: defining the digital divide* that demonstrates that race, location, gender, age, and income are controlling factors in the question of access to electronic information resources.[8] Since then, hundreds of articles and books have discussed the digital divides within societies and between societies and nations from technical, sociological, commercial, and political points of view. Even those who state that the forces that initially tended to increase the divide are decreasing and the divide along with it acknowledge that the divides exist and steps should be taken to lessen them.[9] Members of minority groups, the poor, the less educated, and disadvantaged children—particularly those who live in rural areas or in the inner city have limited or no online access. One answer, of course, is to use libraries—particularly public and school libraries—as centers of online access and places in which people can obtain instruction and assistance in the use of online resources. This may seem a peculiarly modern phenomenon, but there is a striking similarity to the history of the nineteenth-century public library in Britain and the United States. In the last third of that century, the rich had their books delivered to their houses, the upper-middle class purchased their books from upscale bookshops, the middle class paid fees to borrow their books from private circulating libraries, and the legions of the working class used public libraries. These public libraries, besides providing wholesome recreation, became "the universities of the poor" and, often, a major path out of poverty.

The modern equivalent of the nineteenth-century public library could be the fully integrated library that preserves the best of the past and present of human interaction with the human record in all the forms it takes and uses technology efficiently and wisely to facilitate that interaction. It would be easier and cheaper to surrender to the all-digital dispersed vision and to abandon the library as place, but the difficulties of achieving the fully integrated library should not prevent us from trying to achieve that ideal. One difficulty is that the library as place and digital technology exist in wildly divergent time frames. Buildings are measured and used in multiples of decades; manifestations of digital technology are measured in years, if you are lucky. The latter is subject to the sheer pace of technological innovation, but it is also the product of the techno-lust of IT departments and commercial imperatives (the need of Big Technology to produce new products and improvements incessantly just to remain viable—see, for example, the six-monthly Apple dog and pony shows replete with oohs and aahs over the latest thing and revulsion from the things the audience was oohing and aahing over six months before). For whatever reason, the fact is that librarianship and IT exist in separate worlds, each with its own ethos and timetables—and, like it or not, an equal coexistence must be forged and maintained. In Breeding's words:

> Refreshing technology is a key aspect of maintaining a library's physical facilities as well as its virtual presence. While great architecture can endure for centuries, any given round of technology ages rapidly and loses its utility and appeal all too quickly. Through routine equipment

upgrades or opportunities to remodel, rebuild, or reconfigure facilities, new approaches to technology can be leveraged to improve use and strengthen the effectiveness of library facilities.[10]

My view of the integrated library as place is that it could be as powerful a social force as were those early public libraries. This is not just for the simple reason that a library is a perfect place in which to provide a service in that it is usually centrally located and already contains professionals who are skilled in helping and advising seekers of information and knowledge. I believe there is a subtler reason. Integrated libraries can demonstrate that access to electronic data and information is not the only way—or even, in many instances, the best way—to find the knowledge and information you need. It is true that many will come to, and bring their children to, a technologically advanced library because of the lure of free online access, but it is not difficult to see how innovative librarians can use that lure to open eyes to the wider picture. The idea of critical thinking is already commonplace in instruction programs in academic libraries, and the object of many such programs is as much to educate students about the perils as well as the advantages of online resources as it is to enable students to steer their way through them and evaluate them.

How can a library work to promote "traditional" library programs and services at the same time that it works to integrate electronic resources into those programs and services? The first step is to ensure that everything about the library demonstrates the comprehensive nature of the service. Immediately on entering the library, even the first-time visitor should be able to see books, reading areas, technological devices, and service points. Even someone who has come to the library only to use online resources should instantly be aware of the other services the library offers. The second step is to work actively to promote the whole range of library services, particularly to the young. One ideal occurrence in an integrated library would be to bring a class of young children to the library for a session introducing them to online resources and then have them stay for storytime or a book discussion. The third, and most important, step is to staff the library with librarians and other library workers who are technologically knowledgeable and enthusiastic about—and skilled in—the whole range of library collections and services.

BUILDING THE IDEAL TWENTY-FIRST-CENTURY LIBRARY

The library building boom of the 1990s and early 2000s showed signs of easing during the Great Recession. The *Library journal's* overview of library construction and reconstruction makes for sobering reading.[11]

NEW LIBRARY BUILDINGS	ADDITIONS, RENOVATIONS, ETC
Financial Year 2008: **90.**	Financial Year 2008: **88.**
FY2009: **80.**	FY2009: **90.**
FY2010: **70.**	FY2010: **55.**
FY2011: **62.**	FY2011: **89.**
FY2012: **34.**	FY2012: **73.**
FY2013: **27.**	FY2013: **47.**

However, the ALA 2013 *State of America's Libraries Report* contains this statement:

> Even with an economy still staggering under the impact of the Great Recession, library construction and renovation continued apace in 2012, concrete evidence that libraries still bring solid economic dividends to the communities they serve[12]

and goes on to describe a number of public, school, and academic library building projects. The *Library journal* article "Year in architecture 2013" featured four academic library and seventy-seven public library construction projects completed between July 1, 2012, and June 30, 2013.[13] All this despite free-floating doubts and anxieties about the future of libraries. No community or institution makes such a long-term investment on a whim. It is clear that these building projects are in response to the user community's call for expanded services as well as more-suitable—and more-inviting—library facilities.

Given the fact that such massive expenditures of public funds have to be justified in terms of use over many years, and given the perception that libraries are changing rapidly, it is more important than ever that such construction projects are carefully planned for the long haul.

NEW ISSUES

Some factors relating to library buildings have been with us forever: materials storage, study areas, and so on. In building, expanding, or renovating library buildings for the twenty-first century, we face new societal, technological, and legal issues that must be fitted into the complex of decisions to be made. They include:

- accommodating the differently abled user
- creating the technologically integrated library, providing flexibility to accommodate changes in library use and ever-changing technologies
- integrating the library with other services and institutions—again, accommodating changes in library use

The Library and the Differently Abled User

The Americans with Disabilities Act (ADA) was signed into law in 1990 (amended in 2008) and all libraries have made adjustments of various kinds to ensure compliance with the Act. Those adjustments were welcomed by the great majority of librarians, not least because easy access to all is a common library value. There have been a number of articles and books on the ADA and there are official guidelines that have been used by many librarians and architects who are eager to ensure maximum accessibility for all. However, Karen Stone, in a brief but illuminating article written from the point of view of a wheelchair user, made an eloquent plea for libraries to be planned in consultation with persons with disabilities on the very reasonable grounds that "what works for the disabled, works for others."[14] She described a model library in a small town on the west coast of Sweden that provides effortless, easy access to "a totally integrated, relaxed environment." The ideal is, in her words, "universal access for the very small, the big, the blind, the deaf, the young, the old, the physically able and not-so-able, and more." Her fundamental point is that the Swedish library, and another that she praises in Corrales, New Mexico, were planned not just to conform to legal guidelines but also in consultation with people with disabilities. As Stone writes, "Asking 'what would be most useful for you?' is certainly cheaper and far more accurate than solely hiring non-disabled architects to analyze accessibility solutions." We should always communicate with users, but the need to do so in this case seems even more urgent than in others.

Back to the Table?

We progressed from being unwired to wired and then to being wireless. The answer—for the present and near future, at least—seems to be wireless networks within libraries (and beyond). Thus, using these means, library patrons are able to bring their own devices into the library, or borrow devices from the library, and have access to the library's online systems and resources from anywhere in or outside the library. Could it be that all those workstations and terminals we spent so much money on and remodeled our libraries for will be consigned to the anteroom of history and replaced by . . . library tables and carrels?!

Libraries and Multiuse Buildings

A striking library building phenomenon of our days is that of dual use. By this I mean the new library building that shares a roof with other community facilities, or with other kinds of library, or—most exciting of all—with other cultural institutions. At the very least, many new library buildings and extensions, while remaining primarily a library facility, incorporate rooms and areas devoted to other purposes: community auditoria, meeting rooms, college computer labs, and so on. (These additional facilities should be distinguished from amenities—coffee shops, etc.—added to library buildings.) The combined academic and public library on the campus of San Jose State University in San Jose, California, was funded and is staffed jointly by the San Jose Public Library and San Jose State University. This was a bold and exciting project that may well presage many such developments, though the potential bureaucratic, logistic, economic, and administrative complexities are hair-raising. Dual-use school and public libraries are relatively common and have existed in the United States for at least the last three decades.[15] Though collaborative use of the same building by two different types of library may be logical, we should also consider dual use of buildings by libraries and other public services. One example of this is the combined public library and senior center in Hanson, Massachusetts, described by its architects as "intended to reinforce the role of the library as a social focus for the town."[16] Then, and most inspiring to my mind, are the buildings called "culture houses" in Europe—multiuse buildings incorporating art galleries; performing arts venues; arts and crafts workshops and the like; and auditoria and meeting rooms for cultural and artistic events. It has long seemed to me that libraries would make a natural part of such cultural centers, and such buildings incorporating libraries can be found in Scandinavia (see, for example, the Copenhagen Nordvest Culture House and Library, completed in 2011[17]), Germany, and the Netherlands. The Door County Central Library in Sturgeon Bay, Wisconsin, shares its building with the Miller Art Gallery in a particularly attractive and harmonious piece of architecture. It is obvious that, in an age of escalating building costs and straitened budgets, public and private institutions will look to creative and efficient collaboration as part of the solution to the library building problem. Let us hope that those constraints will lead to ever more creative and innovative spaces.

WHAT WILL THE IDEAL LIBRARY BUILDING OF THE TWENTY-FIRST CENTURY BE LIKE?

Because of the range of types of library and the varying missions of those libraries, it is impossible to prescribe the appearance and contents of the ideal library building. A new Library of Congress building will be as different from a new public library in a small Iowa town as the latter is from a major extension to a California academic library. All three have their own individual features, users, and purposes, but all are libraries—places dedicated to facilitating interaction with the human record for their users and providing appropriate services and space for that purpose. Where a commonality of purpose and function exists, there must be some basic similarities in the buildings in which those functions and purposes are to be effected.

External Appearance

Years ago, anyone could see that the design of libraries was heavily influenced by church architecture. From the choice of materials—often granite or another stone—to the style of architecture, many libraries built in the latter half of the nineteenth and the first half of the twentieth century clearly set out to impress, if not awe, at first sight. Public libraries built in the center of towns great and small, and college and university libraries built in the middle of campuses, had a solidity, magnificence, and sacred appearance that made it clear that here was something important, something to be reckoned with, something of permanence and permanent value. Inside, the church analogy seemed even stronger. Vaulted ceilings, dark woodwork, high windows—one was almost tempted to genuflect when approaching the card catalogue in the center of these magnificent edifices. Later generations took to using contemporary architectural fashions for new libraries. This was not always to great aesthetic effect. One acerbic critic said that the metal and glass "X Public Library and Information Center" built in Illinois in the 1970s should have been called the "X Public Library and Car Wash." (The offense was compounded by the fact that the new building replaced a lovely stone building in the Greek Revival style.) Another 1950s academic library in California, now no more, was described as looking like a Bulgarian police station. Sometimes, contemporary architecture is unappealing at first but proves to have enduring appeal over the decades. In other cases, the initial lack of appeal proves prophetic. The aesthetics of extensions to existing libraries are particularly tricky. The dilemma is, of course, whether to ape the original style and materials, or to build something that harmonizes, or to build something that is clearly different. Each of these can have both fortunate and unfortunate outcomes.

Another important matter about the outward appearance of a new or remodeled library is how it fits into the place in which it is situated—both in terms of the topography and the community served. In the words of one library architect:

> Each new or rehabilitated library needs to take into account what I call the community topography: that is, the particularities of the neighborhood it would serve.[18]

What we should seek (and often find) in a library building is harmony, both in terms of its appearance and its siting. This does not mean that each new library should be neoclassical or look as if it were designed by Thomas Jefferson. Modern architecture has brought us many fine buildings, and times and tastes change. However, harmony of appearance and harmony with its surroundings and purpose should be the minimal requirements of a new or remodeled library building.

Inside the Library Building

Harmony and proportion should characterize the inside of the library building. Spaces should be easy to navigate for everyone (including those with disabilities) and should be suitable and adequate for their particular purpose. Furniture should be chosen with care, pleasing in appearance, and suited to its purpose. Light—natural as well as artificial—should be abundant but not glaring, and should contribute to the aesthetic quality of the building. For a superb example of lighting created for a particular building and particular purpose, you need look no further than the reading room of the New York Public Library, in which the lights are a distinct and positive design element. The colors and decorations of walls and ceilings, carpets and other floor coverings, artworks, plants, and other decorative elements are necessary features of public places. Those features must be chosen, planned for, and maintained as carefully as anything else in the building in order to preserve the harmony and aesthetics of the total space.

Library Materials

Two of the great breakthroughs in the democratization of library use were open stacks (accompanied by subject classification) and public access catalogues. The early open stacks held printed texts (books and bound journals) only. There was a reluctance to give the same access to newer forms of communication as they came along. There are reasons, in some cases, for storing and displaying different resources separately, but there is no reason at all that most of them should not be openly available to be browsed. There is certainly every reason why the records for online resources should be integrated into the catalogue. By that means, a subject search yields not only a variety of titles but also a variety of materials—including online resources. This is not the place to discuss the cataloguing of digital resources, but suffice it to say that the fact that we cannot integrate electronic resources with the rest of the collection physically makes it even more important to integrate them into catalogues. In the ideal library building, the physical collections will be easily available for perusal and use (irrespective of their format), and the digital collections and resources will be easily available through all available devices.

The Use of Library Spaces

No matter whether you are dealing with a one-room library or the Library of Congress or all the libraries in between, there are certain uses for space that all have in common. All libraries use space to:

- house tangible materials and machines that give access to tangible and digital resources
- provide study, meeting, and consultation areas
- house points of assistance and consultations
- provide places for staff to work

Individual libraries will contain special spaces for particular purposes. Typically, larger academic libraries will include rare book or special collections reading rooms, areas for format-specific collections (e.g., maps), areas for subject-specific collections (e.g., law), and instructional rooms equipped with appropriate technology. Public libraries often contain separate children's libraries, newspaper and magazine reading areas, and format-specific collections. It is impossible to generalize about special libraries, but they, too—depending on their subject coverage and clientele—will use space in particular ways. School libraries often include activity areas for class projects that are related to library use.

Children's Libraries

From one point of view, children's libraries are the most important libraries of all. They are places that provide the basis for lifelong literacy and learning, places that live in the memory long after we have ceased to be children. For that reason, it is very important that the space, furnishings, and so on allotted to the children's library do not just facilitate the efficient delivery of library service to children but also provide an environment of ease and peace that is conducive to the love of reading and to exploration of the human record. Children's libraries should be bright, welcoming, comfortable human spaces that children enjoy visiting and remaining in. Storytimes and other activities should intrigue and entice small children, and the children's library should be a place into which children can grow so that they keep returning long after they have outgrown storytimes. I admire children's librarians and their unswerving devotion to service, their willingness to use every means to provide that service, and their openness to innovation (including technological innovation).

Housing Collections

The concept of open access to all library materials is, I believe, one of the controlling ideas of modern librarianship. Another is contained in one of Ranganathan's Five Laws of Library Science: "The library is a growing organism." Those two factors—open access and growth—involve many issues, the chief of which is space, which, for most libraries, translates into money. Open access demands far more space than closed access, and allowing for growth over a long period (remember, there are no short periods in library lives) means that unfilled space has to be maintained for decades. I maintain we must accept the need for expenditure on space and the creation of places called libraries, while using any means to lessen unnecessary space expenditures. Before we go on, it is important to recall that housing collections is not the only demand on library space, and that classrooms, study areas, reference areas, and so forth also consume considerable square footage in library buildings.

The British Library in London (which was thirty-plus years in gestation and full the day it was opened) and the tragic San Francisco Public Library (famous for its concentration on technology at the expense of access to its collections) are salutary examples of the perils of ignoring Ranganathan's law. Buildings must be planned in such a way that the collections and services they house are able to grow over many decades. Some measures can be taken now, and new ideas and new technologies will undoubtedly offer more as libraries grow and change.

THE PLACE OF IDEALS

Library buildings come in all shapes and sizes. From the monumental to the unassuming, their styles and purposes are as varied as their communities of users. However, it is also true that all these buildings should embody enduring values: service, stewardship, the love of learning, and the others described in this book. A library building should work efficiently, but it should also have higher qualities. It should be a place that inspires respect and encourages the pursuit of truth by scholars and children, by the high and the low, by the powerful and the powerless—because all these people come to the library with common aims and shared dreams. A library building should also be a good place in which to work, because harmony in the workplace generates joy in work, and joy in work leads to productive and effective service to society. The foregoing may seem impossibly idealistic and out of kilter in the age of technology, the age of materialism, and the cult of information. My answer is a question: Without ideals and values, what is the point? The truth is that we all seek meaning in all aspects of our lives, and the creation and maintenance of useful, harmonious library places and spaces are a crucial step toward finding meaning in our work as librarians.

NOTES

1. Van Slyke, Abigail A. "The librarian and the library: why place matters." *Libraries & culture*, volume 6, number 4 (Fall 2001), pages 518–523.
2. Jackson, Heather Lee and Hahn, Trudi Bellardo. "Serving higher education's highest goals: assessment of the academic library as place." *College & research libraries*, volume 72, issue 5 (September 2011) pages 428–442.
3. Freeman, Geoffrey T. "The library as place." In *Library as place: rethinking roles, rethinking space.* Washington, DC: Council on Library and Information Resources, 2005. page 9.
4. Breeding, Marshall. "Using technology to enhance a library as a place." *Computers in libraries* (April 2011) pages 29–31.
5. *Institutions as a fulcrum for change.* Issued by Partners for Livable Communities. Washington, DC, 1996: quoted in Pierce, Neal. "The Magic of Community Assets." *National journal* (September 21, 1996) page 1707.
6. Ibid.
7. Aabø, Svanhild and Audunson, Ragnar. "Use of Library Space and the Library as Place." *Library and information science research,* vol. 34 (2012), pages 138–149.
8. National Telecommunications and Information Administration. "Fact sheet: rural areas magnify 'digital divide.'" www.ntia.doc.gov/legacy/ntiahome/digitaldivide/factsheets/rural.htm (consulted August 19, 2014).
9. See, for example: Hilbert, Martin. "Technological information inequality as an incessantly moving target: the redistribution of information and communication capacities between 1986 and 2010." *Journal of the association for information science and technology* (November 19, 2013). http://onlinelibrary.wiley.com/doi/10.1002/asi.23020/abstract.

10. Breeding, "Using technology to enhance a library as a place." page 31.

11. Fox, Bette-Lee. "Year in architecture 2013: six-year cost summary." *Library journal* (November 15, 2013). http://lj.libraryjournal.com/2013/11/buildings/year-in -architecture-2013-six-year-cost-summary/ (consulted August 20, 2014.

12. American Library Association. *State of America's Library report 2013: library construction and renovation.* www.ala.org/news/state-americas-libraries-report-2013/ library-construction-and-renovation (consulted August 19, 2014).

13. Fox, "Year in architecture 2013."

14. Karen G. Stone, "To roll into a library." *American libraries*, volume 27, number. 5 (May 1996) pages 41–42.

15. See: Haycock, Ken. "Dual use libraries: guidelines for success." *Library trends,* volume 54, number 4 (Spring 2006) pages 488–500.

16. Schwartz/Silver Architects. "Hanson combined library and senior center." http:// schwartzsilver.com/portfolio/hanson-library-senior-center/ (consulted August 20, 2014).

17. ArchiTravel. "Copenhagen Culture House and Library." www.architravel.com/ architravel/building/copenhagen-culture-house-and-library/ (consulted August 20, 2014).

18 Mays, Vernon. "Double duty." *Architecture*, volume 84, number 6 (June 1995) pages 84–88.

CHAPTER 5

STEWARDSHIP

Littera scripta manet.

—Horace.[1]

WHAT IS THE MEANING OF STEWARDSHIP?

"Steward" is a word that derives from two Old English words, *stig* ("house") and *weard* ("warden")—that is, someone with responsibility for ensuring the safety and orderly functioning of a house or, by extension, any small community. It is still found in that narrow meaning. Its wider, metaphorical meaning goes back—at least—to the King James Bible and refers to someone or some entity who preserves the value of something and ensures that future generations enjoy the legacy that comes to them with an equal or enhanced value as a result of that stewardship.[2] Someone who inherits an estate and improves it during the period she is a guardian before giving it to inheritors can fairly be said to have exercised stewardship.

WHAT IS THE RELATION BETWEEN STEWARDSHIP AND LIBRARIES?

Stewardship in the library context has three components:

- the preservation of the human record to ensure that future generations know what we know
- the care and nurture of education for librarianship so that we pass on our best professional values and practices
- the care and maintenance of our libraries so that we earn the respect of our communities

PRESERVING THE RECORDS OF HUMANKIND

> The task of the librarian, then, is to rescue the past for the enlightenment of the present, to preserve the past not for its own sake or for the curiosity of the antiquarian, but for the meaning it has for today and tomorrow.[3]

The inheritance of which we are stewards is no less than the complete cultural and historical legacy of the records of humankind—the "human record." The value of stewardship is one of our most important duties and burdens—one that we must honor if we are to carry out our mission of preserving the human record and transmitting it to future generations. It is interesting to see how infrequently the question of preserving recorded knowledge and information in digital form is raised during discussions of the future of libraries. If raised, the question is usually dismissed as something that technology and cooperative action will solve, as if by magic and at some yet to be determined time. Somehow, it seems that historic role of libraries is being ignored, simply because all-digital enthusiasts dare not face up to the reality of the immense practical and technological problems posed by digital archives.

Librarians and archivists (whom I regard as members of the same church, if often in schism) have a unique role in preserving and transmitting the records of humankind on behalf of future generations. I do not use the word "unique" lightly. Many of our values and missions are shared with other groups and interests, but we alone are dedicated to the preservation of recorded knowledge and information—the human record. Publishers, booksellers, teachers, researchers, museum keepers are among the people who benefit directly from the fact that the records of the past are available to them, but only librarians and archivists are engaged in the wholesale preservation of those records. If a substantial amount of the world's recorded knowledge and information were to be available in digital form—and only in digital form—we would be facing a crisis in the preservation of the human record that would dwarf anything that we have seen since the dawn of the age of printing. It is imperative that librarians work together to produce a grand plan for future stewardship that contains practical and cost-effective means of ensuring that future generations are able to know what we know.

The All-Digital Age?

Some say that the age of print will, at some time in the future, yield to an all-digital age. In contemplating that possibility, it is instructive to look at the transition to the age of print from the age that preceded it—the age of script. Thomas Jefferson wrote:

> How many of the precious works of antiquity were lost while they existed only in manuscript? Has there ever been one lost since the art of printing has rendered it practicable to multiply and disperse copies? This leads us then to the only means of preserving those remains of our laws ... that is, a multiplication of printed copies.[4]

In her magisterial work on the transformational effect of printing, Elizabeth Eisenstein discusses three attributes of the printed book that distinguished it sharply from the manuscript or, to use her terms, distinguish the print culture from the script culture. They are standardization, dissemination, and fixity. In many ways, her analysis of the script culture closely parallels a modern analysis of what I will call, for the sake of symmetry, the digital culture. This is especially true in the case of fixity. Manuscripts of the same "work" differed greatly one from the other to the same degree that various versions of e-texts differ from other versions—for the same reason (each copyist introduced change and error) and with the same deleterious effect. It is tempting to see the history of human communication as one of constant progress. Humankind has advanced from no recorded communication in prehistorical days through a variety of media, from clay tablets and stone to paper and digital media, each medium being more extensive and less durable than its predecessor. Because of the increasing numbers of communications made possible by digital technology, and because we retain the older media for the sake of their durability (using, for example, stone for memorials and vellum for important historical documents), it is tempting to buy the "onward and upward" theory. Could it be that the story is not one of progress? Could it be that future historians of communication (if there be any such) might look back on the five-hundred-plus-year period in Western history that began with Gutenberg and ended (on some as yet undetermined date) with the "triumph" of digital technology as an aberration—an island of fixity and transmission of the human record arising from the swamp of the age of script and declining into the digital swamp? Adrian Johns ties print to such concepts as "veracity" and "civility."[5] The point is that the stability of print and the standardization of publishing created an intellectual climate in which there is a bond of trust between the author, publisher, and reader. That implicit contract has the following parts:

- A book published by a reputable publisher is what it says it is.
- Reputable publishers publish books that can be trusted.
- A book by a reputable author contains facts that have been verified to the best of the author's, editor's, and publisher's ability.
- A book by a reputable author contains opinions and interpretations that are the author's or are clearly labeled as the opinions or interpretations of others.
- Citations, sources, and the rest of the scholarly apparatus in a book published by a reputable publisher clearly indicate the origins of the facts and opinions contained in that book.
- Each manifestation of a clearly labeled edition of a text is identical to all other manifestations of that edition.

Not a single one of those elements of the unwritten contract between publishers, authors, and readers is guaranteed to be present in the digital world of today and the foreseeable future. Take, for example, a "source" such as Wikipedia. It lacks all the characteristics of authenticity, fixity, and the rest that can forge a bond of trust with the user. There is nothing to stop anyone from gaining access to many digital resources and changing them to his heart's delight before disseminating them as something they are not. That is the heart of the dilemma faced by authors and readers in a digital world devoid of fixity, standardization, and verifiable veracity.

Stewardship of the Human Record in Action

How, then, should we exercise stewardship over the records of humanity? The simple answer, and the truest, is that we should do everything we can to preserve significant recorded knowledge and information in such a manner that it is available in an authentic and fixed form not just to the next generation—or even the next few generations—but for the indefinite future. The key word in the foregoing sentence is "significant." One of the ironies of the present predicament in preservation is that we have solved the issue without having to make the kind of value judgment that "significant" implies. It is beyond question that the best—indeed, the only proven—way to preserve recorded knowledge and information is to print it on acid-free paper, make many copies, bind those copies well, and distribute them to libraries throughout the world. In that system, it is the publisher or printer or both who make the judgments as to what is published. After that decision to print, publish, and distribute, the rest is automatic. There has never been any better preservation system, and it imposes on libraries only the expense—the very considerable expense—of providing space for all those bound volumes. I will return to the question of value judgments based on assessment of "significance" later, but first will sketch the preservation issues that face each broad medium of communication today.

Books and Printed Journals

There are a number of enemies of print on paper, including damp, heat, quality of paper, and inappropriate or poor binding. That being said, there are two massive advantages: (1) the many duplicates of each publication, and (2) the seemingly limitless life of a well-bound text printed on acid-free paper and preserved in favorable conditions.

Manuscripts

These are the mirror images of books in that drawings and writings on paper and other media are, by definition, unique, and very likely to have been stored, for at least some of their existence, in less than optimal conditions. I well remember the collection of the manuscripts of a world-famous poet with which I had the pleasure of working. Many drafts of the poems were written on the backs of bill envelopes, and the collection had been stored in various boxes made for holding shoes and comestibles and transported from one venue to another in the course of a peripatetic and adventurous life. Technology—particularly digitization—offers an excellent means of preserving, protecting, and disseminating unique manuscript collections.

Maps and Music Scores

Many of the circumstances that apply to printed books apply to these materials, but it should be noted that single maps are more fragile than printed books and that many maps and scores exist in fewer copies than most books.

Sound Recordings

From wires to wax cylinders to 78s to tapes of various kinds to EPs and LPs to digital tape and compact discs to streamed music held in a "cloud" by commercial concerns—it appears that we have moved through various stages of fragility and potential loss. A cautious person will note that we have no proof of the longevity and durability of any medium of sound recording; the use of each is subject to the future availability of listening devices. My grandmother had a phonograph on which she used to play her 78s of the beloved (by some) Irish tenor Count John McCormack. The sleek CD players of just yesterday are beginning to look as quaint as her phonograph looks and is today. Who knows how comical and peculiar streaming and iPods will look in twenty years' time?

Films and Videos

It is known that at least one-third of the feature films made in the more than one-hundred-year history of moving pictures are gone forever. The situation with shorts, newsreels, and the like is even worse. To quote a *New York times* journalist:

It's bad enough, to cite a common estimate, that 90 percent of all American silent films and 50 percent of American sound films made before 1950 appear to have vanished forever. But even the films we have often live on in diminished states. An astonishing number of famous titles—like "King Kong" and "His Girl Friday"—no longer exist as original camera negatives, but survive only as degraded duplicates and damaged release prints. A great deal of important material—not just features but shorts, newsreels, experimental work, industrial films, home movies and so on—remains on unstable nitrate stock, and must be transferred to a more permanent base before the films turn to goo. And once the endangered material has been stabilized (the preservation step), it often must undergo an even more expensive process of restoration to recover its original luster: the removal of dirt and scratches, the replacement of lost footage or missing inter-titles, the cleaning up of degraded soundtracks.[6]

Many of the films that remain are on a brittle medium, are in colors that have faded, or depend on a process or projector that is no longer available. We have seen a number of video formats fail and others survive, at least for the moment. It is hardly likely that all or any of the currently used video formats (and the machines on which they are played) will be around, say, fifteen years from now. What about all those films that are available to be streamed from the "cloud"? Who will preserve them, especially those that are of little or no commercial value?

Artifacts and Artworks

Many libraries contain artifacts and artworks that embody or contain recorded knowledge and information. The wise librarian takes guidance from museums, art galleries, and other specialists on the preservation and special treatment of such materials. This is yet another argument for the closer collaboration between libraries and other cultural institutions that I argue for elsewhere in this text.

Microforms

The story of microfilm, microfiche, microcards, micro-opaques, and the other variations of the medium that first surfaced during the Franco-Prussian War of 1870 is salutary. For most of the twentieth century, microforms were perceived as the salvation of libraries in terms of library space and of preservation. One variation—ultrafiche—contained so many images that it was predicted we would all be "carrying the Library of Congress around in a briefcase." Nice try. Microforms have several drawbacks, chief among them the fact that most library users hate them. There is also the instability of some earlier forms of microfilm; the lack of standardization of reading machines for some microforms (microcards, ultrafiche, and the like); and doubts about the long-term durability of even the established microforms. There are many preservation and digitization of microforms projects (often lacking coordination and complete funding) that seem to offer hope that much of the parts of the human record that are found only in microform will be preserved and transmitted to future generations.[7]

Digital Resources

There are so many intractable issues concerning the preservation of digitized recorded knowledge and information—and so few proposed practical solutions—that it is tempting to do what many digital enthusiasts have done: ignore them. However, it may be worth listing a couple of them here.

- The vast majority of digital information is worthless, of only temporary usefulness, or of very local interest. How is all that chaff to be separated from the worthwhile wheat? And who will undertake that Sisyphean labor?
- The hardware used to gain access to digital resources and the formats in which those resources are kept change radically and frequently. This means that preservation programs must also involve considerations of the hardware needed for access and constant refreshing of the formats.
- Even selective digital archives will be massive. Who is to ensure that governments and organizations will maintain those archives for centuries in the future?

Which Documents Are "Significant"?

This is a difficult and, in many ways, unanswerable question. As I have pointed out previously, librarians have largely left it to publishers and booksellers and, to a lesser extent, to the law and to library book vendors. After all, it is not librarians who decide what is or is not to be published and what is or is not a legal publication. Add to that our almost universally held belief that library users are entitled to everything that is available and you can readily see us as professionals who are reluctant to employ such criteria as significance and worth. All libraries, great and small, practice some degree of selection; but that selection has been, first, from a known and limited universe—the universe of published items—and, second, mostly confined to questions of suitability for the community that the library serves. In short, most librarians not only do not generally practice selection based on the significance or value of one publication as compared to another, but also actively shy away from such questions for fear of being accused of censorship. There is one shining exception to this pattern: the children's librarian. I have always admired children's librarians for many reasons—chief among them being their willingness to distinguish between "good" books and those that are inferior and to make selection choices based on their principles and values. The rest of us are reluctant and, anyway, out of practice. What then are we to do when faced with the Internet and digital resources of all kinds? There are really only three basic strategies, and none of them cause the librarian's heart to leap with joy.

- We can ignore the question and give as much access to as many resources as we can without regard to value. This, of course, means ceding the preservation issue before we start.
- We can choose the digital resources that we give access to with care and choose the links we make from our bibliographic architecture with care and simply not bother about the rest of the digital swamp.
- We can consciously set out to choose, evaluate, give access to, and preserve those things that we find significant and of value. A noble endeavor—but one that calls for expenditures few of us are prepared to make—is based on the exercise of skills that few of us possess, and requires policies that none of us has, as yet, formulated.

To illustrate how tricky such discriminations can be in the digital realm, we need look no further than an example from the orderly world of print.

More than three decades ago, *New Yorker* writer Frances Fitzgerald published a fascinating book about the way in which the United States constantly revises its history.[8] This influential and widely read work was based almost entirely on the study of high school textbooks from the past one hundred years. There must be few, if any, research librarians who would put outdated schoolbooks high on their lists of significant types of publication.

There are abundant other examples of the significance of the insignificant, and they all illustrate the immensity of the problem. That immensity should not discourage us from attempting to be good stewards of all our resources (including digital resources). On the contrary, it should energize us in our pursuit of the twin goals of preserving what we have and establishing systems that will enable us to preserve the future records of humankind.

The Modern Language Association, in a statement issued in 1995, reaffirmed the continuing importance of reading and the book and their primary role in scholarly enquiry.[9] Though we all play a part in the preservation and provision of books, the fact is that the multimillion-volume research library has the lead role in that endeavor. We have done a fairly good job over the centuries of preserving almost everything of value in the print record. Absent malice and malevolent neglect, there is no reason why that almost total success rate should not continue. On the other hand, we have scarcely even begun to preserve digital resources. Vague plans have been drawn up; much has been said and little done. Success in that preservation effort is, at best, a very long shot indeed.

BEYOND THE PRESERVATION OF THE HUMAN RECORD

In his seminal article, Lee Finks defines stewardship as "a responsibility for the destiny of the library as an institution."[10] He stresses that the survival of the library and its collections is crucial to the futures of culture and society. This grand task is obviously centered on the preservation of the human record but also involves the survival and development of the library and of librarianship. In my opinion, that latter mission has two important components:

- preserving the knowledge of librarianship for future generations of librarians by means of library education
- assuring the bond of trust between the library and the society we serve by demonstrating our stewardship and commitment, thus strengthening the mutuality of the interests of librarians and the wider community

The second component depends on us acting with responsibility and ethics in the service of our particular community and of society as a whole. We have the implicit respect of most of the people we serve, which is a good foundation. However, that generalized good feeling needs to be intensified if it is to be of practical use. If we are to continue to earn the respect and support of our communities, we must demonstrate that our mission is relevant to their lives and to the wider culture. There is no better way to do that than to make that mission plain and to work hard on being good servants of the culture and good stewards of its records.

LIBRARY EDUCATION

I honestly believe that libraries, on the whole, are doing a good job of preserving the records of humankind. I also believe that a certain lack of assertion is our only failing in demonstrating to our communities that we are good stewards. Modesty is an admirable trait, but excessive modesty can be a political mistake of the first order. We do good work and should not be afraid to proclaim it, especially to those who fund our activities. Library education, on the other hand, is a disaster verging on a catastrophe.

There are many villains and numerous failures in the sad story of American library education. Practitioners blame educators. Educators blame practitioners. Teachers, students, practitioners, the American Library Association (ALA) and other professional organizations, and writers of books and articles on libraries are all complicit in this train wreck. Almost the entire debate centers on "the 'L' word" (an annoying trope modeled on euphemisms for curse words), referring to how the majority of "library schools" (a term that they disdain) do not in fact use the word "library" in their name. This last is a particularly fatuous thing to do, as most of the renamed schools and programs produce graduates who seek employment in libraries. Though such semantic discussion is as futile as it appears, it is symbolic of the deep ill, the existential crisis, that has gripped our profession. (It is odd, is it not, that some librarians are fleeing from the word "library" as outmoded, when computer types happily use the word "computer" for the machines that are far more than the calculators the name implies?) Speaking for myself, I have lived most of my life as a librarian, love libraries, and will die proud of having been a librarian, without ever wishing to change the word "library" or any of its cognates.

The sad facts behind "the 'L' word" wars are these:

- A huge gulf exists between the interests of LIS educators and library practitioners.
- Three of the former intellectual powerhouses of American librarianship (the schools at Columbia, Chicago, and Berkeley) are dead or malignly transformed.
- Many LIS program graduates lack basic education in the central processes of librarianship.
- Many library programs contain two mutually irreconcilable cultures—a (female-dominated) culture of librarianship and a (male-dominated) information science culture.[11]
- Many practitioners and employers cannot or will not accept their role of training new librarians and fail to distinguish between education and training.
- The ALA accreditation process has become a farce gleefully exploited by LIS and "I-school" administrators.

Let us go to the basic issue. An enlightened employer—the consumer of the product of LIS programs—wishes to hire librarians who have been educated in the core competences of our profession.[12] Is there a single employer in a library of any kind who wishes to hire someone in a professional position who lacks an education in any one of the following (under these or other terms): bibliographic control, reference work, collection development, library systems, and digital resources? I have noted previously that "education" is the key word here—not "training." It is the role of the enlightened employer to provide training in, say, cataloguing, reference work, or collection development, but even the most enlightened employer cannot do that in the absence of a foundation of knowledge and understanding provided by a good education.

Information Science and What It Has Wrought

The adverse impact of information science on library programs cannot be overstated. Although a sadly overlooked article demonstrated and documented the fact that there is really no such thing as "information science," this bogus discipline has a stranglehold on many of our LIS schools.[13] Many

of the courses that would add to the education of librarians are being el-
bowed out by IS and IT courses that have little or no relevance to the real
work of real librarians in real libraries. The reason for this is that academics
(mostly male academics) are pursuing their own interests, grants, and promotion or tenure at the expense of useful library education. Many of them
are not librarians but refugees from other disciplines, or have little interest
in libraries and their mission—indeed, think that the library has no future.
It is a free country, and everyone is entitled to her views—no matter how
wrongheaded. However, people with those beliefs should found their own
schools and programs and not work to the detriment of the supply of future
librarians. They certainly should not receive the imprimatur of ALA accreditation. If the profession is weakened and sickened in this manner, our
mission of preserving "the library and its fruits" (Lee Finks's words) will fail.

Accreditation

About the same time as ALA was finishing the long-drawn-out process
of formulating approving its *Statement of core competences*, it was going
through the process of revising its accreditation standards. Since the core
competences are, in essence, a statement of what a graduate of an LIS master's program should know, it would seem logical that accredited master's
programs should be required to teach those competences. Logic, unfortunately, had nothing to do with the case and ALA's revised accreditation
standards and proposed revisions of those standards contain no such requirement.[14]

The accreditation process, essentially, now works like this: The persons
designated by ALA's Committee on Accreditation (COA) ask the library
program what it is trying to accomplish and then assess how well it is doing in that self-defined task. Thus, if the master's program of the School
of Information Studies at X University states that it is in the business of
"educating information professionals for the new millennium" and that process does not involve the study of bibliographic control but does involve
webmastery, that program will be judged on how well it produces webmas-
ters. In this way, the American Library Association is saying, in essence,
"Teach what you like and we will still certify your graduates as worthy to be
employed in libraries." One of the criteria for being a profession is that the
professional body controls the education of persons wishing to enter that

profession. This is true of, for example, the ABA and the AMA. Alas, it is not true of ALA.

Almost all advertisements for librarian positions contain the magic words "MLS (or equivalent) from an ALA-accredited program." Until the past two or three decades, a prospective employer could assume a common body of knowledge in an applicant who was a graduate of an ALA-accredited program. No longer. Because ALA turned the process into what amounts to self-accreditation, the alert employer needs to look at the degree (by no means are all master's degrees from LIS programs the "equivalent" of an MLS), the program, and the program's curriculum—all of which is more work than we are used to, or should be asked to do.

It is difficult to imagine the American Medical Association accrediting a medical school that allowed its graduates to become doctors without having studied surgery. It is equally difficult to imagine the American Bar Association looking with approval on a law school that neither taught nor intended to teach constitutional law. Why, then, is no one puzzled by ALA's acceptance of master's programs that do not require their graduates to have more than the most elementary knowledge of, for example, cataloguing? What is the point of a list of core competences if there is no mechanism to ensure that they are taught in library programs and that their graduates possess them on graduation?

Accreditation is in crisis in other ways. Library schools have died, faded away, or become something else. Others are perennially said to be on the verge of leaving the accreditation process. This is generally assumed to be a very bad thing and library education to be on the verge of suffering mortal wounds. It may well be, but not because of high-profile defections. After all, an earlier crisis in library education was supposed to be fatal because fifteen library schools folded between 1978 and 1993—including the famous examples of Columbia and Chicago. They are much missed, but life goes on and what ails today's library schools has little to do with the absence of those fifteen schools. My guess is that the same would apply if the soi-disant I-schools walked the information science plank. The key issue for them would be the employment prospects of their graduates who wish to work in libraries. Perhaps there will be none such and the defectors will, like Berkeley, cease to be LIS schools in fact as well as in name. On the other hand, I do hope that a "library program" that walked away from accreditation would not expect its graduates to be considered for jobs for which an "MLS (or equivalent) from an ALA-accredited program" is a requirement.

Another problem with accreditation today is the perception that the Committee on Accreditation (COA) carries out its work inconsistently and in the shadows.

Control of professional education is at the heart of professional identity and remains the connection between practitioners and educators. Our lack of it leaves us ailing, weak, and confused. Few librarians really understand the accreditation process, but they do understand its effect on new colleagues (and the lack of new colleagues). If the system collapsed or was outsourced or just faded away, where would we be? In that dread future, we would find ourselves trying to weigh the suitability of a person with an "MLS" from the Jack Daniels School of Information Economics against that of someone with a "master's of information management" from the Millard Fillmore College's School of Library and Media Center Studies. In a world in which no program is accredited, *all* programs are accredited. That is why our stewardship of our profession must revivify library education by

- insisting on education in the core of our profession and the necessary penumbral skills and knowledge;
- creating a core curriculum;
- accrediting MLS (or equivalent) programs on the basis of how well they teach that core curriculum; and
- ensuring that the accreditation process is firmly in the hands of ALA and is carried out by a radically reformed successor to the ALA Committee on Accreditation in an explicit, standardized, clearly understood, and overt manner.

BEING A GOOD STEWARD

If we are to succeed, individually and collectively, as stewards of the human record and our profession, we will do three things:

- Ensure that future generations know what we know by designing and implementing effective collaborative schemes to preserve recorded knowledge and information, irrespective of format. In particular, resolve the problem of controlling and preserving significant digital resources.

- Do good work and earn the trust and respect of the communities we serve.
- Revive, strengthen, and maintain library education by defining our profession, ensuring that LIS master's programs educate new librarians according to an agreed core curriculum, and devising an effective and fair accreditation system controlled by ALA.

NOTES

1. "The written word remains."
2. Bible. New Testament. Gospel of Luke, 16:1–13.
3. Shera, Jess H. "Apologia pro vita nostra." *In* Shera's *Knowing books and men: knowing computers too.* Littleton, Colo.: Libraries Unlimited, 1973. page 120.
4. Quoted in Eisenstein, Elizabeth. *The printing press as an agent of change,* volume 1. Cambridge: Cambridge University Press, 1979. pages 115–116.
5. Johns, Adrian. *The nature of the book.* Chicago: University of Chicago Press, 1998.
6. Kehr, Dave. "Film riches—cleaned up for prosperity" *New York times* (October 15, 2010) page C2.
7. See, for example, the University of North Carolina SILS Microform Digitization website: www.microfilmdigitization.com/about.html (consulted August 22, 2014).
8. Fitzgerald, Frances. *America revised: history schoolbooks in the twentieth century.* Boston: Little, Brown, 1979.
9. "MLA Statement on the Significance of Primary Records." *In* Profession 95. New York: MLA, 1995. pages 27–28.
10. Finks, Lee W. "Values without shame." *American libraries* (April 1989) pages 352–356.
11. Hildenbrand, Suzanne. "The information age versus gender equity?" *Library trends,* volume 47, number 4 (spring 1999) pages 669–681.
12. American Library Association. *Core competences of librarians* (adopted January 2009). www.ala.org/educationcareers/careers/corecomp/corecompetences (consulted August 22, 2014).
13. Houser, Lloyd. "A conceptual analysis of information science." *Library and information science research,* volume 10 (January 1988) pages 3–34.
14. See: American Library Association. "Standards, process, policies, and procedures." www.ala.org/accreditedprograms/standards (consulted August 22, 2014).

CHAPTER 6

SERVICE

The service culture, soft-edged and traditional, represents the historical culture of librarianship, carrying with it our traditional social commitment and service responsibility. By contrast, the entrepreneurial infotech culture is future-oriented, scientific, material, and hard-nosed. The first is linked to personal service, the second to impersonal technology. The first is linked to free access to information, the second to information as a commodity. The first is squarely in the public sector, the second works closely with or is situated in the corporate sector. The first is feminine and the second is masculine.

—Sheila Bertram and Hope Olson[1]

WHAT IS THE MEANING OF SERVICE?

"Service" is a complex word with many meanings and nuances within meanings. For example, *Webster's Third* contains twenty main definitions of the word "service"—most with a number of subdefinitions.[2] The definitions that best express my interpretation of service are

- duty done or required;
- professional or other useful ministrations; and
- effort inspired by philanthropic motives or dedicated to human welfare or betterment.

Read those last few words carefully. They sum up the ethos, motivation, and goals of our profession. In doing so, they tell us that a profession based on service is altruistic at its heart. A librarian's mission is to serve individuals and, in doing so, to serve society and humanity as a whole.

THE RELATIONSHIP BETWEEN SERVICE AND LIBRARIES

Without being pious, one can state that the concept of the duty and service inspired by professional values and a desire to better humankind can be a guiding light for all librarians and library policies. It is hard to imagine a productive and effective library that is not imbued with the idea of service; it is easy to envisage a happy work life for an individual in such a library.

Librarianship is a profession defined by service. Every aspect of librarianship, every action that we take as librarians can and should be measured in terms of service. It is important to get away from the negative aspects and definitions of the word (it is unfortunate, in this respect, that the word "service" has cognates with such associations as "servile" and "servant"). Our service can be as large as a successful integration of library use with the undergraduate curriculum, or as small as a single, brief act of helpfulness to a library user. Whichever it is, the value of service can and should pervade our professional lives so that it becomes the yardstick by which we measure all our plans and projects and is the means by which we assess success or failure of all our programs. A successful library multiyear plan measures any proposed change or innovation against its impact on service to that library's users. Any such plan that ignores service will fail.

SERVICE IN ACTION

One of the most important changes in the wider economy, and one with great (not all benign) implications for society, has been the change from an industrial to a service economy. More than three-quarters of the people in the American labor force work in services; more than half of family incomes is spent on services; and good service is seen to be an important criterion in judging the effectiveness of all organizations.[3] Many things that used to be made in the developed world are now made for the developed world in less-developed countries. Insurance salespersons are more easily found than industrial workers, and communities that used to supply muscle power for a manufacturing industry are now facing the difficult transition, through retraining, to supplying service workers. In the new economy, the search for a service edge is an intense part of competition, especially when the service deals with commonly encountered goods. To put it bluntly, in the rare cases in which a company is the only supplier of a widely consumed item, cost and service are of marginal importance. The much more common situation, however, is that of competition between companies that sell similar smartphones, similar inexpensive clothing, seats in identical multiplex cinemas showing identical films for teenagers of all ages, and all the other homogenous items consumed by an increasingly homogenous society. The edge is to be found in two areas: cost and service.

It is striking that many of the most successful companies, nationally and globally, are noted for their service and attention to the individual customer. Further, that emphasis is growing as it becomes more difficult to find striking price differences in bands of company type (e.g., inexpensive apparel, chain restaurants, computer vendors).

Improvements and innovations in service in the commercial world have been achieved by two, sometimes antithetical, means—technology and human contact. Well-designed technology can lead to great increases in service and consequent customer satisfaction. The more successful enterprises in online commerce (Zappos, e-Bay, Amazon, etc.) are eloquent testimonials to technology driven service. On the other hand, technology used to replace human contact for cost-cutting reasons (e.g., electronic banking, seemingly endless multiple choice telephone systems) has, in many cases, led to a customer backlash. In those instances, customers perceived the elimination of the human factor as a loss of service and have often caused companies to reverse their strategy.

The vast majority of libraries operate in the public sector and, even when they do not, are seldom judged in terms of price. (They are increasingly subject to cost-efficiency and cost-benefit assessment, but that is different from being concerned with the unit price of services.) Of the two ways to get an edge, therefore, service is the one that applies to most of us. We, too, have to balance technology and the human factor in our drive to achieve better levels of service.

The test of service in libraries lies not in its definition or philosophical underpinnings but in our practical applications of that value. To understand those practical applications, we have to create and apply evaluative procedures. There are many ways to measure service (e.g., tallies of online use, number of reference questions answered, number of materials requests filled within two months, number of students completing formal library instruction programs) but some dimensions of service—particularly those connected with the human element—are difficult or impossible to quantify. Measuring the quantity of questions answered is infinitely easier than assessing the quality of those answers. Measuring the number of students reached in an outreach program is a cakewalk compared to assessing the outcomes of that outreach. In libraries as in all aspects of life, it is easier to count items, transactions, and so on, than to assess quality.[4] This is not to say that we should abandon the attempt to evaluate in terms of quality, but to emphasize that human-to-human transactions are, by definition, complex and multidimensional.

What is the universe of service in libraries? It is all too easy to concentrate on the service element in what most libraries used to call "public services"—reference and user services,[5] branch library service, special and subject library work. We should not forget that service may be direct or indirect, and that a service rendered indirectly is equal in importance to direct human-to-human service.

Processing Services

A technical processing operation that identifies the materials needed by library users and ensures speedy and timely accession and cataloguing (even in the debased form of metadata) to make those materials available for use is just as much in the business of service as is a busy user service point. Indirect service by technical processing is also just as involved with the human aspect of library use as is a more direct public service unit. Ensuring that library users have timely and efficient access to the materials they want is an important component of the service role of the library. So is the construction of user-friendly bibliographic control systems that enable users to locate the resources they need. In the past, it was too easy for bibliographic control work and systems work to become ends in themselves, without regard for the users of catalogues, other finding tools, and online systems—thus leading to the stereotypes of the rule-obsessed and usually reclusive cataloguer and the technology-obsessed library techie. I am certain that, for a variety of reasons, those attitudes are fading and user-friendly systems are becoming commonplace, as are service-oriented procedures in processing and systems. The service rendered by technical processing and systems units includes the following:

- selecting appropriate resources
- working with materials vendors to establish plans to ensure the speedy delivery of needed items, both classes of material and individual orders
- establishing contracts for continuing access to online and e-resources
- cataloguing and classifying materials using national and international standards to make them accessible to library users
- building and maintaining local catalogues and contributing quality bibliographic data to regional, national, and other shared databases
- contributing to the design and implementation of advanced, user-friendly online systems that integrate access to the whole range of resources

Given these necessary contributions to user service, it is especially regrettable that library administrators who know the cost of everything and the value of nothing are busily dismantling cataloguing departments, trusting in the chimera of keyword searching while increasing the funding of bloated IT departments. This is like a botanical garden ceasing to buy seeds and plants and spending the money they "save" on shovels and hoes.

The Service Encounter

The human service encounter is at the heart of every service. Everything flows from it. A service encounter is an event at which a user of service interacts with a service provider and a commodity (tangible or linguistic) is exchanged. Service encounters are rich and complex, involving personalities, perceptions, value judgments, verbal and nonverbal communications, and, above all, the ability of the humans involved to reach an understanding of the requirements of the user and to match the service required with those requirements.[6]

Just as in a commercial service enterprise, it is easier for the library user to see the direct service element than to discern the many activities of those in back rooms. It is easier to grasp the service dimension of public services than it is almost any other library activity. Though those services have expanded beyond "the person at the reference desk" and may take place in person or online, they still maintain that vital component of human interaction—that moment of truth—at the center of their service, however, wherever, and whenever that service encounter takes place.

One text contains a service matrix of which the axes are willingness/unwillingness to serve and ability/inability to serve, leading to four categories of service personnel: those who are willing and able; those who are willing but unable; those who are able but unwilling; and those who are unwilling and unable.[7] Good management is aimed at getting all personnel into the first category and discovering, as a preliminary to retraining and reorientation, why the negative characteristics of those in the other three categories exist. This is vitally important as the person delivering a service represents the whole entity (the service provider), and the provider (the library in this case) is judged by the qualities, positive and negative, of that person.

As has been shown in many department stores, banks, travel agencies, and other commercial concerns, people in need of assistance want the person from whom they seek help to be

- approachable,
- knowledgeable, and
- comprehensible.

Approachability does not involve the mindless friendliness of the "Hi, you guys" and "Have a nice day" variety, but it is seriously compromised by a grim or arrogant demeanor. The very furniture and layout of a service area can influence whether library users use the service that is offered. The stereotype of the drearily aloof librarian behind a high desk looking down on enquirers is potent precisely because it matches the secret fears (and, alas, experience in some cases) of library users. One should never forget the fact that asking a question (in person or online) involves a major vulnerability—

the fear of being judged to be stupid. Another factor in approachability is simple presence. Is an initial question posed online answered promptly? Is there always someone at the service point? How long does the library user have to wait before asking his question? How busy does the librarian appear to be when approached? How genuinely friendly is the response from the librarian? How good is the librarian at dealing with people of different ages, ethnicities, educational levels, and so on with the same level of courtesy and dignity? It is difficult, though by no means impossible, to use these and similar questions as part of the assessment of the service encounters in your library. Another potent approach to evaluation is simply to put yourself in the place of the library user and ask, which characteristics would you like to see as a user of this service?

Being *knowledgeable* is obviously a minimal qualification for a service librarian. The level of knowledge and the areas in which the librarian is knowledgeable are most important. A good service librarian knows

- the maps of the bibliographic universe provided by catalogues and classifications
- the collections in her library
- the strengths and limitations of online resources available to the library's users
- how to conduct the service encounter in person or online
- the type and quantity of information that is appropriate to the needs of the library user

There are recurring patterns in inquiry that are known to the expert service librarian. They have been summarized by the estimable author and Library of Congress reference librarian Thomas Mann as:

- patterns in the types of question that people ask, and in how they ask them
- patterns in the usually unconscious assumptions they hold about what can be done
- patterns in the bad advice they are sometimes given by teachers, employers, and colleagues
- patterns in the mistakes and omissions that reduce the efficiency of their research[8]

Mann goes on to write, "Viewed collectively, these patterns tend to suggest the areas in which most people need the most help. . . ." Though Mann lays out those patterns in a book aimed at helping individual researchers to be their own "research librarians," the patterns he describes play an important part in the service encounter and its outcomes. Skilled librarians take them into account and render their best service by complementing the problems they pose and giving the library users what they need, irrespective of how well those users have formulated those needs.

Mann was writing in the late twentieth century, and it is easy to see that conditions in which service encounters take place in libraries, the nature and quantity of those encounters, and other factors have changed. That is so; but the fact remains that service encounters—however and wherever they take place—are subject to the same human factors as they were twenty years ago and a hundred years ago and as they will be as long as librarians are facilitating human interactions with the human record.

I wrote earlier that good service librarians should be *comprehensible*. I am not referring only to their grasp of the English language—though here, as in all aspects of librarianship, the ability to communicate in clear, direct language is a decided asset. When considering the desired abilities in a reference librarian, knowledge at various levels is clearly very important, but it is also important to remember that knowledge can be negated by an inability to communicate it. Zeithaml et al. provide a definitive brief explanation of the purpose of communication in service: "Keeping customers informed in language they can understand and listening to them."[9] The important points here are the matter of using language that the service user can understand and the two-way nature of the communication. Just as the amount and type of information in an answer should be appropriate to the needs and nature of the questioner, so should the language used in answering.

A service librarian—particularly one in a large general library—is going to encounter all kinds and conditions of people. That it is imperative for librarians serving diverse populations to be able to communicate at a variety of different levels and to recognize the appropriate level to communicate in each service encounter.

The need to listen in the service encounter cannot be overstressed. All experienced librarians know that the initial question in a service encounter rarely contains all that the questioner wishes to know. Most commonly, the first question is couched in much more general terms than the person really intends. For example, the question may be "Where can I find census data?" but the intention is to discover the number of Native Americans in California. Another example is "How can I find information on budget deficits?" when the intention would be better conveyed by "I am writing a term paper on the deficits of the 1980s and would like some relevant information." Discerning the intention behind the question requires careful listening and probing—skills that the most knowledgeable may not always possess instinctively.

My former colleague Dave Tyckoson is the author of an important general article on reference published in the 1990s.[10] In it he reviewed the various alternatives to "traditional" reference desk services that had been proposed in the past fifteen years and found each of them wanting. Those alternatives include expert systems (the use of technology as a substitute for human contact); e-mail interaction; "tiered" service, in which different levels of staff categorize questions and deal with them accordingly; team staffing of reference desks; replacing immediate access to reference librarians by "appointment" systems; and eliminating reference service altogether. Tyckoson dissected each of these solutions and found them wanting, the last coming in for some justifiably harsh criticism involving, as it does, drivel about "access engineers," "knowledge cartography," and the former reference librarian as market researcher.[11] His conclusion was that the only thing that was wrong with reference service carried out by means of the human-to-human reference encounter is that it was underfunded and undersupported.

It seems to me that Tyckoson's analysis still stands, with the single and significant exception of online reference (through "chat," e-mail, instant messaging, etc.), which has benefited from technological and other developments not present when his article was written. It should be noted that this positive online development still rests on the requirements for all human service interactions being met. See, for example, the study of "query clarification" on online chat reference service by Radford and others,[12] which, in essence, refers to the same issues of communication that arose when face-to-face interactions were the only service encounters.

Service librarians are under stress, but that stress is not inherent to the service encounter. It is caused by overwork and doing more with less. Library administrators who wish to run libraries that function at a high level of service have to fund and support this most visible of all library services.

Comforting the Afflicted

> A service philosophy should be promoted that affords equal access to
> information for all in the academic community with no discrimination
> on the basis of race, values, gender, sexual orientation, cultural or ethnic
> background, physical or learning disability, economic status, religious
> beliefs, or views.[13]

Perhaps the most obvious manifestation of the altruistic service ethic that
pervades librarianship is our historic mission to help everybody, but especially the poor, societally disadvantaged, and powerless. In all kinds of
libraries, you can, should, and must see a concentration on service to those
who need it most.

Knowing the Library User

It is an axiom in business that, in order to succeed, a company must have,
identify, and maintain a customer base and provide the services those people want and need. For that reason, most companies not only do expensive
research into groups to which they wish to sell a product or service, but also
pay large sums to maintain the information in that database in order to
keep the information current. It seems easy to define the community served
by any given library: a municipality; a university community; a company;
a nation; pupils in a school; patients, nurses, and doctors in a hospital, and
so on—but that ease of definition is often illusory. Almost all libraries also
serve people who are outside their "natural" constituencies, and that phenomenon increases as libraries cooperate and create more and larger alliances. However complicated arriving at that definition may be, the definition of
the community served is essential if the library is to focus its services where
they are needed. It is also important to define a core community and peripheral communities in order to apply budgeting and service priorities to each.

Public Libraries

The primary community served by a public library is defined by political
boundaries and is funded on the basis of service to those who live in the
political entity. Except in the case of small homogenous towns and sparsely
populated rural counties, a public library will serve a wide range of people

and differing groups defined by age, income, ethnicity, language, and so on. This is complicated further because, in addition to service to library users who live in the community served, modern public libraries have other users. Almost invariably, cities today are surrounded by separate political entities (suburban communities) that house large numbers of people who work in those cities and use their public libraries. Most public libraries are involved in cooperative arrangements that facilitate mutual acceptance of library privileges from other public libraries, interlibrary loan, cooperative purchase of online services and databases, and other means for users of other libraries to use their services and resources. All the groups—within and without the political entity that funds the public library—have to be taken into account in formulating a service plan, including the priorities assigned to each group.

The heaviest users of public libraries are the young and poorer senior citizens—the least powerful groups in our society. As described in chapter 4, public libraries were created in the nineteenth century for the poor and, in many cases, evolved into "the people's universities"—the means for poor people to escape the bondage of poverty through self-education. In addition to the users in the library's buildings, public libraries have often reached out beyond their walls to provide services to the housebound and the incarcerated and to those in remote areas by means of mobile libraries. Bringing library services to the sick and the lonely and the desperate is another demonstration of higher levels of service. Almost all communities prize the children's library and its services above all other programs offered by the public library.[14] It is important in this context to note that children share with the poor and the old the characteristic of less mobility than other groups (the least mobile are poor children and poor old people). A number of libraries have successful outreach programs for both groups because of that lack of mobility.[15] If service to children is a political and moral priority, the funding argument that rages in many places about local versus centralized public library service should be heavily weighted in favor of local service.

Academic Libraries

Libraries that serve higher education at all levels—community colleges, liberal arts colleges, universities—almost always have a defined service community on which they concentrate. That community may be central;

but it does not include all those served by those academic libraries. To begin with—and especially for publicly supported institutions—there is also the population in the wider community: the "town." Colleges and universities, particularly large institutions in small towns ("college towns" such as Urbana, Ill.; Bloomington, Ind.; and Ithaca, N.Y.), are a major cultural, political, and societal presence in their communities. They cannot, even if they wish, stand aside from the community and neither can the academic library. Publicly and privately supported institutions that hold depository collections of federal and state documents are obliged by law to make those collections available to any member of the public. Publicly supported institutions cannot deny access to their facilities to taxpayers and their families. They may withhold access to certain library services—borrowing privileges, interlibrary loan services, access to online databases—that they offer to their students and faculty, but they may not or cannot withhold other services and access.

On a mundane—though important—level, we should note that few academic libraries are funded to provide services or to persons who are not members of the academic community. Those users from outside that community cannot easily be persuaded that they are not entitled to the use of facilities and services that are largely paid for with tax revenues. Nor would it be in the political or moral interest of the academic library and its institution either to make that case or to act on it. To take a common example, many urban academic libraries are used heavily by high school students, particularly in the evenings and on weekends. There are numerous instances of librarians in those libraries reporting that they are inundated by requests for assistance from high school students, sometimes to the detriment of the service they give to "their" students. Similarly, many public terminals in those libraries are used in the evenings and on weekends by high school students trying to meet assignment deadlines. Not a penny of the library's funding is based on the provision of reference service to, or terminals for the use of, high school students. However, state universities and colleges that seek to recruit high-quality students have a particular interest in encouraging the kind of student who is diligent or intellectually curious enough to pursue an assignment in an academic library. On the one hand, the library is being asked to provide services for which it is not funded. On the other hand, the library is serving the educational goals of the high school students and the institution by providing those services. The answer, I believe, is a more imaginative approach to cooperation and funding for mutual benefit among all educational levels. Is there any reason *in principle* for opposing an integrated approach to funding library services for students from kindergarten through graduate school using state and local funding sources? Is there any reason *in principle* why public, school, and academic libraries in a community should not integrate their funding in search of maximizing the total library service for that community? The answer to both questions is no, but that does not explain away the enormous number of practical and bureaucratic obstacles to such a service-oriented approach.

Academic libraries spend a large and increasing amount of money on online and human-to-human library instruction—a service that, by definition, disproportionately benefits disadvantaged students. The reason for the latter is very simple. There are three broad classes of entrants to state universities: high school graduates, community college transfers, and "re-entry" students. The high school graduates that need library instruction most are those from deprived backgrounds, because the current method of financing public education means that the better schools are found in rich neighborhoods and the poorer schools in poor neighborhoods—the latter containing higher numbers of minority students. A high proportion of community college attendees are from the less-wealthy population (because of the far lower fees those colleges charge). "Re-entry" students are those adults who return to college, usually with the objective of improving their job prospects after they have been divorced or downsized or have undergone some other life-changing experience. Such library skills as they have are likely to be outmoded. All three groups add up to substantial numbers of people who really need library instruction to empower them to profit from higher education. I would suggest that one could not find a better expression of the service ethic than bringing familiarity with the human record and how to use it effectively to those who really need it.

School Libraries

School librarians have a well-defined primary clientele: the children and young adults learning in the school the library serves. They have an important role in education, standing in the same relation to the school that the academic library does to the university or college. Their role is to provide another dimension complementing classroom instruction in giving access to recorded knowledge and information in all formats. They also have a strong instructional role—teaching young people how to use libraries and, even more important, helping in literacy teaching and the acquiring of a love of reading and learning. These heavy tasks require a variety of professional skills combined with dedication and empathy. The fact is that they are too often exercised in environments lacking necessary resources.

One of the sadder manifestations of the "crisis" in public education has been the decline of the school library in many states. When budget cuts hit, school administrators cut those functions that they regard as less essential. Given the hype about the "age of information," it is easy to see that such administrators, clutching at technological straws, class libraries (and the space they occupy—important to the distressing number of space-strapped schools) as "inessential," together with the arts, music, and other intangible benefits that are undervalued in a materialistic age. Just consider the Los Angeles public school system. It is reported that, in 2014, 87 percent of schools in that system have no credentialed librarian and half of the schools that have libraries have no trained staff of any kind to run them. This in a system that is continuing to pour money into an iPad program that has already cost more than a *billion* dollars.[16] This is but one particularly egregious example among far too many across the country.

Far from being inessential, school libraries and school librarians are vital to education, not least because they can be—and are—the basis for literacy and lifelong learning. Does anyone doubt that today's lower levels of young people's proficiency in reading and writing are linked to the underfunding of school libraries and their services? Even when schools have maintained their "libraries," they have often done away with their librarians. A "library" without professional assistance is just a room with books and other resources in it—not much of an advance on no library at all. If we want strong public education—something that even its severest critics favor (at least nominally)—and believe it to be a mainstay of democracy, we must support and encourage strong school libraries and our colleagues who work in them.

Companies and Institutions

There are many types of for-profit and nonprofit concern—from museums to research laboratories to software companies to foundations to law firms to auto manufacturers—that possess libraries. Those libraries are as various as the organizations they serve, and their services are tailored to particular clienteles. It is relatively simple for the librarians of those libraries to define their user groups and their mission. It is also relatively easy to gauge the success or otherwise of the service they offer. Because many special libraries are in for-profit entities and because their users are so clearly defined, it is not surprising that special libraries have been leaders in innovation in librarianship and the use of technology. This has benefited the profession as a whole as those innovations have often been transferable to libraries with more diffuse missions and user groups.

Other Kinds of Library

Some of the most rewarding and demanding jobs and opportunities to serve available to librarians are found in hospitals, hospices, retirement homes, and prisons. Without library values (particularly that of service), work in such libraries would be difficult if not impossible, and the difficulties of the users of those libraries would overwhelm the librarians who work in them. In some cases, the local public library is responsible for library service to the ill, the institutionalized, and the incarcerated. In many others, the library is part of the institution itself. Reading and other library services can be consolations and blessings to all of us; how much more are they consolations and blessings to those in extreme circumstances? Those who are ill or alone treasure reading matter that will take them out of themselves, that will provide insight into their condition and the human condition, and that will enable them to pass the days. Those who are imprisoned (vastly too many in the United States today) read for those purposes, too, but they also read for more practical reasons—to learn the law and to become more educated. The rate of illiteracy in the prison population is far higher than among those outside, and increasing literacy is a proven antidote to recidivism. A prison librarian can turn a life around—an awesome responsibility but one that is in the best traditions of the service ethic of our profession.

SERVICE—THE BOTTOM LINE

Libraries exist to serve their communities and society as a whole. Librarianship is suffused with the idea of service. It is very important that we continue to seek innovation in service, from any source we can. It is equally important that our service be informed with humanistic values as opposed to materialistic values. Business practices may well offer us some good ideas and approaches, but they should be used and adapted with caution. Our work is to serve the individual, groups of individuals, communities, and society, acting idealistically in a materialistic age. Those ideals, though, need to take reality into account—no one is served by impractical goals and visions divorced from reality.

NOTES

1. Bertram, Sheila and Olson, Hope. "Culture clash." *Library journal*, volume 121, issue 17 (October 1996) pages 36–37.
2. Webster's *Third new international dictionary*.
3. Gutek, Barbara A. *The dynamics of service*. San Francisco: Jossey-Bass, 1995.
4. Baker, Sharon L. and Lancaster, F. Wilfrid. *The measurement and evaluation of library services*, second edition. Arlington, Va.: Information Resources Press, 1991.
5. Some libraries seem to be in a contest to come up with the most inane substitute for "reference librarian." My least favorite is "interpretive services librarian," which summons nothing so much as a vision of white-faced mimes.
6. See: Ventola, Eija. "Revisiting service encounter genre: some reflections." *Folia linguistica*, volume 39, issues 1–2, pages 19–43.
7. Zeithaml, Valarie A., et al., *Delivering quality service*. New York: Free Press, 1990. page 136.
8. Mann, Thomas. *The Oxford guide to library research*. New York: Oxford University Press, 1998. pages xvii-xviii.
9. Zeithaml, *Delivering quality service*. page 22.
10. Tyckoson, David. "What's right with reference." *American libraries*, volume 30, number 5 (May 1999) pages 57–63. The article is a response to: Miller, Bill. "What's wrong with reference: coping with success and failure at the reference desk." *American libraries*, volume 15, number 5 (May 1984) pages 303–306; 321–322.
11. Campbell, Jerry. "Shaking the conceptual foundations of reference." *Reference services review*, volume 20, number 4 (Winter 1992) pages 29–36.
12. Radford, Marie L., et al. "Are we getting warmer?" *Reference & user services quarterly*, volume 50, number 3 (Spring 2011) pages 259–279.

13. Association of College and Research Libraries. "Intellectual freedom principles of academic libraries." *Principle* 10 (June 1999). www.ala.org/Template .cfm?Section=interpretations&Template=/ContentManagement/ContentDisplay .cfm&ContentID=8551 (consulted August 25, 2014).

14. *Buildings, books, and bytes.* Issued by the Benton Foundation. Washington, DC: 1996. The report states that children's services were by far the most valued library service by the focus group they assembled. See *Library trends*, volume 46, number 1 (Summer 1997) pages 178–223.

15. See, for example: Swell, Kim. "Beyond library walls" *Children & libraries: The journal of the Association for Library Service to Children*, volume 10, issue 1 (Spring 2012) pages 27–29.

16. Hing, Julianne. *The nation*, February 10, 2014. page 6.

CHAPTER 7

INTELLECTUAL FREEDOM

WHAT IS THE MEANING OF INTELLECTUAL FREEDOM?

The phrase "intellectual freedom" is widely used to describe the state of affairs in which each human being has the freedom to think, say, write, and promulgate any idea or belief. In the United States, that freedom is protected by the First Amendment to the Constitution, which states, in part, "Congress shall make no law respecting an establishment of religion or prohibiting the free exercise thereof; or abridging the freedom of speech, or of the press." There is, of course, no such thing as an absolute freedom outside the pages of fiction and utopian writings; for that reason, intellectual freedom is constrained by law in every jurisdiction. Here the initial and simple concept becomes tricky because, of course, there are just laws and unjust laws, and to put it simply, times and opinions change.

Over the centuries, laws have banned certain kinds of political, social, sexual, literary, and religious expression. To complicate matters, some of those laws have been at the national level, some at the state level, and some at the local level, and they have often been at variance each with the other. Over the centuries, one or more of blasphemy (divergent views on religious doctrines), sedition (expression of views in opposition to governments), and obscenity (unlawful sexual expression) has been the target of government restriction. It seems that, today in the United States, only sexual expression deemed to be "obscene" is banned by law and—theoretically, at least—all political, literary, social, and religious expression is free of government restraint. It does not help that "obscenity" has never been defined clearly and hence has been ruled to be a matter of local mores and values, so that something that circulates freely in Greenwich Village may be forbidden in a small rural California community.

WHAT IS THE RELATION BETWEEN INTELLECTUAL FREEDOM AND LIBRARIES?

It is noteworthy that the American Library Association has never defined "intellectual freedom," particularly given the existence of ALA's Office of Intellectual Freedom (reason, in and of itself, to be a member of ALA) and given the fact that ALA has made many statements and taken many positions on many aspects of the topic. The most concise statement on the topic is to be found in the Association's *Intellectual Freedom Manual*:

> The First and Fourth Amendments to the U.S. Constitution are integral to American librarianship. They are the basis of the concept librarians call intellectual freedom. Intellectual freedom accords to all library users the right to seek and receive information on all subjects from all points of view without restriction and without having the subject of one's interest examined or scrutinized by others.[1]

For libraries, intellectual freedom begins with opposition to censorship of books and other library materials—hence the activities and publications centered on the annual Banned Books Week. From there the topic expands to include ALA's stand on the library user's right to gain access to all library materials, which, in turn, is connected to the librarian's duty to make all library materials available to everyone. The librarian not only has a duty to library users but also has rights that are personal to her or him. Those rights include—but are not limited to—freedom of expression, the democratic process in the workplace, and the right to pursue any chosen lifestyle. Related to all this is the concept of the library as an advocate of intellectual freedom. That notion is not without elements of controversy, because it sets up the clash between those who believe in advocacy and the minority who think that the library should be neutral in all social conflicts—including those that relate to the First Amendment.

It can readily be seen that intellectual freedom begins as a question of a basic and, to many, inalienable human right that is opposed in principle only by those who do not believe in social equality and democracy; but it soon leaves that relatively simple field of argument. The fact is that many quarrels about intellectual freedom are not between those who are for it and those who are against it. They are often between people who believe in different applications of intellectual freedom, while all professing to be for it. There are those who are "absolutists" and would deny no one the right to create, disseminate, say, see, or read anything at all. There are those who agree broadly with that notion, but would restrict access to certain materials by certain groups—for example, children. There are also those who use the "protection of children" as a stalking horse for their comprehensive censoring agenda. Therefore, in considering intellectual freedom issues, we should always be aware that we are not dealing with good and evil—though both may well be present—but with a complexity of views, many of which are sincerely held. After all, the debate over "protecting" children from the evils of cyberspace is about what is best for children. Some may believe that the intellectual development that comes from free access to all recorded knowledge and information is worth the risks. Others wish to shelter their children from unpleasant reality. Even the absolutist will admit that cyberspace can be a very unpleasant place. Yet others wish to restrict the reading and viewing habits of all children, including those for which they have no direct responsibility.

Librarians believe in intellectual freedom because it is as natural to us, and as necessary to us, as the air that we breathe. Censorship is anathema to us because it inhibits arbitrarily our role in life—to make the recorded knowledge and information of humankind freely available to everyone, regardless of faith or the lack of it, ethnicity, gender, age, or any other of the categories that divide us one from the other. I strongly believe we should hold fast to intellectual freedom and carry out our tasks without reference to our own opinions or the opinions of those who want to restrict free access to knowledge. I used to be an academic librarian, and, as such, was comparatively better off than fellow librarians in other areas. After all, academic librarians work in institutions that are overwhelmingly dedicated (in principle if not always in action) to the idea of academic freedom; tend to work for people who share that ethic; and are usually not professionally isolated. Compare that context to the lonely battles that are fought by librarians in small, rural public libraries and by solitary school librarians battling obscurantist school boards. If you look at the lists of challenged and banned books that are issued each year, you will see that those are the people in the front lines. All the more reason to support our library associations' offices of intellectual freedom in the great work they do on our behalf to protect this most important professional value.

INTELLECTUAL FREEDOM IN ACTION

Most library associations and related professional bodies have a statement on intellectual freedom that exhorts their members to apply the concept of intellectual freedom in all the activities of the library. One of the best of these is the Canadian Library Association's statement, which reads:

- All persons in Canada have the fundamental right, as embodied in the nation's Bill of Rights and the Canadian Charter of Rights and Freedoms, to have access to all expressions of knowledge, creativity and intellectual activity, and to express their thoughts publicly. This right to intellectual freedom, under the law, is essential to the health and development of Canadian society.
- Libraries have a basic responsibility for the development and maintenance of intellectual freedom.
- It is the responsibility of libraries to guarantee and facilitate access to all expressions of knowledge and intellectual activity, including those which some elements of society may consider to be unconventional, unpopular or unacceptable. To this end, libraries shall acquire and make available the widest variety of materials.
- It is the responsibility of libraries to guarantee the right of free expression by making available all the library's public facilities and services to all individuals and groups who need them.
- Libraries should resist all efforts to limit the exercise of these responsibilities while recognizing the right of criticism by individuals and groups.

- Both employees and employers in libraries have a duty, in addition to their institutional responsibilities, to uphold these principles.[2]

I have pointed out previously that intellectual freedom is a complex matter with many dimensions. In practical application in libraries, the use of even the CLA's innocent seeming admonitions can and do create problems. There are no problems for the absolutist and the censor, of course. The first would allow everybody to have access to everything. The latter would choose what is made available and to whom, based entirely on individual preferences and convictions. For the rest of us, the world is infinitely more complex and one to be negotiated in the light of both principle and practicalities. Here are some real cases:

- A school board orders two novels on contemporary Latino life to be withdrawn from a class reading list and limits their availability in the school library.
- A public library board is taken over by an organized group of conservative evangelicals that orders filtering software to be installed on all library public terminals used to give online access for both adults and children.
- A group of citizens calls for a nineteenth-century work of literature to be withdrawn from the library because of race-insensitive terminology.
- A religious group donates copies of its publications and then cries "censorship" when they are deemed outside the scope of the collection and not added to the shelves.
- An anarchist group wants to meet monthly in a public meeting room in the library and display publications calling for militant opposition to the government.

Suppose that your work life, job, and even career may depend on how you deal with these issues. This is the point at which one might well see a clash of values. There is the value of intellectual freedom in the first instance, but there is also the value of service to a community. You will notice that most of these real-life examples occurred in small towns, school districts, and public library systems. A person who genuinely believes (and with good reason) that she is personally important to the health of library services in a small community may well feel inclined to make small accommodations to the forces pressing on her in order to preserve the greater good of the library and its users. If you are inclined to decry those small accommodations, please weigh your own circumstances against those of the librarian in question. Please also consider the value of taking a stand against the value of a useful, productive career. Let us also consider this practical question: If the librarian in these cases stands on her principles and is fired, whom do you think the people who fired her will hire? Do you think it would be another First Amendment absolutist? I will yield to no one in my admiration for those who take the moral high ground and I would never advocate a spineless truckling to power, but I do want to make the following fundamental points. Life is never as uncomplicated as it appears from a distance. Small sacrifices may well, on occasion, benefit the majority of library users. One does not have to be perfect to be able to live with one's conscience.

FIGHTING ONLINE EVILS

The American Library Association and the Freedom to Read Foundation have been waging the just war against censorship for many decades. They have stood for freedom of access to recorded knowledge and information for everyone, without regard to their age, gender, ethnicity, religion, or any other distinguishing characteristic. Many of the battles fought by ALA and its members center on the relatively simple (and constitutionally protected) issues of the freedom of the press. It says it right there in the First Amendment, and, though some can and do argue that there should be limits on what you can print and read, the overall issue is very clear to most Americans, and, if only in the long run, the good guys usually win. If only the Founding Fathers had the prescience to include "online freedom."

When you think of all the battles waged over freedom of the press, banned books, and censorship in the print age, it is not difficult to believe that we may come to look back nostalgically on that time because of the appalling complexities introduced by digital resources of all kinds. Despite the digital divide, almost the entire country has the ability to gain access to online resources. Schoolrooms and public libraries contain computer terminals and give Wi-Fi access more or less as a matter of course. Many children have ready access to smartphones and tablets. The widespread use of cyberspace is surpassed only by hype about all-digital futures. The world is awash in online information, misinformation, disinformation, opinion, vituperation, tweeting, trolling, and solipsistic disquisitions. The products of established journalistic sources and scholars jostle with those of pornographers, spinners, bloggers, basement-dwellers, mountebanks, fraudsters, and hucksters.

It is hardly surprising, therefore, that those who favor censorship in general are much exercised about cyberspace and advocate measures to prevent unlimited access to those resources, particularly by children and young adults. It is difficult, when the censorious winds blow so hard, to step back and have some historical insight, but it is well worth doing. Almost every new means of communication in the past century and a half has been greeted as being, in itself, an assault on the morals of the nation, particularly the young. (I write "almost" because I cannot recall newspaper stories about microfilms destroying the morals of the young.) Just think of the havoc that silent and pre-Code talking pictures wrought on the flappers; the awful toll on the morals of young, unmarried people dancing to gramophone records; the "howling wilderness" of television; and the modem evils of misogynistic gangsta rap and movies that drive children to homicidal mania. There was even a popular book in the 1950s that denounced the corrosive effect of the "hidden messages" contained in comic books[3] (the same comic books that now supply the screenplays of half of the Hollywood movies made today). Violent movies are not new, but pervasive online access is, and librarians have to deal with hyped-up attacks on online resources and those who give access to them. In the words of one commentator, "Children have always looked for forbidden books, magazines, and other media, and guardians of public morals have often blamed such sources for a decline in juvenile behavior."[4]

Let us face an important fact. When censors and filterers talk about "culture" and "moral decay," they mean the dreadful duo: sex and violence. Those, too, are nuanced. To some people, any depiction of, or writing about, sex is offensive. To others, it is only images and writing about sexual variations that offends. Then there is the Tarantino Problem—which, stated succinctly, is: If violent images are harmful, why is the violence in Quentin Tarantino's films acceptable? Because Tarantino is a cult director? Surely, the example of violence in a critically acclaimed film is as harmful as the violence of a trashy videogame. If it is not, then the often advanced "cause and effect" argument is confounded or, at least, shown as the unbearable complexity it is.

Every "threat" posed by a new means of communication has been met by calls for legislation to make the world—especially children—safe from the perceived iniquity. The federal Children's Internet Protection Act (CIPA) and Neighborhood Children's Internet Protection Act (NCIPA) went into effect in 2004 and 2002 respectively. They both mandate filters to block "visual depictions" that are obscene (as defined by law), are child pornography (as defined by law), and are "harmful to minors" (persons who are not yet 17) in that the depiction:

A. taken as a whole and with respect to minors, appeals to a prurient interest in nudity, sex, or excretion;
B. depicts, describes, or represents in a patently offensive way with respect to what is suitable for minors, an actual or simulated sexual act or sexual contact, actual or simulated normal or perverted sexual acts, or a lewd exhibition of the genitals; and
C. taken as a whole, lacks serious literary, artistic, political, or scientific value as to minors.

Failure to abide by the prescription to install filters that block such depictions is punished by withdrawal of federal money available through the Library Services and Technology Act, Title III of the Elementary and Secondary Education Act, and on the Universal Service discount program known as the E-rate (Public Law 106–554).

Thus we have moral panic enshrined in a law written in language that a country lawyer could take apart in seconds. Let us disregard for the moment that children and minors have First Amendment rights—and all filters will block constitutionally protected speech for minors, as well as potentially block that speech for adults—to contemplate, for the moment, a mind-set that thinks sixteen-year-olds need protection from having an interest in nudity and sex—an interest that legislators call "prurient" but that will seem to most to be both inevitable and normal. The filters mandated by these laws are devices as ineffective as they are philosophically offensive.

Before going on to discuss filters as such, let us see what they are designed to achieve. The central concern of those who genuinely wish to protect children (as opposed to lifelong censors who are using the Internet as the latest weapon to achieve their social aims) is that children may see or read images and texts that are morally harmful. It is very easy to find stuff online, advertently or inadvertently, that is aesthetically repulsive, inherently sordid, or exploitative of humans. None of those constitutes an offense to morality—unless, that is, you believe that your own morality is or should be universal. The latter is only acceptable to those who use statements beginning "The American people believe . . . ," thinking that they are equipped to decide what the majority of this vast, diverse nation believes on every issue. I do not eat meat. Pictures of factory farms and of meat being cooked are repulsive to me. Does that mean that I should do everything in my power to stop others (who may or may not eat meat) from seeing those pictures? That may seem absurd, but is it really any more absurd than me seeking to stop people from seeing pictures of people engaged in sexual variations that do not appeal to me?

Then there is the question of the assumed superiority of those who would censor. The idea is that such people can read texts or view images that will have no effect on them but will be "harmful" to other, presumably more suggestible, people. Someone once defined a censor as someone who does not want you to know or read what he knows or has read. Could it be that the effects of texts and images on the individual psyche are simply incalculable—as unpredictable as any other effect on individual behavior? Anyone who is honest with herself will acknowledge that some sexual or violent images and texts stay in the mind for years and exercise power over that mind. These are images and texts that have been ignored or forgotten in minutes by millions of viewers and readers but, for some reason, hold sway in one mind for a lifetime. It is difficult for me to believe that online violent or sexual images do much good to anyone, but it is equally difficult to imagine that they do much harm either. Millions of people around the world have watched the horrific violence of many mainstream Hollywood movies, but the worst that happened to 99.999 percent of them was that they wasted their time.

Japanese popular culture is saturated with vividly violent and searingly sexual images and texts—manifest, among other places, online. Japan's level of violence is lower by many magnitudes than the level of violence in the United States. Further, there is no evidence at all that sexual mores in Japan are inferior to those in the United States. What does that tell us? First, that Japanese society and culture are very different from the society and culture of the United States. However, it also tells us that exposure to violent and sexual images and texts is not a determining factor for the nature of a society. Denmark and the Netherlands are well known for their permissive attitudes toward, among other things, sexual writings and images. Is there anyone who would seriously argue that Danes and the Dutch are morally inferior, as a whole, to American people? Well, yes—those who think that sexual writings and images are inherently wrong. In other words, the argument has turned in on itself, and we are no longer discussing the "harm" that is alleged to be done, but the imposition of one morality on those who may or may not share it.

Children and Adolescents

ALA has rendered itself unpopular with a vocal minority by stating a constitutional fact: children and young adults share the First Amendment rights of those over age eighteen. (One would have thought this might be obvious in states in which, under certain conditions, people can marry at age sixteen.) Even if you believe that viewing and reading can harm those under eighteen, you still have to come to terms with the necessity of abridging those rights in order to prevent that "harm." That being so, it seems to me that it is important to define that harm and gauge its extent. There have been thousands of studies of the effects of television watching on children. (Television watching and online use are very similar activities, though the latter seems different because of its potential for interactivity—despite the fact that most online use is as passive as television viewing—and because it is the newer, "hotter" medium.) Many of the studies reinforce the obvious—that spending many hours a day watching programs with little intellectual content and social value is not good for the minds and bodies of children. Some seek to show that watching programs with sexual or violent content can do psychological harm. The evidence for the latter is much less conclusive. Many researchers believe that there is no direct and strong correlation between acts of violence and watching acts of violence on television and that television programs are a minor part of a web of social factors that lead to antisocial behavior by some children. "On balance, it seems likely that any relationship that may exist between watching television violence and perpetrating actual violence is likely to be a complex one, and a number of contributing factors must be considered."[5] In addition, it appears that children are more affected by the violence they see in news programs than in fictional representations of violence.[6] There are numerous studies of the effects on children and adolescents of violence in online music videos and video-games. They do not add up to a consensus on the nature of the harm or even if there is any harm.

If the connection is difficult to discern between violence on television, in videogames, or online and violence in life, how much more difficult is it to define the connection between online sex and sex on television and . . . what? Most children and adolescents are intensely interested in sex and seem to have a natural ability to cope with the level of truth about sex that is appropriate to their age. Many sexual writings, scenes, and images found online or on television are tawdry and unedifying. What else is new? Most portrayals of anything online and on television are tawdry and unedifying. No, the objection to children having access to sexual materials through modern media is the same as the decades-old objection to sexual content in books, films, and other material. It is rooted in a morality and an ideology that wishes to protect the "innocence" of children from the "corruption" of sex. It is the duty and obligation of parents to guide and advise their children in their reading and viewing habits; they—and they alone—should police those habits in the light of their own morality and convictions. I would much rather young people were reading *The joy of sex* than listening to violent rap, watching slasher movies, or playing violent videogames, but that is my morality, and I would neither seek to ban nor seek to impose anything on the basis of it.

Filter Fever

The most commonly proposed remedy to protect the young from the online ills perceived and actual ills is called "filtering." Filtering programs purport to screen out "undesirable" sites. Filtering advocates are those who wish to make those undesirable sites unavailable. They are opposed by those who claim that filtering is an unconstitutional infringement on the liberty of the individual. With all due respect, I would maintain that this enduring clash is completely irrelevant. The truth is that filtering systems do not work, and they never will work. They do not work because they are based on the same keyword searching using an uncontrolled vocabulary that gives you 648,332 "relevant hits" after an online search. Any librarian with knowledge of bibliographic control knows that controlled vocabularies and close classification are the only way to ensure precision and comprehensive recall.

The mirror image is that the only way to have filtering systems that work would be to catalogue and classify cyberspace fully. ALA is on record as opposing filtering (principally on First Amendment rather than practical grounds) and has, therefore, drawn the ire of would-be cybercensors.

The Heirs of "Dr. Laura"

"Dr. Laura" [Schlessinger], now mercifully forgotten, was a leading figure in the social atavism movement. Unlike many of the mail-order "Reverends" and "Doctors" who infest that movement, she actually had a respectable, if irrelevant to her public persona, academic background.[7] She made a minor career out of attacking ALA as "smut peddlers" and the like before her fifteen minutes of fame were up. Unfortunately, she has not lacked successors, and ALA—a body devoted, inter alia, to First Amendment rights and intellectual freedom—is still being attacked as a promoter of pornography by the ignorant and the malign (not mutually exclusive categories).

Combating Filter Fever

ALA has been staunch in its opposition to filters, but it is not easy to deal with what is, fundamentally, an irrational proposal. Of course, we need to fight this battle on philosophical and moral grounds. To quote an ALA report:

> Given increased demand and the mission to provide free and open access to information for all, libraries find that Internet filtering poses fundamental challenges to intellectual freedom. Filtering also conflicts directly with core professional values of librarians as articulated in ALA's Library Bill of Rights. As Internet filters, by design, block access to content, not only are they incompatible with library values, but for many librarians they also constitute censorship.[8]

We also need to fight filters on practical and political grounds. First, it is essential to make the point about the inutility of filters. It is certainly not difficult to demonstrate that blocking by keywords does not work. Most online users understand that keyword searching is ineffective—regular encounters with thousands of irrelevant and marginally "relevant hits" using search engines are the background noise of the online life. All we need to do is to demonstrate the reason why such events happen (the use of keyword full-text searching) and then to make the connection with exactly the same technique used in filters. Second, we need to continue to put out positive messages about the use and limitations of online sources, the need for parental involvement in the use of libraries by minors, and the need for minors to read more books. Third, we should continue to emphasize that filters fail to block the materials at which they are aimed and do block things that are constitutionally protected. For example, a *Consumer reports* study of Internet filters (June 2005) found that

> while Internet blockers have gotten better at blocking pornography, the best also tend to block many sites they should not. . . . [and] found the software to be less effective at blocking sites promoting hatred, illegal drugs or violence . . . The best porn blockers were heavy-handed against [i.e., blocked] sites about health issues, sex education, civil rights and politics.[9]

The last thing we need to do is to squander the accumulated capital of goodwill that libraries and librarians have built up over the years—particularly not in a fight in which librarians can be portrayed as the enemies of morality and as ivory-tower purists eager to sacrifice children and families (not to mention our colleagues in many small libraries) on the First Amendment altar. The opponents of intellectual freedom managed to demonize the American Civil Liberties Union in the 1970s and 1980s, partly by misrepresenting that excellent organization's beliefs and activities.

This is no war of shadows without consequences, nor is it a war between good (ALA) and evil (the Filterati). ALA does act from good motives and is philosophically, morally, and intellectually on the correct side. The filter fans may be led by demagogues and bullies, but they include many people holding sincere convictions and with serious concerns about the culture and the future of their children. Those people can be reached and should be the targets of our arguments about the filter fallacy, the need for parents to participate in library use, and the uses and value of literacy. We should also have a good deal of sympathy for our colleagues in the kinds of communities in which the filter wars are being fought. Many of them simply cannot understand why those of us in different circumstances appear not to know about the pressures that are being applied.

Filtering is just the latest front in the censorship wars that have been going on for decades. Despite this, we must never forget that filtering is a powerful symbolic representation of the real fears of many people who are not particularly ideological. On their behalf and on the behalf of colleagues caught in the filtering cross fire, we, as a profession, must devise an effective and successful strategy to counter filtering. That strategy will do the following:

- Stress the positive contributions that librarians and libraries make to society.
- Make reasonable accommodations to concerned parents.
- Demonstrate the ineffectiveness of filtering.
- Stress the importance of reading.
- Stress the constitutional underpinnings of the First Amendment rights of children and adults.
- Stress parental duties to guide, advise, and monitor the reading and viewing habits of children.
- Use all available public relations and marketing techniques to get these messages to the widest possible public.

We should use advertising and all other means of mass communication to build on the generally favorable view that the public has of libraries and librarians. We have a good story to tell and have earned the respect and esteem of the public. We will add to that respect and esteem if we manage to persuade the majority of parents that we are reasonable. We need to place great emphasis on the importance of sustained reading to intellectual development. A child reading a good book is the positive answer to the fears to which filtering and the V-chip are negative answers. We should never yield our belief that children have rights, too, and that those rights include the right to free enquiry. Surely we could find common cause with most concerned parents in stressing the preeminent role of parents as guides and mentors. None of this will persuade the censors and culture warriors, but it will reach the sensible mass of people as a counter to their propaganda. If it is a propaganda war, then let us fight it as such.

Libraries and censors have been around for centuries. The grounds change, the causes change, media of communication change, but the idea of liberty of thought and expression is the same as it was in the age of Tom Paine.

NOTES

1. American Library Association. *Intellectual freedom manual,* eighth edition. Chicago: ALA Editions, 2010.

2. Canadian Library Association / Association canadienne des bibliothèques. *Position statement on intellectual freedom* (approved June 27, 1974; amended November 17, 1983, and November 18, 1985). www.cla.ca/AM/Template.cfm?Section=Position _Statements&Template=/CM/ContentDisplay.cfm&ContentID=3047 (consulted August 26, 2014).

3. Wertham, Frederic. *The seduction of the innocent.* New York: Rinehart, 1954.

4. Dessart, George. "Barring *Rambo* from the Potemkin Village." *Television quarterly,* volume 28, number 3 (Summer 1996) pages 37–41.

5. Hough, Kirsten J. and Erwin, Philip K. "Children's attitudes toward violence on television." *Journal of psychology,* volume 131, number 4 (July 1997) pages 411–416.

6. Walma van der Molen, Juliette H. *Pediatrics,* volume 113, issue 6 (June 2004) pages 1771–1775.

7. A PhD in physiology from Columbia University.

8. Batch, Kristen. *Fencing out knowledge.* Washington, DC: ALA OITP, 2014. www.ala.org/offices/sites/ala.org.offices/files/content/oitp/publications/issuebriefs/ cipa_report.pdf (consulted September 13, 2014).

9. American Library Association. "Filters and filtering." www.ala.org/advocacy/ intfreedom/filtering (consulted November 12, 2014).

CHAPTER 8

RATIONALISM

Only reason can convince us of those three fundamental truths without a recognition of which there can be no effective liberty: that what we believe is not necessarily true; that what we like is not necessarily good; and that all questions are open.

—Clive Bell

WHAT IS THE MEANING OF RATIONALISM?

Rationalism is simple to explain. It is the practice of being guided by "emphasizing the role or importance of reason . . . in contrast to sensory experience . . . feelings, or authority."[1] In short, basing one's opinions and actions on what is considered reasonable in light of the evidence. The philosophical belief that reason is a source of knowledge in itself—independent of emotions, faith, and the senses—is the basis for the rational approach. In one sense, rationalism is the antithesis of religion in that it relies on evidence and reasoning while the latter relies on faith (beliefs not based on evidence). By contrast, rationalism is the basis of the scientific method, in which conclusions are always tested against existing and new evidence, and discarded if found wanting. As with most values, rationalism is not and should not be an absolute. Paradoxically, a total reliance on reason is quite unreasonable, and one should always be wary of those Gradgrinds who exalt reason above everything and lose their humanity in the process.[2] However, in the practical matters of the world, a tilt toward reason over emotion is always to be preferred.

RATIONALISM UNDER ATTACK?

There is a great tide of fundamentalism, superstition, and plain craziness in the world today. From faith healers to militants of all stripes, the world is full of people who are convinced that they know the One True Way and are aggressively intolerant of those who do not share or, worse, who mock their irrationalism. It sometimes appears that the classical conflicts of most of the twentieth century are being deemphasized, to be replaced by a broad single conflict between the forces of internationalism and secular rationalism on the one side and what one writer describes as "atavistic social movements" that oppose both.[3] This is not to espouse the notion proposing that the triumph of democratic capitalism over communism means that we have reached "the end of history"[4] (something that even its propounder appears to have abandoned). Rather, I wish to place the various forms of irrationalism in a global context. Nor would I state—most simply because I do not believe it—that internationalism and particularly its manifestation known as "globalization" are preferable to their alternatives in all instances. Insofar as they mitigate the many evils that nationalism and fundamentalism (of all kinds) have visited upon the world and its inhabitants, surely we can argue that movements that bring people together are to be preferred to movements that set one class of person against others. Further, surely we can argue that rational, logical, and humanistic beliefs have proven to be more beneficial than irrational and antihumanitarian beliefs. I would stress here that I do not use "rational" as the opposite of "spiritual" but as an antonym of "irrational." It is, it appears, possible for a person to be both rational and spiritual, and reason and rationality are not necessarily the foes of faith, if they are seen as belonging to different aspects of life.

Libraries are children of the Enlightenment and of rationalism. In the words of one scholar-librarian:

The philosophical and political principles of the European Enlightenment provide the philosophical foundation of American academic and public libraries. The values of the Enlightenment should seem very familiar to Americans. The Enlightenment belief that scientific investigation of nature and society leads to improvements and progress has been a constant American refrain since the early republic. American political rights are numerous: individual human rights, liberty, democracy, equality, the freedom to believe what you like, behave how you want as long as others are not harmed, study what you want, share your beliefs or insights freely with the world. These rights are commonplaces of American identity. Also derived from the Enlightenment is the belief in the necessity of education in a democratic republic and the obligation of the state to improve the lives of all its citizens, not just the lives of the rich and powerful.[5]

Libraries stand, above all, for the notion that human beings are improved by the acquisition of knowledge and information and that no bar should be placed in the way of that acquisition. We stand for the individual human being pursuing whichever avenues of enquiry she wishes. We also stand for rationalism as the basis for all our policies and procedures in libraries. Our bibliographic architectures, online systems, collection development, public service, library instruction, and so on are all based on rational approaches and the scientific method. Librarianship is a supremely rational profession and should resist the forces of irrationalism both external and internal.

WHAT IS THE RELATION BETWEEN RATIONALISM AND LIBRARIES?

As far as libraries are concerned, rationalism is important in two different ways. First, all the practical aspects of librarianship—what older writers used to call "library economy"—benefit from the application of reason. Cataloguing, service, library instruction, collection development, materials processing, online systems—all must be guided by policies that are firmly based on the rational method. Second, there is no better antidote to the forces of unreason than a well-stocked, well-organized library—the natural home of someone seeking objective information and well-founded knowledge and with the willingness to discriminate between them and the ill-founded and the unreasonable.

I will examine here three aspects of library work in the light of rationalism:

- the ways in which we organize libraries
- library instruction as a rational process primarily aimed at imparting the rational approach
- bibliographic control as the ultimate library expression of the rational approach

ORGANIZING LIBRARIES

One important application of rationalism and belief in reason in libraries is—or should be—the way in which we organize libraries in order to carry out our mission. Too often, organizational structures have grown by accretion—like coral reefs—in which the original, long-forgotten organization has been shaped and added to for different reasons at different times. Why does one library have three public service divisions when another library of similar size and mission has one? The most likely explanation is that the three departments were created around long-gone personnel issues or to respond to long-solved issues and problems. The other problem with long-established organizational patterns is the Old-Shoe Syndrome. Most people are more comfortable staying with the familiar than working with new people in new work patterns. If one has the power and is determined to apply the rational method, one might think that such accidental organizations should be swept away and replaced with more efficient structures. Surprisingly often, that is not the best answer. Rationalism calls for a clear appraisal of the practical effects of each policy and procedure. It might be that an organization that has grown unplanned would, on examination, prove to be working quite well. Accepting a productive organization that may appear to be illogical is a very rational thing to do. On the other hand, we should not accept ineffective organizational structures because they are familiar and comfortable. Sensible change may, on occasion, have bad effects on morale in the short term but yield increased morale in the longer term, because effective organizations make people more productive, and most people are happier when engaged in productive work than when they feel their work is ineffective or even futile. Probably the best weapon the rational reorganizer has is that most rational of all maxims, Occam's Razor: "Entities should not be multiplied without necessity."[6] In other words, a library should have the smallest effective number of departments and other organizational units, the smallest number of steps in the hierarchy, and the smallest number of staff and types of staff in each unit that is consistent with effectiveness.

Let us try to adduce some principles of organization derived from rational analysis of work in libraries and the functions that units within libraries are designed to perform. I would propose the following:

- The ideal organization should be as "flat" as possible. That is, it should have the least number of steps in the hierarchy that is consonant with the library's mission.
- No one should have an impractical number of people reporting to her or him. The late Hugh Atkinson used to invoke the minyan as a model for the upper limit of the number of people reporting directly to an administrator, though even that number seems high to me.[7]
- Organization of work should follow my "drift down" theory of library organization, which states, aphoristically, that no librarian should do what a paraprofessional can do, no paraprofessional should do what a clerical staff member or student assistant can do, and no human being should do what a machine can do.[8]
- The units of the library should have a clear mission and explicitly defined and demarcated responsibilities.
- Each unit should be staffed with enough and no more than enough people at appropriate levels.
- No organizational unit or structure should be based on either personalities or temporary exigencies.
- The organizational structure should be flexible enough to allow for the formation of temporary groupings (e.g., task forces) to deal with specific projects and temporary challenges.
- Units concerned with the general functions of the library should be organized around those general functions (e.g., collection development, reference, cataloguing) and not around types of material. The exception to this is the case of materials that either need machines to be useful (e.g., sound recordings) or need special handling, storage, and conservation (e.g., manuscripts, archives).

- All organizations should permit and encourage cross-training leading to flexible deployment of human resources.
- Organizations should facilitate and encourage individual development and advancement.

It is apparent that, in practice, some of these prescriptions may conflict. For instance, it is difficult to create and maintain a "flat" organization and an organization in which no one has a lot of people reporting to her or him. The flattest organization, after all, is one in which everybody reports to one person. This is illustrative of the central problem of organization, which is that theory and practice can conflict—and usually do. Another manifestation of that problem is that most administrators have to deal with existing structures and work patterns and seldom have the luxury of sweeping change or—luxury of luxuries—the chance to build a new organization from scratch. That practical realization does not mean that administrators have to abandon the rational approach any more than the rational approach means that all libraries must, willy-nilly, be forced into impractical, theory-based structures. As with so many philosophies and values, rationalism is an approach, not a prescription, and the successful administrator is one who achieves balance between theory and practice, between pragmatism and ideals.

TEACHING THE RATIONAL APPROACH

One of the more controversial duties of the librarian is the duty to instruct. Melvil Dewey stressed the teaching role of librarians.[9] Others have called that role a fiction.[10] From the earliest days of public libraries, in which the role of the librarian as raiser of the cultural level of the community was taken for granted by most, to the most modern technologically advanced library of today, there has been considerable discussion and debate about whether it is proper for librarians to see themselves as teachers. Public librarians have largely abandoned that idea, but school librarians in most states are teachers in name as well as fact. The history of librarians teaching in academic libraries is complex and difficult to untangle. It revolves about the central question of whether it is better to deliver the recorded knowledge and information that a user wants and needs or to teach that user to find what she needs herself. The mock-Oriental cliché about the superiority of teaching people to fish rather than giving them fish has been invoked often. This seemingly sage remark does not, of course, take into account the person who just wants a fish to satisfy his immediate and temporary hunger and, consequently, resents the time-consuming process of learning how to fish. It is difficult to imagine a less service-oriented approach than that of denying a simple request for help in the interest of educating the requester in a skill that she may never need again.

Why Library Instruction Developed

Teaching about libraries used to be called "bibliographic instruction" (BI) in academic libraries. BI had a long and interesting history arising in great part from two phenomena of thirty to forty years ago:

- the movement that established undergraduate libraries on major college campuses in the 1950s and 1960s[11]
- the manifold deficiencies of bibliographic control in the age of the mammoth card catalogue and successive layers of unsatisfactory cataloguing rules

The first phenomenon segregated undergraduate library users in designated places physically apart from the "main" or "graduate" library. (This latter was by no means an unintended consequence for the senior faculty who encouraged the undergraduate library movement.) It also created a subspecialty within academic librarianship of librarians devoted to the special needs of undergraduate students. This contrasts with smaller university libraries and college libraries, in which reference service, collection development, and bibliographic control are directed to the full range of library users, from freshmen to internationally renowned scholars.

Card catalogues became virtually unusable at a yet undiscovered size (it will never now be defined, as these behemoths no longer exist). Many millions of volumes arranged by the LC or Dewey Decimal classifications are, to put it mildly, difficult to navigate. Printed indexes to periodical literature were, at best, slow and tedious to use and, worse, months if not years out of date. These negative factors defined the environment in which a student was supposed to do library research in research libraries before the advent of the online catalogue and online indexing an abstracting services. It was hardly surprising, therefore, that the relatively new specialty—undergraduate librarianship—should focus on programs that were dedicated to help undergraduates find their way through the shockingly unfriendly bibliographic maze that lay outside the more user-oriented confines of the undergraduate library. Bibliographic instruction (BI), in short, sought to make up for the many and manifest inadequacies of bibliographic control in large academic libraries until the early to middle 1980s.

BI evolved from that simple aim, however. It sought to become a new branch of librarianship in itself. Its more avid adherents seemed almost happy to deny easily bestowable help to the library user in need in favor of making that user jump through some BI hoops. They were accused of seeing BI as a subject in itself rather than a tool to help library users and of ignoring the real needs of library users. BI was even accused of being a cloaked attempt to raise the image and status of academic librarians by equating them with teachers. (Remember that this was a time in which the arguments about "faculty status" for librarians raged unchecked.)

Why BI Was Transformed

Time may not have been a great healer in this instance, but it was certainly a great transformer. As online catalogues and online indexes and abstracting services became more sophisticated and easier to use, the need for that kind of "bibliographic instruction" became less and less. The introduction of rationality to bibliographic standards (MARC, ISBD, AACR[2], etc.), their widespread adoption, and the consequently high level of second-generation online catalogues and union databases made instruction that was specifically "bibliographic" less important to library users. The result was that BI was reborn as "library instruction" (LI)—programs devoted to teaching people how to use the library, to find what they need, and to evaluate what they had found (critical thinking). In other words, the emphasis swung from the negative (making up for the deficiencies of rotten systems) to the positive (how to make the most of the library and its services). These LI programs were, in turn, transformed by the widespread availability of online resources in libraries. Given the seductive power of online resources and the ease with which one can find "something" online, it is hard to argue that library users do not require some instruction aimed at understanding the value and limitations of online resources. In fact, in academic libraries, that need is so manifest and universal that it has—for the time being, at least—settled the old "information versus instruction" debate. Today's student needs both help and instruction, and both in great quantities.

"Library Instruction" and Public Libraries

Before I go on to discuss the application of rationalism to instruction in libraries, I wish to touch on the question of "library instruction" and the lack of it in public libraries. Schools and institutions of higher learning have, in varying degrees, captive audiences. Leading university librarian Hugh Atkinson once said, "An ounce of help is worth a ton of instruction." It is hard to argue that it is practical to deny public library users their ounces of help when they are simply not available to receive their ton of instruction. Formal programs of library instruction are inappropriate in almost all public library settings, so the discussion tends to revolve around using reference work not only to answer the questions of the moment but also to inculcate the best way to find desired information in the future. In the guise of "information literacy," some public libraries and librarians are addressing the need to teach public library patrons how to navigate the modern, technologically advanced public library; others are not.[12] Roma Harris's research in the 1980s indicated that there was a very high level of agreement among public librarians that reference work should involve an element of instruction, even when it was not requested by the patron.[13] That was some time ago, but surely the need has increased not lessened. It would stand to reason that the influx of online resources into public libraries in years since—and the provision of new services, technological or otherwise—will have, if anything, strengthened that agreement. Every public library is now an important gateway to the "information age," especially in the poorest areas of the country. Poor areas are inhabited disproportionately by those with less education than most. Given those circumstances, it is almost impossible to think that people should not be taught how best to make their way in that brave new world. Call it what you will, "library instruction" is not just for colleges anymore.

Rationalism and Teaching the Library and Its Resources

Once a library of whatever type has accepted the need for teaching the use of the library and its resources (which I will continue to call "library instruction" for want of a better, more inclusive term), it must formulate and understand the rationale for such a program. Given the fact that the human resources available are likely to be limited, it is vital that the program be focused on the most pressing needs. In most libraries, the most obvious need is for instruction and assistance in the use of online resources. It is likely, however, that one problem in online use is that it blinds the uninformed to other sources of knowledge and information that are available in the library. A primary skill crying out for instruction is the identification and choice of the most appropriate and effective sources in any format to fit individual questions and problems. Many people need to be taught that no one type of resource can supply the answers to everything. In an age of rampant commercialism, cyberpropaganda, "everything on your smartphone," and the rest of the hype, that is not an easy point to make. Devising a rationale for an instruction program depends, in the first instance, on defining the skills that are most important to the library's users.

People use "information competence" as if it were a substitute or development of library instruction; on examination, it turns out mostly not to be so. Many of the information competence programs that I have seen are concentrated entirely, or greatly, on online resources. They are, therefore, based on the idea that the all-digital library is an emerging reality and that authoritative recorded knowledge of the kind found in print is no longer relevant to the concerns of library users. I see information competence as a part of library instruction, and believe that both are in need of augmentation.

The instruction program of the future, whether carried out by formal instructional means or integrated with individual library use, should have three ascending components:

- basic library and online skills
- how to identify and locate appropriate sources
- critical thinking

At the first level, library users will learn about libraries—what they are and what they contain. This may seem to be self-evident, but elementary facts about libraries can come as a revelation to a person unused to public library use and with only scant, involuntary involvement with a school library that had no librarian to advise and teach. This first level of instruction would also contain introductory facts and strategies to enable the technologically challenged to be at ease in computer use and, thereby, able to use online resources to their advantage. This last may be the one opportunity for public libraries to attract large numbers of their users to formal classes.

At the second level, library users will become aware of the bibliographic structure of the library and the ways in which we organize recorded knowledge and information for retrieval. At this stage, it is vital that instruction should differentiate between the three concentric rings of organization:

- the highly organized and structured environment of the library, featuring authority control, controlled vocabularies, bibliographic standards, the artificial language of classification, and so on
- the less-organized environment of journal indexes, abstracting services, and the like, featuring a lack of standardization between different indexing entities but vocabulary and name control within a particular service
- the unorganized online environment, in which the user has to rely on random aggregations of sites and search engines based on keyword searching

At each level, both *relevance* (the match between the search terms and the documents retrieved) and *recall* (the percentage of relevant documents retrieved) are degraded. In other words, one of the most important lessons that must be taught is that the same search using the same terms will yield very different results in different environments. This matters a lot because a search that yielded a few highly relevant documents in a catalogue or index will, in all probability, yield a large number of mostly irrelevant documents online. (This is greatly complicated by systems that jam together the catalogue, other finding aids, and online access, all subject to default keyword searching—the predictable result being the lowest common denominator.) The temptation for the uninitiated is to take whatever is found without even knowing that there are far more relevant documents among the large number retrieved. The instruction here should be dedicated to ensuring that library users cannot just locate something but can locate and identify the materials that are most relevant to their needs. The strategies that must be imparted are dedicated to distinguishing the strengths and weaknesses of each medium and the various paths by which the most relevant of them can be located.

The third level is that of critical thinking. The ability to distinguish the true from the false, the relevant from the irrelevant, the wise from the meretricious, and the deep from the shallow has always been a part of enlightened education. It is probably fair to say that, until recent decades, librarians were happy to leave such instruction to school and college teachers. After all, we all knew which publishers were reputable, which newspapers and journalists were authoritative, and which journals ranked highest in their fields. A librarian had obviously done her job well in giving a direction to a library catalogue or indexing service that led a user to a book published by Oxford University Press or Random House, an article in the *New York times* or *Le monde*, or an article in the *Journal of the American Medical Association* or *Nature*. Today, all bets are off. Just telling someone to look something up online can scarcely be accounted a job well done. It is clearly impossible for a librarian to be there to help each library user lost in the wasteland in which, for example, the *Washington post* and *BuzzFeed*, an NIH paper and a quack cure, *Citizen Kane* and a kitten video are on equal footing. That being so, librarians must do their best to ensure that the user's online struggles are not completely unequal contests. The equalizer in that struggle is critical thinking—the ability to evaluate and judge resources in all forms and from all sources.

The rational approach to librarianship demands that we dispense instruction and, in so doing, enable library users to be empowered by knowledge and relevant information.

BIBLIOGRAPHIC CONTROL

Apart from their physical plant, libraries have three major assets: their resources in all formats, their staff, and the architecture of bibliographic control. Good buildings, resources, and staff count for nothing without bibliographic control. A place with well-housed resources with bibliographic control but no staff is a glorified warehouse. The best staff and the best organization in the world cannot make up for inadequate collections. A Russian riddle asks, "Which is the most important leg on a three-legged stool?" thus aphorizing the interdependence of the three pillars of a good library. Collection development and the hiring and care of staff have more of art than science about them, but bibliographic control is the epitome of rationalism and the "scientific approach" in librarianship.

Standards

The modern age of librarianship began in the late 1960s and culminated about ten years later. In some respects, that golden age provided us with the foundations of libraries for many years to come. The breakthrough events that characterized that period were the spread of library automation and the concurrent and linked spread of effective and accepted bibliographic standards. MARC—still the globally accepted standard for electronic bibliographic records—was born in the age of the card catalogue and is present today as an essential element of the most advanced Web-based library system. The *Anglo-American cataloguing rules*, second edition (AACR2) made national and international standardization of the content of MARC records possible and achievable, not least because it incorporated the *International standard bibliographic description* (ISBD) global standards. AACR2 was the de jure or de facto standard in all English-speaking countries—and in many that are not—for more than thirty years. It is also the basis for many codes written in other languages, a fact that makes the adoption of the misbegotten *Resource description & access* (RDA) all the more unfortunate. We have national standards for classification (the Dewey Decimal and Library of Congress systems) and subject headings (the LC *List of subject headings* [LCSH]), but they are not as widely accepted internationally.

The point of this near-global bibliographic standardization is not that cataloguing has improved (though it almost certainly has) but that it has made some longtime dreams realizable. Librarians have been building union catalogues and aspiring to a universal union catalogue since the middle of the nineteenth century. Two things made those goals impractical until thirty years ago: the technology of the time and lack of standardization. It is impossible to create and maintain a *current* union card catalogue, book catalogue, or microform catalogue. Until 1979, not even Britain and North America shared a common cataloguing code, still less the rest of the world. Computer technology and standardization made massive current union catalogues possible and even made the dream of Universal

Bibliographic Control (UBC) achievable.[14] UBC is a program that states, in essence, that we should use technology and standards to ensure that each document is catalogued once in its country of origin and the resulting record is made available to libraries and researchers throughout the world. Viewed in this light, the various international and national cooperative cataloguing schemes of the Library of Congress and the gigantic world union catalogue that OCLC and others have created represent a harmonic convergence of rationality and dreams. We have come to a point at which the rational approach typified by cataloguing, standardization, MARC, and cooperation will enable the creation of a seemingly fantastic dream: the World Catalogue.

What about Electronic Resources?

It would be a great irony if, on the verge of achieving the World Catalogue, we were to use it mostly for access to tangible documents (books, maps, journals, etc.). It is imperative that we ensure that this universal bibliographic resource includes records for, and links to, worthwhile online resources. The rub lies in those last few words. What is worthwhile? Which online resources? I have written of the value of stewardship and the consequence of deciding what is or is not significant in chapter 5 of this book, and now wish to apply that criterion to online resources and their peculiar problems.

To simplify, there are two basic problems with online resources as far as bibliographic control is concerned. The first is that the majority of such resources or aggregations of data are of no value, little value, very localized value, or temporary value. The second is that online resources are inherently unstable and shape-shifting. These two simple points add up to a massive complexity that may, at first, seem to defy rational analysis and a rational set of answers. It is clearly neither rational nor efficient to catalogue a mass of online resources that are valueless or of limited value. It is clearly not efficient to catalogue something that may have a completely different shape and content in the future. It might be natural to despair and hope that, left alone, the great online swamp will somehow resolve itself. I think such a course of action would violate the two important values of stewardship and rationalism, and I believe there is another—much more difficult and expensive—plan for the future.

One part of that plan would be to blend traditional cataloguing and "archival" cataloguing. By the latter, I mean the cataloguing of aggregations of resources rather than the resources themselves. Some electronic resources will be of sufficient importance to be catalogued on their own; others (including but not limited to websites) should be catalogued in groups with their individual components listed briefly, if at all.

Another much-discussed issue is that of "metadata"—a pompous word meaning "data about data" which, when you come to think about it, applies to any form of cataloguing.[15] The most popular manifestation of metadata is "the Dublin Core," an ill-defined subset of the MARC format that deals with a minimal structure of the bibliographic record and hardly at all with its content. In a way, metadata is a panicky response to the perceived immensity of the problem and a solution from the "anything is better than nothing" school of thought. The point is that, in considering the cataloguing (by whatever name) of electronic resources, we do not need new structures and new standards (and certainly not those as ill articulated and skinny as the Dublin Core). It is possible to catalogue any document in any format using even the spavined RDA, a major classification, the LC subject heading list, and MARC. The question is not *how* to catalogue electronic resources but *which* electronic resources to catalogue. My proposal, first made many years ago, is to devise a system in which electronic resources would be evaluated in terms of their value and whether that value is general and permanent (as opposed to local and temporary) and, thereby, sorted into the following categories:

- those to be catalogued fully, using all bibliographic standards
- those to be catalogued using an agreed-upon, enriched, better-defined set of "metadata"
- those to be catalogued using the skeletal Dublin Core
- those to be left to the mercies of search engines and keyword searching

These categories are in descending order of permanence and value. They are in ascending order of number of resources in each category. The first category would comprise no more than a few percent of electronic resources (though even that seems a high estimate of the proportion of permanently valuable items). The second and third categories might add up to another ten percent, and all the rest would be dealt with as they are today.

Those percentages are pure guesses, of course, but even if they are roughly correct, foretell a massive and sustained cooperative cataloguing effort over many years.

If all the political, strategic, and financial questions were answered and this grand plan were to be implemented, libraries would still be faced with the fragile nature of online resources and the need to preserve those that had been catalogued. Such digital preservation schemes as have been proposed or implemented lack credibility and scale. Those who care at all about preservation (as all librarians should) are either fatalistic or optimistic that some technological solution as yet undreamed of will show up. Even if it does, what about the resources of today, which may well be lost by the time the Great Solution appears? The fact is, there is only one certain way to preserve electronic texts and images and to ensure their transmission to future generations. That is to print them on acid-free paper, make many copies, and distribute those copies to a number of libraries. When you have eliminated the implausible, whatever remains—however low-tech—must be taken seriously.

NOTES

1. *The Oxford companion to philosophy*; edited by Ted Honderich. Oxford: Oxford University Press, 1995. page 741.
2. Dickens, Charles. *Hard times*. 1854.
3. Tax, Meredith. "World culture war." *The nation* (May 17, 1999) page 24.
4. Fukuyama, Francis. *The end of history and the last man*. New York: Free Press, 1992.
5. Bivens-Tatum, Wayne. *Libraries and the Enlightenment*. Sacramento: Library Juice Press, 2013. Preface.
6. William of Ockham (1285–1349) is best remembered for Occam's Razor, which states, *"Entia non sunt multiplicanda sine necessitate."*
7. "minyan" (Hebrew: "number") plural "minyanim" or "minyans." "In Judaism, the minimum number of males (ten) required to constitute a representative 'community of Israel' for liturgical purposes." *Encyclopedia Britannica Online*. s.v. "minyan." www.britannica.com/EBchecked/topic/384689/minyan (consulted August 27, 2014).
8. Gorman, Michael. "A good heart and an organized mind." In *Library leadership: visualizing the future*; edited by Donald E. Riggs. Phoenix: Oryx, 1982. pages 73–83.

9. "The time is when the library is a school and the librarian in the highest sense a teacher." Melvil Dewey, "The profession." *American library journal*, number 1 (September 30, 1876) pages 5–6.

10. Wilson, Pauline. "Librarians as teachers: an organizational fiction" *Library quarterly* 49 (1979) pages 146–152.

11. The first undergraduate library was established at Harvard University in 1949. Harvard College Library. "Lamont Library: history." http://hcl.harvard.edu/libraries/lamont/history.cfm (consulted August 27, 2014).

12. Hall, Rachel. "Public praxis: a vision for critical information literacy in public libraries." *Public library quarterly*, volume 29, issue 2 (April–June 2010) pages 162–175.

13. Harris, Roma. "Bibliographic instruction in public libraries: a question of philosophy." *RQ* (Fall 1989) pages 92–98.

14. Kaltwasser, Franz Georg. "Universal bibliographic control." *UNESCO library bulletin*, volume 25 (September 1971) pages 252–259.

15. For an unusually good discussion of metadata and cataloguing, see: Diao, Junli and Hernández, Mirtha A. "Transferring cataloging legacies into descriptive metadata creation in digital projects: catalogers' perspective." *Journal of library metadata*, volume 14 (2014) pages 130–145.

CHAPTER 9

LITERACY AND LEARNING

In these days, when more of us run than read, and when what we know exceeds what we understand, let me urge a return to the book. The book remains that small handy instrument that we call a key. We can all carry it and with it we can unlock most of the doors to the unimaginable beauties that lie somewhere beyond the TV set, to the east of the movies, and to the west of the moonshine that flows from too many media of communication. Best of all, the book is not a fleeting fancy. It is steady. It remains ready for reference, for reassurance, and paradoxically for the comfort of companionship as well as the luxury of solitude. I am for it.

—Walt Kelley[1]

WHAT IS THE MEANING OF LITERACY AND LEARNING?

Read: *verb.* To take in the sense of, as of language, by interpreting the characters with which it was expressed . . . To learn or be informed of by perusal . . .

Peruse: *verb.* To read carefully or critically . . .

Literate: *adj.* Instructed in letters; able to read and write . . . n. One who can read or write . . .[2]

These are suspiciously simple definitions. It is obvious that deciphering a child's ABC book is a very different activity from reading at a high level, yet we call them both "reading." It may be significant that another dictionary adds the description "archaic" to the word "peruse," as if reading carefully and critically were such a rare activity that a word describing it is no longer necessary. The matter of reading is both complicated and critical to the future of the life of the mind, and we cannot understand libraries or human learning unless we place literacy in context and explore its meaning thoroughly.

Learning to Be Literate

In the common course of human development, a child will learn to speak and then learn to see more than random squiggles when presented with letters or characters. She will then learn that those letters or characters are capable of being linked in words, phrases, sentences, paragraphs, chapters, and, ultimately, complete texts. This process, which is usually accompanied by improvements and extensions in speech and vocabulary, can be described as "learning to decode." It is the necessary precursor of understanding (though, of course, the dawning of understanding often accompanies rather than derives from the process of learning to decode). If you think of the process of learning a foreign language after childhood, you will see that, in learning, say, French or Spanish, you have a knowledge of most of the characters, and very little else. Even if the words assembled from those characters look vaguely familiar, you probably have little idea of how to pronounce them or what they really mean. Thus, the process of learning a foreign language is a process of proceeding from the basic characters through decoding to understanding, in the same way as acquiring the ability to read one's native language. It is a long road from:

The cat sat on the mat.

to

Where the shadow is regarded as so intimately bound up with life of the man that its loss entails debility or death, it is natural to expect that its diminution should be regarded with solicitude and apprehension, as betokening a corresponding decrease in the vital energy of its owner.

This sentence from Sir James Frazer's *Golden Bough* (1890) not only contains some words not commonly found in everyday speech, but also expresses a complex thought that requires analysis and understanding. Also, it is but one sentence in a mammoth twelve-volume exposition of a complicated and multidimensional subject. A person needs more than the ability to read in order to read that book with intellectual profit. She needs the basic decoding skill but, beyond that, the ability to interpret, think critically, understand, and learn.

According to David Wood, a shift in learning occurs typically between the ages of eleven and thirteen.[3] At that time, it appears that students begin to learn more and absorb more from the written word than they do from speech and observation (this effect is true regardless of the level of reading ability). This observation reinforces the central importance of being able to perform sustained reading and use that activity to learn. It is interesting in this context to observe that the great majority of people learn more from and retain more of the knowledge contained in lectures if they take notes. In other words, it is important to be able to read even an abbreviated version of a spoken communication in order to reinforce that mouth-to-ear-to-brain experience by a supplementary eye-to-brain experience. In the same passage, Wood also emphasizes the importance of advanced reading to speech and the ability to achieve true literacy (his words apply to schoolchildren but surely have force for all of us of whatever age):

> The child who is fortunate enough to achieve fluent levels of literacy has at her disposal a whole new range of words, linguistic structures, and skills in planning which [sic] enable her to create interesting, informative, dramatic, and coherent narratives . . . she has command over a range of literary devices and structures that can be exploited in speech to make what she says dramatic, flexible, variable, versatile, and, should she so wish, fast and efficient.

Literacy is not just a question of reading and writing—even at the highest level—but also an ability to express oneself fully. Some see the three abilities (reading, writing, and speech) as inextricably intertwined. I think that reading is the central portion of this complex in that one could live the life of the mind in isolation with printed texts—not the most highly recommended way of life, but certainly possible—whereas, it is safe to say, writing well is impossible for someone who cannot or does not read, and expression through speech may be vivid but will lack depth and substance unless it is accompanied by sustained reading. (Some might dispute these assertions with reference to preliterate and illiterate societies and the oral tradition. Though I can see the force of their argument, I would counter with these facts. What we know of, say, the *Odyssey* and *Beowulf* comes from the written record. For good or ill, we live in a time and society in which the oral tradition is not in any way central to the culture and life of most people, except in the bastardized and malign form of entertainment television.

As stated earlier and broadly speaking, human beings learn in three ways:

- They learn from experience.
- They learn from others (teachers, gurus, guides) who are more knowledgeable and learned than they in at least one area of human knowledge.
- They learn by interacting with the records of humankind found in books and other tangible and intangible documents created by other human beings.

The records of humankind (whether carved on stone, printed in a book, or contained in an e-book or other digital resource) consist of words, images, and symbols. To profit from those records, one needs to be skilled in understanding words and symbols and interpreting images. When skilled, we are able to interact with the minds of long-dead men and women and—adding a miracle to the miracle of the onward transmission of human knowledge—create new knowledge and record that knowledge for those yet unborn.

Reading, an activity that is routine to most of us, is in truth miraculous and should be cherished and encouraged. We speak of "learning" and "literacy" as if they were separate ideas, but they are inextricably linked. Literacy is more than a means to learning—although it is one of the most important means. In a real sense, literacy is learning and the sustained reading of complex texts as necessary to the developed mind as are air, water, and food to the healthy body. Reading at a level above the practical is a way of developing the mind, and the interpretation of texts is a rewarding intellectual activity in itself.

Despite many changes in the reading environment and all the discussions about various other "literacies," it is evident that certain verities about reading are eternal even when the topic is twenty-first-century literacy:

> Competent readers must also come to the reading act with an understanding of knowledge and knowing that fosters their engagement and heightens their abilities to think critically and analytically.
>
> Moreover . . . such a critical eye and a facilitative epistemic orientation must be aided by the continued and lifelong pursuit of expertise in reading, by principled knowledge of the domains or topics encountered, and by perceptiveness and the ability to see relations within the flood of information that unrelentingly assaults us all.
>
> Reading competence cannot be achieved within the first years of schooling; there is simply too much to be learned, to be honed, and to be experienced. Further, reading competence must be founded on a base of knowledge that permits the reader to navigate the hazards of irrelevant, inaccurate, and misleading content. And competent readers must be able to quickly and effectively grasp the similarities, contradictions, and conflicts within the ideas and voices that informational deluge contains.[4]

Lifelong Learning through Literacy

Modern neuroscience teaches us that various types of neuroplasticity mean that the old idea about brain structure—that it was relatively unchanging after childhood—is no longer accepted, that the brain undergoes physiological and functional organizational development, and that it can profit from learning at all ages. Neuroplasticity is the mechanism for development of the mind and for learning.[5] In short, the habit of sustained reading of complex texts throughout a life can, using literacy as a tool, leads to understanding and wisdom—the ultimate goals of learning

How Literate Are We?

There is a general idea that literacy rates have been climbing over the decades and centuries and that our society today is more literate than any of its predecessors. This fits with the "onward and upward" view of human history that, in essence, equates advances in technology with advances in culture and the health of society. Also, the presumption is that more than a century of mass education must have produced a literate society. A check in catalogues and indexes will reveal masses of titles over many decades on the question of literacy and society, all betraying an unease about where we are and where we are going. We can see a lack of satisfaction with the state of literacy and learning from the famously anxiety-producing *Why Johnny can't read*,[6] through Neil Postman's book on "amusing ourselves to death,"[7] to contemporary cris de coeur.[8]

Why is this so? The simple answer lies in what one means by "literacy." If the word means "the ability to read at some level," then we have mass literacy. If, however, to be literate means the ability to read and interpret complex texts (sustained reading) and the habit of doing so regularly, then the United States consists of two nations (not divided by class, race, or economics, in this case). The first nation contains the majority of people who can read enough to be able to function in society and in their work but seldom read other than for uninstructive recreation or out of necessity. The second nation contains a minority that reads to learn and elevate their consciousness.

The National Assessment of Adult Literacy defined four levels of literacy:

> **Below Basic:** (no more than the most *simple* and *concrete* literacy skills)—
> 14% of the US adult population
> **Basic:** (can perform simple and everyday literacy activities)—29%
> **Intermediate:** (can perform moderately challenging literacy activities)—44%
> **Proficient:** (can perform complex and challenging literacy activities)—13%[9]

Alan Purves calls the proficient "scribes"—people who not only have the ability to code and decode text, but also have a rich basis of reference that enables them to understand and create complex texts.[10] In his estimation, "the ratio of readers and non-readers is probably the lowest ever in American life since the time of the Massachusetts Bay Colony." This last quotation demonstrates one of his points: in order to be truly literate, one needs not only to be able to read and understand the words in a text but to share in the scribal nexus of knowledge that enables the reader to realize the meaning behind the decoded words—in this case, knowing that the Colony existed in the seventeenth century and was made up of people fleeing religious discrimination, and that dissenters of that time were avid readers of the Bible and religious texts. Another analysis finds three groups: a well-informed "reading elite"; a large and growing group of people who can read but rely mostly on television and other media for information and entertainment; and an underclass of the illiterate and uninformed.[11]

Two big questions arise if we come to believe that we live in a society that is made up of two (or three) nations—the aliterate/illiterate and the truly literate. They are:

- Has anything changed?
- What are the consequences for society and for individuals?

It is tempting to see our present situation as simply a contemporary version of the societies of the past. There have always been elites and masses, the learned and the ignorant, the educated and the uneducated. The civilization of Ancient Greece, from which comes almost all that is good about modern civilization (democracy, the rule of law, education, philosophy, and on and on), was based on a small proportion of educated, prosperous people supported by a large number of uneducated slaves and serfs. More than a hundred years ago, Oscar Wilde wrote that twentieth-century technology would make possible a utopia—a re-creation of classical Greece with machines replacing helots and all citizens able to enjoy the fruits of the world and the pleasures of the intellect.[12] Wilde got it right about the technology (just look at modern agriculture, which combines unparalleled productivity with a small number of human farmworkers), but was obviously wrong about society. At the end of the twentieth century, almost everybody in the developed world had unprecedented levels of material prosperity and freedom from drudgery, but can we really say that the general level of culture had increased? The forces that dominate society—cyberspace, infotainment. streaming media, television, mass marketing, advertising, Big Technology—seem to be more powerful than the drive to learn and live the life of the mind for the majority of people.

Are we worse off than we were fifty, one hundred, two hundred years ago? Are we better off? Perhaps neither is the case and only the details of society change. Optimists would point to the large number of books and magazines that are still published each year in print and online. Pessimists would invite you to look at the *New York times* list of best-sellers, dominated as it is by self-help manuals, shopping and romance novels, vilely partisan political books, ghostwritten biographies of television nonentities and sports people, rubbishy fantasy, and hyped-up drivel tied to movie deals. Optimists would point to "the promise of the all-digital future." Pessimists would suggest you look at the mass of online content—online porn and violence, paranoid ravings, celebrity "journalism," stultifying personal trivia, enormous accretions of transient and local information, and the odd golden nugget too often obscured by the mountain of dross. Optimists would point to the high percentage of people who can read and write. Pessimists would point to the relatively small percentage who do read and write at anything beyond a functional level. Such an argument is almost endless, as are the facts that can be adduced to support either side. What does not seem to be in dispute is that the understanding and power over one's life that come from literacy and its exercise are of great benefit to the individual, both materially and psychically. Those who deal with the world by reading and writing in order to understand are better off in almost every way than those who do not.

What Are the Consequences of Two Nations on Either Side of the Literacy Divide?

This is a most important question for all of us because the health of society depends on there being a balance of interest between the elites and the mass of people. The former may well be the driving force in society, empowered by their knowledge to dictate—or, at least, heavily influence—the lives of others and the ways in which society is developing and changing. However, in the words of John Oxenham:

> To those who hold democratic values, it is also important that the majorities of people should have an adequate understanding of what the minorities [the elites] are up to and be able to exercise some intelligent and informed control over them. Already it is arguable that even very literate citizens in relatively democratic polities find themselves unable to maintain a satisfactory grasp of the workings of their societies.[13]

Notice that the power elites overlap with the literate elites but are not identical. In other words, there are a number of truly literate citizens who have little control over the politics and economics of society. How do we ensure that everybody in a society has, at least, the chance of being as knowledgeable and informed as those in power? Literacy and the ability to deal with the torrents of information are, surely, essential prerequisites.

WHAT IS THE RELATION BETWEEN LITERACY AND LEARNING AND LIBRARIES?

We have seen that literacy is not a simple question of being able to read or being unable to read. Literacy is best seen not as a state of being but as a process by which, once able to read, an individual becomes more and more literate throughout life; more and more able to interact with complex texts and, thereby, to acquire knowledge and understanding. It is a key element in the enterprise—learning—to which all libraries are dedicated. Instead of accepting the world as permanently divided between the illiterate, aliterate, and literate, we should see literacy as a useful tool with which to end that state of affairs. Viewed thus, literacy becomes an open-ended range of possibilities in which librarians, educators, and students work together to learn and become more learned using sustained reading of texts as a central part of the life of the mind. In this respect, the distinctions between kinds of librarian become unimportant—a children's librarian or school librarian is as important to the early stages of literacy and learning as a public librarian or academic librarian is to the later stages. We are all involved in the same process: providing the materials, instruction, and assistance that enable individuals and societies to grow and to thrive intellectually. Incidentally, it is not a question that is of marginal importance to academic librarians. (I am not speaking here of the reading abilities or willingness to read of the average high school graduate—that is a separate matter of concern, though a manifestation of the direction society is taking.) Whether a librarian accepts the existence of two nations divided by literacy is not crucial to this discussion. The fact is that, whatever your view of the state of literacy today, literacy is important to individual well-being and societal achievement and a goal to be pursued by all libraries.

WHAT SHOULD WE DO?

All librarians can and should be involved in promoting literacy to one extent or another. The most important thing that we can all do is to build and maintain collections of texts in all formats that are as rich and rewarding as possible, considering the mission of the library and the resources available. We should also encourage reading and the love of the self-improvement and pleasure that reading can bring. In all but the most specialized libraries, some (maybe a large proportion) of the library's actual and potential users will not be interested in reading and will need encouragement to raise their levels of literacy. This means that it is no longer enough to build the collections and hope that they will come. Active steps to guide users to reading are called for, and the more methods (large and small) that the library employs the better. Simple things such as displays and new acquisitions lists sent to library users by e-mail, available on a web page, or communicated via social media can raise the consciousness of even the most educated users. Lectures, other public events, and publications can also be used to promote reading. Some kinds of libraries can create formal literacy programs using teachers, peer counselors, and advisers. Others may only be able to use more indirect means. Two things need to be emphasized, irrespective of the type of library. First, literacy programs, formal and informal, should not be limited to teaching the mechanics of literacy but should also aim at instilling the lifelong habit of reading. Second, all libraries are in the literacy game and should work together, formally and informally, to advance the cause, each in its own way.

School and Children's Libraries

I should begin this section by stating that I believe children are better off reading books and other texts than they are watching television, going online, or living any other kind of screen life. I also believe that librarians dealing with children can do no better thing than promoting reading and the love of reading. Children can benefit only from going online when they are firmly established as readers. School and public children's librarians can have a formal involvement in reading and writing classes for children. They can also provide an environment that encourages reading outside the classroom (for schoolwork or pleasure). Displays, talks, storytimes, and contests are all tested and effective ways of bringing literacy to children. The attractiveness of the collection is central to the success of these libraries, because it is difficult to persuade a child to abandon all the many distractions of modern life in favor of old and superficially unattractive reading matter. The popular wisdom says that school and children's libraries should have a major online component to enable children to be in touch with the "information age." I believe this is a tragically mistaken policy that is likely to decrease literacy rather than advance it. There are those who would say "so what?" (see the end of this chapter), but they are people who do not value reading. Unless strictly controlled, the allure of the screen will distract young minds from the relatively difficult but rewarding task of reading texts and seduce them into online vacuity.

Public Libraries

Public librarians can and do play a direct role in adult literacy programs by using their libraries as tutoring centers. There are specific reasons for designating libraries as teaching centers. Not only are librarians people who appreciate the enriching powers of reading and writing—possibly more than any other group—but also libraries are places that adult illiterates can enter with neither shame nor embarrassment. One writer believes that the central feature of successful adult literacy programs in public libraries is the "institutionalization" of those programs—their complete integration into the mission, goals, and programs of the library.[14] An Australian writer states:

> Public libraries, with their focus on intergenerational reading, their informal nature, their popularity across the age span and their prominent location within disadvantaged communities tick all the boxes for the development of adult literacy.[15]

The integration of adult literacy programs into the public library's mission has, of course, great implications for the funding and planning of library operations and for the way in which the library presents itself to the community. In other words, the public library must not just become a convenient home for the adult literacy program but embrace that program as a natural part of what it does. The result is, of course, that a successful literacy program will ensure that the number of people who can take full advantage of the library's programs and collections is increased. Beyond that, in raising the level of literacy in the community, the library is—and is seen as—a valuable community asset. Thus, an integrated adult literacy program is good policy on both idealistic and pragmatic grounds.

Colleges and Universities

Academic librarians can encourage reading and writing through participation in Great Books and other, less formal programs. They can also participate in the regrettably large numbers of "remedial" classes found in all but the most elite, selective institutions. The sad fact is that many students who are accepted into higher education today are the product of a society and a school system that has de-emphasized basic skills, including the most basic skills of all: reading and writing. I am not making a political statement here and am a strong supporter of public education and increased funding for public education. However, I also believe that K–12 education would be transformed for the better if it were based on a syllabus that sought, from the earliest ages, to give intensive instruction in literacy and numeracy based on classroom teaching, supplemented by reading and writing assignments and experiences. The emphasis on technology over reading and creativity over basic writing skills, not to mention the proliferation of new and peripheral subjects, has produced a generation of nonreaders and poor writers. In many states, school libraries have deteriorated to the point of collapse. Is it any wonder that this witches' brew has resulted in the need for remedial education in colleges aimed at bringing students up to competence levels at which they can deal with university-level courses? I have come to believe that the evolving structure of "library instruction" not only must accommodate basic online skills but also should be coordinated with remedial English classes to raise the levels of literacy among incoming students. This is a very different idea of the role of an academic librarian, and one on which many may frown, but altered circumstances call for new solutions and actions.

Special Libraries

The United States incarcerates more of its people per capita than any other nation on earth. Regrettably, there is a huge and growing population in prison—a population that is disproportionately illiterate and semiliterate. This is not the only negative indicator about the incarcerated, but it is among the most telling. The scourge of illiteracy is the ultimate powerlessness of those deprived of liberty and is the antithesis of the freedom and power of the educated and literate elite. If rehabilitation is still an aim of imprisonment, literacy education is a key element. I admire many of my librarian colleagues, but, as a class, I admire prison librarians more than most. Prison librarians can act directly to attack illiteracy and to encourage those in prison not only to better themselves but also to find in reading the antidote to the despair of the lower depths of society. Prison librarians can use the range of methods to combat illiteracy, from the provision of reading matter to actual classes and tutoring in reading and writing. This again is another manifestation of the combination of idealism and pragmatism in the best of librarianship. Not only is it good to open mental doors for those with little help, it is also very practical—what are the chances of an illiterate former convict getting a job on release from prison?

Many special librarians have only the most general involvement with the question of literacy and have little chance to advance reading and writing specifically. However, as we have seen in the case of prison librarians, that is not always the case. For example, librarians in hospitals, particularly mental health facilities, can and do advance reading as a source of pleasure and diversion and, quite often, as an element in the healing and rehabilitation process.

IS THERE AN ALTERNATIVE TO LITERACY?

In the twenty-first century, the question of reading and writing texts is still central to culture and communication. There are those who believe that technology will supply (and is already supplying) at least the possibility of alternatives to reading and writing texts that will enable people to become both educated and fulfilled in a postliterate society. Anyone attending meetings on university campuses will be familiar with chatter about "paradigm shifts" in learning and the importance of other "literacies"—"visual literacy," "computer literacy," and so on. Two European authors have discussed the "literacies" that "encompass different aspects of social, business and technological life in the 21st century, and challenges facing European education systems to adapt to these *new forms of literacy*" [my emphasis].[16] All such talk is an attempt to deal with two facts:

- Most university students write at a level that is inferior to their counterparts of two or three decades ago and, by no coincidence at all, read less and read less well than those counterparts.
- We should face the fact that all educated people have to deal with texts, whether in the form of print on paper or on a screen and, if they cannot read books effectively, will be unable to read texts on screens.

These are stubborn and contradictory realities. There are only two real strategies: bringing students back to sustained reading (against the grain of their pre-university education) or evasion.

Examples of the latter abound and usually center on either the substitution of graphic or visual "information" for text or the birth of "new worlds" and "new ways of thinking" based on cyberspace or virtual reality or both.[17] The prose that encases such proposals is so opaque as to be virtually unreadable. Of course, clear, concise, declarative language is hardly to be expected from authors who are attempting to express in written words an alternative to written words as a means of learning and growing. In a paper that advances, as far as I can tell, the idea that computers will make possible new visual means of storing and imparting knowledge that are superior to text, Pamela McCorduck writes:

> [Text] . . . will be joined by other epistemologies or ways of knowing and high among them will be a return to visual knowledge. But, I suspect, for that way of knowing to be as effective as text, knowledge must be encoded in a way that will demand the same level of attentiveness that text now does.[18]

Well, quite. I read the paper with a suitable level of attentiveness and find no proposal that addresses the problem of encoding knowledge visually in a more intense way than we have for centuries of drawing, painting, photographing, filming, and creating online images. The primacy of text, which McCorduck believes to be coming to an end, is neither an accident nor the result of a slavish adherence to tradition. Attention has to be paid to text because of the depth and richness of its content. No amount of speculation about virtual reality can escape the reality (called, archly, "uppercase Reality" by McCorduck) that words can store and display depths of knowledge and nuance unmatchable by still or moving images or the fake experience of virtual reality. Insofar as we continue to learn from experience, virtual reality is a replacement for real life, not for texts.

The essential thing to remember about literacy is that it is, in Oxenham's words, the "major enabling technology in the development of reason, logic, systematic thinking, and research."[19] Nothing based on sound, images, or symbols, or any permutation of them, can possibly provide a technology that is equal to the written word for those central purposes of the life of the mind. This is far from a purely philosophical statement. Modern education at all levels faces the problems of huge numbers of students, rising levels of aliteracy, and the cost of building new schools and campuses in the face of inadequate funding and deeply mistaken public policy. In Peter Deekle's words:

> College teaching increasingly uses electronic technology to bridge the growing gap between an aliterate population of undergraduates and an ever-expanding knowledge base.[20]

It is not surprising, therefore, that educationalists, politicians, and administrators at all levels embrace online learning (that is, library-less learning) and the "smart" classrooms as panaceas and de-emphasize the importance of reading and writing. Librarians should not be complicit in these intellectually lazy courses of action, but should work with their natural allies—teachers, faculty, and parents—to emphasize the importance of literacy and sustained reading to students.

LITERACY—THE BOTTOM LINE

The civilization that has lurched, with many ups and downs, from classical times to the present day is dependent on literacy and the spread of literacy into the less-privileged classes. It is possible that the spread of online access and the infotainment culture is a serious challenge to literacy and that only the privileged will be literate in the future (as was the case until the last hundred years or so). Libraries and librarians must do their best to ensure that we do not regress as far as literacy is concerned. We must do that by emphasizing that the sustained reading of texts is important to all of us—not least because our civilization may depend on it.

NOTES

1. Kelley, Walt. *Pogo files for Pogophiles*. Richfield, Minnesota: Spring Hollow Books, 1992. page 217.

2. All definitions from *Webster's Third international dictionary*.

3. Wood, David. *How children think and learn*, second edition. Oxford: Blackwell, 1998. pages 210–211.

4. Alexander, Patricia A., et al. "Reading into the future: competence for the 21st century." *Educational psychologist*, volume 47, issue 4 (2012) pages 259–280.

5. Pascual-Leone, Alvaro, et al. "The plastic human brain cortex." *Annual review of neuroscience*, volume 28 (July 2005) pages 377–401.

6. Flesch, Rudolf. *Why Johnny can't read: and what you can do about it*. New York: Harper, 1955.

7. Postman, Neil. *Amusing ourselves to death*. New York: Viking, 1985.

8. Cleckler, Bob C. *Let's end our literacy crisis: the desperately needed idea whose time has come*. Utah: American Universities & Colleges Press, 2005.

9. National Center for Educational Statistics. *National Assessment of Adult Literacy*. http://nces.ed.gov/naal/kf_demographics.asp (consulted August 28, 2014).

10. Purves, Alan C. *The scribal society*. New York: Longman, 1990.

11. Stedman, Lawrence, et al. "Literacy as a consumer activity." In *Literacy in the United States*; edited by Carl F. Kaestle, et al. New Haven: Yale University Press, 1991. pages 150–151.

12. Wilde, Oscar. *The soul of man under Socialism*. 1891

13. Oxenham, John. *Literacy: reading, writing, and social organization*. London: Routledge and Keegan Paul, 1980. pages 121–122.

14. Johnson, Debra Wilcox. "Libraries and literacy: a tradition greets a new century." *American libraries*, volume 28 (May 1997) pages 49–51.

15. Thompson, Sally. "Public libraries: central to adult learning and literacy." *APLIS*, volume 25, issue 4 (December 2012) pages 190–191.

16. Carneiro, Roberto and Gordon, Jean. "Warranting our future: literacy and literacies." *European journal of education*, volume 48, issue 4 (December 2013) pages 476–497.

17. See, for example: *Adolescents' online literacies: connecting classrooms, digital media, and popular culture*; edited by Donna E. Alvermann. New York: Peter Lang, 2010.

18. McCorduck, Pamela. "How we knew, how we know, how we will know." In *Literacy online: the promise (and peril) of reading and writing with computers*; edited by Myron C. Tuman. Pittsburgh: University of Pittsburgh Press, pages 245–259.

19. Oxenham, "Literacy." pages 131–132.

20. Deekle, Peter V. "Books, reading, and undergraduate education." *Library trends*, volume 44, number 2 (Fall 1995) pages 264–269.

CHAPTER 10

EQUITY
OF ACCESS

All societies should allow universal access to libraries, so that they can help citizens to educate themselves.

—John Stonehouse[1]

W e must begin with the basic premise that everyone has a right to have access to library resources and services, irrespective of who they are and where and under which conditions they live. That concept is known as equity of access. Equity does not mean equality, but it does mean fairness. It is a key element in the concept of social justice—the idea that every person in society is entitled to a fair shake. In a world in which social justice prevailed, there would be no barriers to the elementary rights to which we are all entitled. In such a society all would have equal access to library resources and services as well as the universal rights to justice, medical care, employment, education, housing, free speech, and liberty that all humans have irrespective of their status and condition of life. We inhabit a far from an ideal world, and the things that distinguish us each from the other have an effect on our use of libraries as they do on every other service that we need or want. An ideal world of equality of access is out of reach, but it is by no means impossible to achieve a world in which librarians and library users have reached a far greater state of fairness than now.

Equity of access is often referred to as "unfettered access." "To fetter" means "to restrain or confine"—a metaphorical extension of the notion of physically shackling or fettering a human being. The metaphor is continued in the phrase "unfettered access"—that is, access to libraries and their services that is unconstrained and free. The American Library Association's *Statement on equity of access states:*

> Equity of access means that all people [are entitled to] have the information they need—regardless of age, education, ethnicity, language, income, physical limitation, or geographic barriers. It means they are able to obtain information in a variety of formats—electronic, as well as print. It also means they are free to exercise their right to know without fear of censorship or reprisal.[2]

It is a pity that the statement uses the flabby word "information" in the first sentence, when something like "library resources and services" is clearly meant. (The statement shows all the signs of having been written by a committee that had been meeting for a very long time.) It may also appear to be unnecessarily complex, but one can understand why the words "age, education, ethnicity, language, income, physical limitation, or geographic barriers" are there—because, in their absence, one could not deny access to a library to a naked person or one in the grip of homicidal mania. Absent such threats to life, safety, decency, buildings, and the like, no one may be denied access because of her age, gender, economic status, ethnic origin, or any other categorization that does not inhibit her legal, constitutional, and moral rights. In a modern twist to an old story, equity of access to digital resources implies that library users have a right to information, training, and assistance necessary to operate the hardware and software provided by the library. This latter is not a negligible point; it implies that librarians and staff in libraries large and small must possess—in addition to their other professional abilities and skills—up-to-date technological and practical knowledge of all the means by which users gain access to those digital resources (knowledge that needs constant refreshing).

WHAT IS THE RELATION BETWEEN EQUITY OF ACCESS TO RECORDED KNOWLEDGE AND INFORMATION AND LIBRARIES?

Libraries deal with the human record, but are not the only institutions that do so. The ideal is fairness in access to all forms, but we should recall that much of that access is outside libraries and not in the purview of librarians. Purchasing a book, downloading streaming media, using an online resource, or visiting an art gallery are all manifestations of access to recorded knowledge and information. It is important that we play our part; at the same time, we should concentrate on the aspects of this value over which we can have some control: access to library resources and services. We should also work with other agencies to promote all aspects of access because an educated citizenry requires the full range of access afforded by libraries and other cultural institutions.

Equity of access involves removing or minimizing all the many barriers to use of library resources and programs for all library users. Just as with many other contemporary issues in librarianship ("information literacy" comes to mind), many librarians, educators, and others have focused the discussion on—and only on—the technological aspects of library service. I am sure that a cursory examination of the problem will reveal that students in poor rural or inner-city areas with no or poor library service absolutely will not have equity of access to the same universe of knowledge as their better-off peers, even if they have access to online resources. Real library services and collections staffed by librarians are as necessary to all children as are good teachers. This applies to all grades—from kindergarten students who need access to good age-appropriate books, story hours, the attention of skilled librarians, and all the other things that instill an early love of reading and learning, to high school students looking for guidance on what to read and do research into new topics.

Equity of access, then, means that all people deserve and should be given the recorded knowledge and information they want, no matter who they are and in which format that knowledge and information is contained. It means that one should be able to have access (either to a library building or from a remote location), that library services should assist in the optimal use of library resources, and that those resources should be relevant and worthwhile. "All people," of course, includes disadvantaged groups and minorities of various kinds. Take, for example, the question of the right to equity of access of people with physical and mental handicaps. In her study of the provision of library services to young people with disabilities in Western Australia, Denise Barker states:

> In my experience, the greatest barrier facing young people with disabilities comes from not the physical aspect but how others perceive them and at times treat them differently because of their disability. I have heard stories of people over compensating and assistance being offered when it is not required, as well as people with disabilities being ignored or spoken to in a condescending manner. By library staff working with organisations and agencies involved with service provision to young people with disabilities they can encourage them to come to libraries. Library staff will gain invaluable informal training. Also, the young person with the disability becomes more comfortable and may even be led to use more public facilities.[3]

Thus we see that equity of access is not only a practical question but also a way of thinking about library users and how there are many kinds of barrier to that access.

I have already written of the importance of intellectual freedom to libraries. The question of access to library materials and library services is linked to that. It is important to make everything accessible to everybody without fear or favor, but it is equally important to ensure that such access is practically possible and not biased in favor of the better-off or the more powerful. Such equitable access is brought into question by some aspects of technology. For example, in the United States we are seeing a continuing (if little noticed) scandal in the dissemination of government documents (the contents of which are our property to which we are all entitled). It is well known that the information and recorded knowledge generated by the government is not as available to all citizens as it is to some business interests, and the excellent system of depository libraries is being dismantled by a combination of actions and inaction of Congress. In their zeal to embrace the all-digital future, Congress forgets (or chooses not to acknowledge) three major problems with this approach. First, there is no depository library divide—anyone can gain access to government information without payment using them—but there still is a digital divide. Second, the government gives no guarantee that all-digital government information will be preserved for future citizens and scholars and has no plans to give that guarantee. Third, what the government holds digitally, the government can alter, delete, or deny access to at will. Hardly a prospect that should appeal to civil libertarians, Libertarians, or those suspicious of Big Government.

More generally, the idea of charging for access to library materials and library services is much more popular today. There seems to be a difference, in some people's minds, between "free" print and other materials and "cost recovery" access to digital resources. Interestingly, many libraries still pay for digital resources from outside their materials budgets, and that may condition their willingness to charge for what are seen as extras even in budgetary terms. In a world of access being limited by the ability to pay, the all-digital idea is, essentially, an elitist construct that writes off sections of society as doomed to be "information poor."

I am not saying it is inevitable that libraries using technology intensively as an enhancement to their services are going to betray the value of equity of access. However, it is evident that there is an inherent contradiction in society's approach to the use of technology—the disconnect between the idea of technology making more information accessible to more people and the inability of many (because of who they are and their economic status) to take advantage of that accessibility. That contradiction should make us very sensitive to the idea of maintaining libraries that are freely available to all, irrespective of social standing and economic circumstances.. This value is especially important to those libraries that serve a population containing a majority of economically disadvantaged users.

EQUITY OF ACCESS IN ACTION

There are many reasons why one individual may not have equitable access to the recorded knowledge and information that he needs. Not all library resources and services are available to all without distinction, and the factors that inhibit access vary from person to person and place to place. Even someone who is in a library physically may have barriers to his use that are not present for others in the same building. Not all these inequities are eliminated by technology; in fact, as we have seen in the discussion of the digital divide, technology may itself introduce new inequities.

Barriers to equity of access may, broadly, be grouped into three categories: personal, institutional, and societal. Here are the types of barriers in each category.

Personal. Poverty. Physical disability. Lack of mobility. Level of knowledge.
 Level of education. Level of literacy. English language skills. Level of
 computer skills.
Institutional. Location of the library. Layout of library building.
 Type, quantity, and availability of equipment. Helpfulness of staff.
 Availability of staff.
Societal. Education system. Political environment. Unequal funding of
 library services.

If one or more of the descriptions and states of living in the following list apply to you, you are very likely to have lesser or even no access to the library resources you need and to the services that enable you to use them.

> poor . . . ailing . . . member of a single-parent household . . . disabled
> . . . live in a rural area . . . very young . . . live in the inner city . . .
> old . . . member of an ethnic minority . . . wrong side of the digital
> divide . . . have limited English proficiency . . . no or limited computer
> skills . . . incarcerated . . . no or limited private or public transportation
> . . . undereducated

When we contemplate the number and multidimensionality of the barriers to access, it can readily be seen that creating equity of library access for all is a complex and extraordinarily difficult task.

Let us look at some things that are increasing and would increase equity of access. The following is not an exhaustive list by any means; it contains measures that librarians can and do carry out or influence as well as measures that we cannot, and it consists of public policy and purely library steps to be taken. The list is not in order of priority or importance.

- Increase the number of school libraries and of librarians with teaching credentials to work in them.
- Provide more equitable funding for counties, school districts, and other governmental units within states.

- Offer classes in libraries on
  - literacy
  - English-language skills
  - information competence
  - computer skills
- Keep branch public libraries open in rural areas and inner-city areas.
- Ensure that "smart" libraries and schoolrooms are accompanied by personnel trained in computer skills and information competence.
- Go beyond the minimal requirements of the Americans with Disabilities Act in building and retrofitting libraries, particularly by consulting library users with disabilities.
- Work to remove restrictions on the library rights of the incarcerated.
- Take library services to the people by such measures as
  - mobile libraries
  - branches and library services in "unconventional" settings, such as shopping malls, college dormitories, day care and senior centers, and hospitals and hospices
- Ensure that online systems are current, accessible, and user friendly.

STEPS TO EQUITY

If we are to work in a coordinated manner to reduce inequities of access on all fronts, we must recognize that individuals have a part to play, libraries and other public institutions have a part to play, and legislators and others interested in public policy issues have a part to play. I have long thought that the articulation of all these interests and influences will require a major and sustained profession-wide campaign that can be led only by the American Library Association. Such a campaign will be based on the simple idea that it is a societal injustice for access to library resources and programs to be conditioned on any of a variety of states of life. The potential for inequity is great, and the factors that influence that potential are numerous. How can we even begin to remedy the situation? How can an individual librarian or group of librarians influence the world about us and improve access for the disadvantaged? The following steps will set us on the path toward abolishing inequities of access.

- Cease to take inequities for granted.
- Understand the strengths and the limitations of technology so that we can use the former and learn to deal with the latter.
- Understand and analyze the barriers to access and assign them to the following categories:
  - those over which we have control
  - those that we can play a role in remedying
  - those that are outside our control but which we can mitigate
  - those that are very difficult for us to do anything about
  - those that are impossible to change
- Organize within our institutions and professional organizations to work systematically on reducing inequities.
- Keep going so that one barrier at a time is reduced or eliminated.
- Make equity of access a cardinal principle of all innovations and programs.

Stop Accepting Inequity

The first step in this program is a matter of principles and priorities—and a step that is more difficult, ironically, for those who work in libraries in which equity of access is of lesser immediacy. For those librarians in the trenches, faced daily with inequities, the principle of equity is an inevitable part of daily working life. A children's librarian in a poor rural area is confronted by inequity daily when she deals with children who cannot read, who work in the fields with their parents, who may have an imperfect command of English, or who regard a mandated trip to the library as an inconvenience. However, even university libraries are often situated in far-from-affluent communities and serve the members of the wider community as well as those in academe. It is difficult for me to imagine a librarian who could function well in any library while remaining unconcerned about inequity of access. One does not need to be a revolutionary insurrectionist to advocate the removal of all barriers to effective library use.

Understand the Role of Technology

I think that, in the early days, many people—even many librarians—thought that technology would be the great leveler, that it would enable us to give equitable library service to even the most remote user, and that it would, somehow, make up for deficiencies in funding of library services to the disadvantaged. There can be no doubt that technology can help if the following conditions can be met:

- There is universal online access.
- Everyone has online skills.
- The technologically advanced library is accessible.
- Everyone is trained in information competence and critical thinking.
- Libraries can organize to provide services to distant users.
- Technology is integrated with—and not a substitute for—other library resources and services.

It is a fact of contemporary life that every library and schoolroom should provide online access. Now that we have achieved it in almost all cases, there are still questions to be asked and answered:

- Is the provision of online access always backed up by freely available and knowledgeable professional and technical assistance?
- Will a schoolroom equipped with modem computers with high-speed online access compensate for a "library" consisting of twenty-five-year-old books and with no librarian?
- If you are a child or a less-mobile adult public library user, what good is online access in every library if your branch library closed two years ago?
- Even if there is easy access for knowledgeable users, what about all the recorded knowledge and information that is either not available online and/or is better than anything available online?

None of these questions is easy to answer, and their implications are ominous. It is common for those who can implement public policy at all levels to simply install computers and walk away—declaring a victory and going home. How can we explain away a world in which, despite near universal online access, levels of literacy and education continue to decline inexorably? Is it possible that such a state of affairs is because of near-universal online access? There is a natural human tendency to settle for what you have, and we could hardly blame a distant learner or a teacher in a rural school for settling for whatever can be found online in the absence of books and other traditional library resources. In addition, there is an obvious seductiveness about online clicking, flash, and speed and the ability to download what is discovered instantly. This is especially so when compared with the more arduous task of sustained reading and the thought processes it induces. An old gibe about education—that it is "the transfer of information from textbook to notebook without going through human minds"—is daily being recast as "the downloading of online texts and images into term papers without passing through human minds."

I have stressed the importance of providing assistance to library users using online resources. Such assistance is especially important as a means of overcoming the passive acceptance of anything that is available online, not least because of the lack of ability to know what is available only in books and other tangible library resources. As well as helping users in the library and in the schoolroom, we should be aware of what has been called "the virtual patron" and the grouping of those library users into "virtual communities." As one writer puts it:

> These virtual communities require the services and resources of various academic support units much in the same way as traditional campus communities. In order to remain relevant within this milieu, academic libraries are changing rapidly and being transformed to meet the changing needs of the evolving academic communities they serve. To that end, libraries are increasingly providing services and support to virtual patrons, by facilitating access to and navigation of electronic resources and providing value-added support services that optimize effective use of these resources. [4]

Libraries have been giving assistance to distant users at least since the invention of the telephone (or earlier, if you think of postal reference service). However, there are particular and difficult characteristics of online users: they expect the response to be as quick and easy as the request; they pose complex questions that require numerous iterations and interactions (a frustrating process); and they often require technical support and advice that the library or individual librarian may not be able to give. The latter may not be a simple matter of providing only library-related answers. Even if the library's personnel are prepared to answer any questions about software and systems, a user's level of technical knowledge may be so low as to make communication difficult or impossible.

Then there is the perennial question of monetary and human resources. As remote access to library resources and services increases, so will the demands of the virtual patrons. Most libraries will not have new money for new staff to meet those demands and will be back to the same old "reallocation of resources"—another example of technological change diverting staff time from "traditional" services that may be no less important than the new service.

Set Priorities

The crucial factors in the third step toward abolishing inequities of access are careful surveying and analysis, beginning with your own library. The jargon of management and planning includes the useful (if pompous) phrase "environmental scan." That concept is valuable to the librarian who is serious about increasing equity of access. The problems are well on their way to being delineated when you begin by looking around your library and thinking about the factors that lead to inequity of access. It is a truism that defining problems is halfway to solving them, but one of the characteristics of truisms is that they are true. It is also important to conceptualize the process of delineation as a series of concentric circles, beginning with issues over which the library has a high degree of control and ending with issues that are produced by major social forces and over which the library has little or no control.

Inside the Library

Let us begin in the library and look at some of the intangible barriers to access for those who are actually there. I have written earlier in this book of the importance of bibliographic control systems to use of the library. Just as an up-to-date, user-friendly, internally coherent, standardized, and accessible online system is an invaluable aid to library users, a system that lacks one or more of those qualities may present insuperable barriers to effective use of the library. The library has almost complete control over its own online bibliographic system and, therefore, can remove or mitigate barriers in and to that system. The online system of today is also a gateway to a variety of other resources, from the relatively orderly world of indexes, abstracts, and indexed full-text databases to the disorderly world of cyberspace. Obviously the library lacks the control over those resources that it has over its own database, but it can reduce barriers to use by designing or deploying easily usable interfaces and "help" capabilities.

The question of access to the library's online system is also, of course, affected by the physical world. How many public terminals should a library have? One answer is: enough so that anyone can have instant access to a terminal at any time. Few libraries of any size come anywhere near that situation, and most university and large public libraries have dealt for some years with the problem of waiting lists for terminals. Now that almost all libraries are offering online access, use of terminals is increasing apace, and even small libraries have to cope with more would-be users than terminals at peak times. Perhaps the wide availability of smartphones and tablets will solve one part of this aspect of access.

How easy is it for library users to gain access to your online system from their homes or elsewhere outside the library? This may be outside the library's control, but it is hardly likely that someone experiencing difficulty in being a virtual library user is going to blame anyone but the library. Therefore, it behooves us to work as best we can to make remote access to our systems and resources as easy and reliable as possible. This brings up the important and often overlooked question of the public relations aspect of equity and ease of access. Just as a library that is closed when it is expected to be open can be a PR disaster, so can a foiled expectation of access to and ease of remote use of the library's systems.

A poor online system and a good online system to which remote access is difficult or impossible are intangible barriers to access. A library building can also contain tangible barriers, and a good survey of the physical plant from the point of view of all users can yield some surprising and correctable results. Many of the features of a modern library—braille tags on elevators, devices for the partially sighted and the deaf, wheelchair ramps, and wheelchair-accessible workstations—are among the more obvious enhancers of access. There are more subtle barriers: size and layout of furniture at service points, signs that use library jargon that is not understood by the bulk of library users, confusing arrangement of materials, poor wording of interfaces, and many others. Such things can often be discerned only by those who can put themselves in the place of all library users and see the library from all their different points of view.

That last—seeing the library anew—may be the most difficult approach to removing barriers to access within the library, but it is undoubtedly the most productive. What does an academic library really look like to a first-generation student whose first language is not English? Do nonlibrarians know what to do when offered the choice between searching in "browse" or "keyword" mode? Remember that the vast majority of library users use our systems without ever asking for assistance—even when they know they need some assistance.

Outside the Library

All libraries exist in specific environments—the institution or community that they serve. They also live in the wider world—the society of the town, region, state, and country in which they are situated. In an era of globalization, those societies include continents and, indeed, the whole world. There are forces in our localities, countries, and the world as a whole that influence our work and the people we serve. Some of those (e.g., literacy, education, scholarly communication, and information technology) are areas in which we can exert some influence, especially if we act in concert. Others (e.g., Big Technology, the infotainment industry, and federal education policy) are beyond our powers. Still others (e.g., copyright and intellectual property) are insoluble by anyone. If we are to work seriously and effectively on increasing equity of access, we must have the wisdom to distinguish among these types of external forces and to concentrate on those that we can change and affect.

Work Together

I am convinced that the only answer to the equity of access issue—once it is defined and analyzed as set out above—is a concerted multiyear effort in which all libraries and librarians participate. Such a campaign should deal with all the dimensions of access (technological and otherwise), should be politically smart and effective, should use all modern means of persuasion (including advertising and PR), and should go through continuing cycles of proposal, work, achievement, analysis, and evaluation. It should seek to involve librarians from all kinds of libraries, the institutions and communities they serve, and politicians and other public policy experts at all levels—local, state, and federal.

Here is how I see a campaign like this working. ALA should begin by declaring equity of access to be its major external priority. (I use the latter term, as ALA must be effective on two fronts simultaneously: serving its membership and addressing the role of libraries in society.) It should follow that declaration by convening a broad-based Convention on Equity of Access to define the issues and priorities and then to work out a plan of action through a variety of librarian and nonlibrarian task forces and commissions. These latter would be charged with specific areas of inequity (e.g., literacy and language skills; technology and lack of technological competence; rural library service; the correlations among poverty, education, and library use; library service to the old and the young; diversity issues). Their work product would be white papers delineating each issue and recommending priorities for action. Those would be widely disseminated and discussed in a variety of forums (town meetings devoted to specific aspects of the problem, webinars, teleconferences, and so on). Those discussions would lead to the formulation of a grand plan of action to be promulgated by a second Convention on Equity of Access (which, like the first, would be comprised of both librarians and other interested parties). At the end of what would probably be a two-year process, ALA would have a multidimensional master plan that could be advanced on several fronts. The unwinding of the process would be accompanied by a public relations campaign aimed at communicating the enduring value of libraries to society. That PR campaign would first make the point of the value of libraries and then build on and enhance that message with reports on the work of the equity of access campaign and the ways in which librarians are working together on many issues to bring the benefits of library service to all.

Take One Step at a Time

This proposed national campaign would consist primarily of the articulation of many local efforts in many areas. It cannot be stressed too often that, as with many other social movements, equity of access to library resources and services will be advanced step-by-step by individual librarians and libraries as barriers are identified and removed or mitigated—sometimes across the nation, sometimes as the result of local action involving very few people. ALA and individual librarians can supply leadership, and a well-conducted campaign can supply inspiration; but the struggle will be most effective library by library as we work collectively and individually to reach the dream of a world in which library resources and services are freely available to all. That dream should inform all our actions—not just those that are part of the national campaign, but everything we do as librarians and every enhancement to library service that we make.

NOTES

1. Stonehouse, John. "Spirit of the stacks." *New scientist* (March 20, 1999) page 47.
2. American Library Association. "Equity of access." www.ala.org/advocacy/access/equityofaccess (consulted August 29, 2014).
3. Barker, Denise. "On the outside looking in." *APLIS*, volume 24, issue 1 (March 2011) pages 9–16.
4. Moyo, Lesley M. "The virtual patron." *Science & technology libraries*, volume 25, issues 1–2 (2004) pages 185–209.

CHAPTER 11

PRIVACY

Google knows what you're looking for. Facebook knows what you like. Sharing is the norm, and secrecy is out. But what is the psychological and cultural fallout from the end of privacy? We have come to the end of privacy; our private lives, as our grandparents would have recognised them, have been winnowed away to the realm of the shameful and secret. . . . Insidiously, through small concessions that only mounted up over time, we have signed away rights and privileges that other generations fought for, undermining the very cornerstones of our personalities in the process. While outposts of civilisation fight pyrrhic battles, unplugging themselves from the web— "going dark"—the rest of us have come to accept that the majority of our social, financial and even sexual interactions take place over the internet and that someone, somewhere, whether state, press or corporation, is watching.

—Alex Preston[1]

WHAT HATH A DECADE AND A HALF WROUGHT?

In the last years of the twentieth century, I wrote about the mounting fears of invasion of privacy caused by accelerating developments in digital technology. I had seen nothing yet. Those vague fears, that queasy unease were born in a time when we knew nothing of two massive developments in the century yet to come. The events of September 11, 2001, led to the War on Terror and a concomitant expansion of state surveillance, the true dimensions of which are even now only dimly perceived, even after the revelations of WikiLeaks and Snowden. At the same time, large sections of the population became ensorcelled by the twin delights of online purchasing and social media. These two horsemen of the privacy apocalypse offered consumerism and social interaction, each without the tedious and often messy necessities of personal contact. Today's Internet adds online porn, online gambling, and online "gaming"; so, given a pizza delivery company, anyone can live an entire sort of life in the solitary basement of her choosing. The digital Mephistopheles did not demand your soul in return for their "gifts"—just your privacy.

Many have written and spoken about this Faustian bargain. "Privacy is dead, get over it," wrote Scott McNealy. "When you get something online free, you are not the consumer, you are the product," has been attributed to several people, including someone called Andrew Lewis (writing, for reasons known best to himself, as "blue_bottle"). A much more significant person than either, Gabriel García Márquez, told us we all have three lives: a public life, a private life, and a secret life. The public life is open to the world, an environment in which there is no reasonable expectation of privacy. The private life is that which we share with family, those we love, friends, and acquaintances. In olden times, family and lovers were licensed to shrink one's zone of privacy in negotiation with the individual. With friends and acquaintances, the zone of privacy was much larger. Apparently, there is now no distinction between friends and acquaintances; "friend" has become a verb (quite different from the old verb "to befriend"); and a "friend" is, more often than not, a stranger who may or may not read the individual's profundities on social media. The secret life used to be the one in which the zone of privacy was very large and often complete. The lines that used to exist between public, private, and secret lives have become blurred, mutable, and, on occasion, nonexistent. Just consider what many people "share" online or in the unreality of "reality television," and ponder the ways in which the three kinds of lives meld in the online age. The commonly predicted "chip in the brain" will complete the process and abolish the very concept of privacy.[2] Worse, the private and secret lives are the places in which the keenest psychological insights and literature originate—and where will we be without those? While we wait for the brain chips to arrive, let us consider the privacy that we may already have lost in McNealy World.

THE MEANING OF PRIVACY?

The word "private" is defined as "belonging to, or concerning, an individual; personal; one's own."[3] Private things, therefore, belong to the individual; they are her personal property. In a free society, the things that belong to you legally are inalienable and cannot be removed or interfered with without your permission. We all need privacy (a word rarely encountered before the sixteenth century) in a spatial sense and an informational sense. Our spatial privacy gives us the right to be alone, to associate only with those with whom we choose to associate, and to be free from surveillance. Our informational privacy is the right to control personal information and to hold our retrieval and use of information and recorded knowledge to ourselves, without such use being monitored by others. We also have the privacy that is embodied in the term "private property"—those things that we own, which include intangible, intellectual private property. The rights to privacy that once seemed so obvious to us in our daily lives have never been legally guaranteed in all cases or practically achievable.

WHAT HATH TECHNOLOGY WROUGHT?

Technology is neither good nor bad in and of itself. Technological advance may contribute to societal progress or may be a detriment to society; those advances may be both (just think of advances in fertility medicine in a world that contains more than seven billion people) or may be neutral. It is a natural human tendency to personalize both technology in general and specific applications of technology. For instance, the mental enslavement of many in the developed countries by the handheld devices we used to call telephones is a popular subject for cartoons and comedians. Those same devices have been a boon in many developing countries, facilitating commerce and communications in many positive ways. The truth is that, though the sight of a couple in a restaurant bent over their tiny screens in silence is some combination of risible and intensely sad, it is not the technology that is at fault; it is our shortcomings as human beings. Similarly, it is not the devices that create good things in Cambodia or Rwanda; it is the scope they give for human creativity and ingenuity to flower. The human use and misuse of technology arouses the emotions, and it is the human use and misuse of technology that we should observe, study, and seek to profit from the good and avoid the bad.

THE WINDOW LOOKING IN . . .

It seems that almost every advance in technology exacts a counterbalancing price or detriment. There is no such thing as a free technological improvement. One of the most obvious prices that we are all paying is the actual and potential erosion of privacy caused by the compilation of, and easy access to, large and complex databases resulting from our interaction with commercial, governmental, and other institutions. The latter, of course, include transactions between libraries and library users and transactions that take place in libraries. Here are words to make us wary: "Every keystroke can be monitored. And computers never forget."[4] The same article quotes Marc Rotenberg, director of the Electronic Privacy Information Center:

> With the new online services, we're all excited that this is going to be our window on the world, to movies, to consumer services, for talking with our friends. The reality is that this may be a window looking in.

The point is that it is not technology that is the enemy of privacy but our joyful, unheeding use of technology. We give away something of ourselves each time we engage in online transactions. One might wish it were not so, but the inescapable fact is that many of us are willing to trade privacy for convenience and allow commercial concerns to build and profit from huge databases built on that bargain. Most people worry about the security of their credit cards and bank accounts, and reputable providers of services take steps to ensure that security. Many people worry about potential governmental and commercial abuse of the information we are required to supply by law or in pursuit of a commercial transaction. Though these are real concerns, there is a wider picture that goes beyond the economic and governmental. We live more and more of our lives online, and the accumulations of data about us grow ever larger while there is an ever-increasing ability to retrieve and manipulate that data speedily. We are coming to see that the history of society is cyclical and that cyberspace is coming to resemble nothing as much as a medieval village—a place in which privacy was unknown.

Digital technology is now the indispensable vehicle of the relationship between individuals and their government and between individuals and commercial concerns. It also dominates and shapes an increasing amount of social interactions. We are right in being concerned about the integrity of our personal data and should support efforts by governments and others to devise regulations and codes that limit (but can never eliminate) incursions on that data. As long ago as 1973, the Department of Health, Education, and Welfare issued a code on personal data systems based on the following (paraphrased) principles:

- There should be no secret record-keeping systems.
- Individuals should have access to their own records.
- Individuals should be able to prevent data gathered for one purpose from being used for another.
- Individuals should be able to correct or amend their own records.
- Organizations collecting personal data must ensure its reliability and prevent misuse.[5]

Those decades-old principles still hold true in a very different world. They are even more difficult to enforce today than they were then, but they do provide the basis for humane and responsible collection and retention of personal data.

An application of these general principles to an important area of privacy can be found in the Health Insurance Portability & Accountability Act (HIPAA)[6] and in the HIPAA Privacy Rules issued by the Department of Health & Human Services.[7] The Act and the Rule are designed to "assure that individuals' health information is properly protected while allowing the flow of health information needed to provide and promote high quality health care and to protect the public's health and well-being." A balance is struck that permits important uses of information, while protecting the privacy of people who seek care and healing. This illustrates an important tension between the privacy rights of the individual and the need for any system, great and small, to have a free flow of relevant information.

THE HISTORY OF PRIVACY

Privacy emerged as a social issue in the eighteenth century. Before then, people—even rich and powerful people—lived open lives because of the nature of society and the buildings in which they lived. Most people lived, ate, slept, played, and so on communally. Even more important with respect to privacy, there was little or no distinction between domestic life and work life. Reading and copying, for example, were communal activities in the Middle Ages. The concept of privacy and the solitary life of the mind came when communities and extended families gave way to nuclear families with houses with solid walls that contained separate rooms and were situated on private land. In the eighteenth and most of the nineteenth centuries, such houses belonged to the wealthy. Even then, communities persisted in the cohabitation of families and their servants. It was not until the twentieth century that the opportunity for privacy was available to the less well-off in Europe and North America. The important changes in the ways in which people lived and worked—notably the physical and psychological separation of work and "private life"—created a hunger for privacy that has been extended and asserted in a number of steps over the decades. One very important step was the publication of a paper by future Supreme Court Justice Louis Brandeis and a colleague arguing "the right to be let alone."[8] That influential paper (from more than one hundred years ago) was spurred by fears of the intrusive capability of then new technologies—cameras, tabloid newspapers, telephones, and the like. Later, when on the Supreme Court, Brandeis was to argue that wiretapping telephones was the equivalent of opening sealed letters.[9] In the United States, the legal definition of privacy has evolved slowly in the years since Brandeis's plea for privacy. The important Supreme Court case *Griswold v. Connecticut* (which said that a right to privacy implicitly, but not explicitly, contained in the US Constitution, underlies the right of married couples to use birth control) was decided only in 1965.[10] There are those who say that *Roe v. Wade*—the most famous case decided on the basis of an inherent constitutional right to privacy—is constitutionally flawed for that very reason. In other words, they believe that the Constitution protects only that which it lists explicitly. One could not possibly underestimate the effect on American society of an acceptance and application of that extremist view.

There is a considerable body of opinion among constitutional lawyers and philosophers that the US Constitution was framed on the basis of natural law and natural rights that are inherent in an ordered society.[11] Given that is so, it is not difficult to see that the Constitution is capable of interpretation that goes beyond the exact words of that document to place natural rights in a modern context. Privacy is, of course, one of the natural rights that has been understood since at least the late eighteenth century. Privacy has been a matter of great weight to the individual and to society as a whole for more than two hundred years, but the right to privacy is nowhere near as entrenched in law and constitutional thinking as most people believe it to be.

Privacy remained a hot political, legal, and societal issue throughout the twentieth century and, in one form or another, is still fought over today. All social movements have been combated by—among other things—invasions of privacy. All the protagonists of the women's movement, the fight for racial equality, the struggle for literary and artistic free expression, and other such movements have been subject to surveillance and intrusion by governmental and other compilers of dossiers on private lives. It is common knowledge that such outrages still exist, but it would be cynical to ignore the advances in privacy contained in the law. That being said, unless we restrain the effects of technology, those hard-won legal rights are in danger of being vitiated by societal forces that cannot be controlled by law.

THE PRESENT AND FUTURE OF PRIVACY

Technology—in the form of vast records of online transactions of all kinds and the possibility of searching and retrieving personal data from those databases—is morally neutral. As noted before, people can use this technology for good or ill—for their own profit or in service of humanity. Our privacy is invaded daily; the task is to ensure those invasions are controlled and have benign outcomes. We have clear opportunities and dangers and should work to take advantage of the opportunities and reduce the dangers.

Columbia University professor Alan Westin published a list of important trends in the protection of privacy.[12] Those trends include the following:

- Personal information will be owned jointly by individuals and institutions.
- Institutions may use personal data only with the consent of the individuals.
- Collectors of personal data will issue privacy codes.
- Storage and use of personal data will be regulated.
- Theft and misuse of personal data will be criminalized.
- A federal agency dedicated to the protection of privacy will be established.

Many of Professor Westin's forecasts have proved to be accurate, in theory if not always in practice. One of them (the last) has not been realized. It is difficult to see a federal agency of the kind that he envisages being established, not least because of the American distaste for central government oversight of personal matters. What has happened is the establishment of a patchwork of ever-changing mixture of legislation, government regulation, and self-regulation. (Good examples of the latter are the various ALA policies and statements on privacy.)

A number of US federal agencies are actively involved in privacy issues. They include the Departments of Commerce, Health and Human Services, and Labor; the Federal Communications Commission; and the Federal Telecommunications Commission—each addressing medical, financial, telecommunications, Internet, and so on privacy issues in a largely uncoordinated manner. A list created in 2005 listed the following federal privacy laws:[13]

- Federal Trade Commission Act (1914)
- Freedom of Information Act (1966)
- Fair Credit Reporting Act (1970)
- Privacy Act (1974)
- Family Educational Rights and Privacy Act (1974)
- Foreign Intelligence Surveillance Act (1978)
- Right to Financial Privacy Act (1978)

- Privacy Protection Act (1980)
- Cable Communications Policy Act (1984)
- Electronic Communications Privacy Act (1986)
- Video Privacy Protection Act (1988)
- Employee Polygraph Protection Act (1988)
- Telephone Consumer Protection Act (1991)
- Driver's Privacy Protection Act (1994)
- Health Insurance Portability and Accountability Act (1996)
- Telecommunications Act (1996)
- Children's Online Privacy Protection Act (1998)
- Financial Modernization Services Act (1999)
- USA Patriot Act (2001)

All these are complemented by a host of regulations, court decisions, state laws, local ordinances, and pending legislation. Outside the circle of governmental action at all levels, there are many voluntary agreements between and within public sector entities (including ALA and other library organizations). It is obvious that this is a multifaceted problem—one that affects us all to a greater or lesser extent—and that it is, at best, being addressed in a haphazard and uncoordinated manner.

The complexity of the American approach is in stark contrast to the approach of the European Union, which has issued a Directive on Data Protection (effective October 25, 1998) that is binding on all members of the EU. The Directive is being revised to "strengthen online privacy rights and boost Europe's digital economy."[14] The proposed revision is because

> the 27 EU Member States have implemented the 1995 rules differently, resulting in divergences in enforcement. A single law will do away with the current fragmentation and costly administrative burdens, leading to savings for businesses of around €2.3 billion a year. The initiative will help reinforce consumer confidence in online services, providing a much needed boost to growth, jobs and innovation in Europe.

The starkly different approach in the United States means that there is no one agency and no single body of law that mirrors the EU's legal requirements, a problem in a world of globalized trade and constant interaction between the two systems. In the words of the US Department of Commerce: "While the United States and the EU share the goal of enhancing privacy protection for their citizens, the United States takes a different approach to privacy from that taken by the EU. In order to bridge these differences in approach and provide a streamlined means for U.S. organizations to comply with the Directive, the U.S. Department of Commerce in consultation with the European Commission developed a "Safe Harbor" framework and this website to provide the information an organization would need to evaluate—and then join—the U.S.-EU Safe Harbor program."[15] The principles on which that program is based echo some of Professor Westin's 1992 provisions.[16] In summary, the Commerce Department's principles are:

Notice. An organization collecting personal data must inform the individuals involved of what they are doing and their rights.

Choice. Individuals must be able to opt out of their data being transmitted to third parties.

Onward transmission. Personal data can be transmitted only to third parties that subscribe to privacy protection.

Security. Organizations collecting personal data must hold them secure against misuse, disclosure, destruction, and so on.

Data integrity. Personal data may be used only for the purposes for which they were collected.

Access. Individuals must have reasonable access to the data that have been collected about them.

Enforcement. There must be mechanisms (governmental or private) to ensure compliance with privacy principles. Those mechanisms must include recourse for individuals whose data have been misused, follow-up procedures to ensure remedies are being applied, and sanctions against organizations that violate personal privacy rights.

Given the increase in online transactions of all kinds, the great commercial value of personal data databases, and the increase in digital technology capabilities, it is inevitable that privacy will continue to be a major issue and one that is increasingly subject to government regulation and private sector codes and compacts.

WHAT IS THE RELATIONSHIP BETWEEN PRIVACY AND LIBRARIES?

There is a world of difference between the passive accumulation of anonymized personal data for a variety of legitimate purposes and the deliberate, active invasion of privacy. The former has potential for abuse; the latter *is* abuse. To my mind, one of the greatest scandals afflicting the political culture today is the wholesale and largely successful attack on the right to privacy. This is the world of *1984*, the world of mind control, the world of mental totalitarianism. The confidentiality of library records and the confidentiality of the use of library resources are not the most sensational weapons in the fight for privacy, but they are important, both on practical and moral grounds.

In practical terms, much of the relationship between a library and its patrons is based on trust, and, in a free society, a library user should be secure in trusting us not to reveal and not to cause to be revealed which resources are being used and by whom. On moral grounds, we must begin with the premise that everyone is entitled to freedom of access, freedom to read texts and view images, and freedom of thought and expression. None of those freedoms can survive in an atmosphere in which library use is monitored and individual library use patterns are made known to anyone without permission. It is very important that all libraries follow a policy that ensures privacy and that they take steps to educate everyone in the library about that policy. In this context, we should always remember that most people in most libraries today interact with library staff, volunteers, and student assistants far more than with librarians. Knowing this, a library with a privacy policy that is not communicated effectively and completely to all who work in the library is just as bad as one with no policy at all.

For all their faults, preautomated systems were far better at preserving the privacy of circulation and use records than are their automated successors. Old readers may remember systems in which a book card and a user's card were matched for the time and only for the time that the book was borrowed. Once returned, the two cards were separated, and there was no trace of the transaction ever having taken place. Now, our systems will preserve all circulation and use records unless they are programmed not to do so. Most library systems are set to delete user information after the materials are returned or the use is complete, but how difficult would it be for a skilled person to restore those "deleted" records? It seems that digital records are forever—if one has the skill, the desire, and the time to retrieve them. In addition, many systems choose to maintain a record of the last borrower (for convenience if a returned item is found to have been damaged or mutilated)—a small but significant invasion of privacy. Libraries serve communities, and communities breed gossip, nosiness, and prurience. Those who enjoy such things can easily find out who in their community has been reading about divorce, murder, diseases, dieting, dyslexia, and sexual variations. Is such a potential invasion of privacy worth the ability to track down library vandals?

Self-check

One technological innovation that is actually assisting the right to privacy is the "self-check" device. This machine enables the user to check out library materials and gain access to other services on her own. I am not aware of any studies on the circulation patterns of self-check users as opposed to those who take their materials to a circulation desk. However, it would seem reasonable to assume that a library user with access to open shelves might feel freer to borrow "controversial" materials if assured that no one would see what she was borrowing. If this is true, such materials would go far beyond the obvious suspects—sexual content and so on—and extend to, for example, materials on diseases, English professors reading Danielle Steele books, "happily married" people reading materials on divorce, and cinéastes streaming Adam Sandler films. The self-check machine, invented to speed the circulation process, may well be a signal contribution to the library right to privacy.

Privacy and Electronic Resources

I have noted before that there is a serious problem of disparity of access to digital resources. Bromides about "everyone" being online and the ubiquity of online access ignore the facts that ethnic minorities, lower socioeconomic groups, vast populations in the developing world, people living with intellectual and physical disabilities, and rural populations in the developed world lack access to the full range of digital services and, hence, are at an economic, educational, and societal disadvantage. The figures on the digital divide vary from one survey to another, but no one disputes the existence of that gap. The public library is in a position to compensate for that gap (as are academic libraries, particularly state-supported institutions in communities that contain a significant number of the disadvantaged) by supplying free access and guidance in using that access. This means that the question of privacy and confidentiality is an ineluctable and important issue for libraries—like it or not. We provide online access because we believe in giving access to all materials, but this particular case is so important because we are providing access to a vital part of modern life. If we are to come to terms with a society in which computer skills are highly esteemed and rewarded, and if we are to give access to modern communications to those who would otherwise be shut out, we will have to deal with the many consequences of that service. Privacy rights, intellectual freedom rights, parental rights, and other issues attached to Internet access are there and have to be confronted.

There are many age-old problems connected with library privacy, but online resources and digital systems have introduced new dimensions to the struggle for confidentiality. Anyone who wishes can monitor the use of online journals, find out who gains access to which web pages and who has downloaded what, create vast caches of information on sites visited and resources consulted, and do a myriad other things. You do not have to be paranoid to wonder a little, the next time you key in your name, address, and other details when ordering an item or service, about the uses to which those data may be put. Amazon, Facebook, Google, and the rest of the unaccountable lords of Big Technology accumulate vast amounts of individualized personal data for commercial purposes. One would have to be very naïve not to understand that data is open to major violations of individual privacy.

Invasions of privacy are often done with good intentions, but everyone knows which road is paved with those. In the electronic arena, users and librarians have to act to mitigate invasions of privacy and to be always alert to the possibilities for snooping and more sinister uses of data about personal use of digital resources. Given this state of affairs, it behooves us to work even harder to preserve confidentiality at least in the area in which we work. Librarians should never agree to the loss of privacy and should work hard to preserve the privacy of the individual by enunciating principles, creating policies, and putting them into action. We need to develop more detailed privacy codes that are flexible enough to cover all kinds of library use in a rapidly changing technological environment.

PRIVACY IN ACTION

In June 2014, the American Library Association issued an interpretation of its Library Bill of Rights that addresses privacy in very broad terms and provides what is, essentially, an overview of the issues and an ethical framework for library policies rather than specific practical steps to be taken.[17] For instance, the interpretation states that "Users have the right to be informed what [sic] policies and procedures govern the amount and retention of personally identifiable information, why that information is necessary for the library, and what the user can do to maintain his or her privacy. Library users expect and in many places have a legal right to have their information protected and kept private and confidential by anyone with direct or indirect access to that information." Because of this necessary level of generality, a library formulating a privacy policy should not look to this document for the details of such a policy. That said, the document does provide a useful beginning and the following conceptual bases for a policy.

- Each library should relate its policy to the needs of its own community and the environment in which it operates.
- Library users have a right to confidentiality and privacy. The rights apply to minors as well as adults.

The latter point is central to ALA's stance on "filtering" (the attempt to block "undesirable" digital resources by programs) in that, because minors are entitled to the same rights as adults, there is no excuse for depriving adults of access to information deemed "harmful" to minors by would-be censors. Some public libraries have sought to square this circle by using filters on most public terminals and setting aside "unfiltered" terminals for use by adults and minors with parental permission. This is a serious invasion of privacy in that no one should be forced to identify herself or himself in order to use certain marked terminals to gain access to digital resources.

The first step in formulating a privacy policy for libraries in the light of the ALA principles is to define the many issues that center on privacy. In essence, the library has to answer the following questions:

1. Are records of library use always confidential?
2. Is the right to privacy different for different media?
3. Does the age or the status of a library user affect privacy?
4. Have all library users the right to access to all forms of information and recorded knowledge?
5. Under which circumstances can privacy be abridged?
6. How far must the library go to ensure privacy?
7. What are the privacy issues arising from libraries supplying newly introduced services, such as 3-D printing and videogaming?

Let me translate each of these questions into concrete (and actual) examples and essay some answers.

1. Can law enforcement officers have access to records of library use?
   A: Those records should be made available only on production of a subpoena.

2. Does the right to privacy on the use of tangible library resources extend to use of digital resources?
   A: Yes, and any automatic tracking of use should be deleted or anonymized and aggregated so that details of individual use are lost. It is acceptable, indeed recommended, that library use data be aggregated so that statistics on the use of the library by classes of persons (children, graduate students, etc.) can be retained and analyzed, even though the use patterns of individuals are erased.

3. Is a parent entitled to know about her child's library use?
   Is a college professor entitled to know her students' library use (of, say, reserve materials)?
   A: The first question is tricky, but a parent is not entitled to access to library records to gain knowledge of that child's library use. The library is neither a child's guardian nor a monitor, and parents should gain their knowledge about their children's reading and online habits

from the children in an atmosphere of mutual respect. The second question is easy. No.

4. Can any user of the library use any library materials and resources (including sequestered collections and the like) in privacy and without supervision?
A: Libraries have often kept collections of controversial materials in supervised places for reasons of security (it should never be for reasons of morality). Access to those collections should be as freely available to all users as possible. The only reason for monitoring library computer use is in cases when a time limitation is imposed because demand for access exceeds supply.

5. If a children's or school library holds a reading competition, can it publish the list of books read by the winners?
A: Yes, but only with the permission of the winners themselves. This illustrates the point that mutual consent is a necessary precondition of any breach of the confidentiality compact between the library and its users, even for benign reasons.

6. Should a library install barriers, screens, and the like or special furniture (even if they involve significant expense) to ensure that only the person using online resources can see what he is viewing or reading?
A: Yes. Just as a library user can read any library book without others knowing what he is reading, that library user should also be given reasonable accommodation to ensure privacy of online use.

7. Do such new library services as the provision of maker spaces, 3-D printers, and video-gaming pose privacy problems? Are the library user's expectations of privacy different for such new services?
A: Yes, but users of such services have the same rights to privacy as the users of more established services. In addition, the library adding a new function may be opening itself up to new challenges. For example, there is a growing use of library spaces and amenities as "offices" for the self-employed. See, for example: "For the growing ranks of freelancers whose alternatives range from a

cramped corner of their bedroom to a $500-a-month, private coworking space, the new library work zones are a boon. Decked out with fast Internet, 3-D printers, meeting rooms, whiteboards, and plenty of space to spread out, they're much better suited to getting work done than jostling for counter space at a noisy coffee shop."[18]

Supplementary question: Is the library, so used, responsible for safeguarding the privacy of the freelancers?

A: Library privacy plans should be built on a combination of principle (the natural law right to privacy) and experience (the case studies that illuminate and exemplify a principle in changing and different circumstances). The example of law enforcement access to library records is a perfect example of principle and experience in balance. The principle is that library records are confidential. Experience and the greater good of society tell us that confidentiality can be breached if—and only if—a formal legal instrument, such as a subpoena, is invoked and produced. Some years ago, FBI agents interrogated a number of academic librarians about the reading habits of foreign scientists working in this country. Quite properly, librarians were not awed by the flashing of a badge and, in almost all cases, refused to answer such questions in the absence of a proper instrument of authority.

As can be seen from the preceding questions and answers, privacy and confidentiality issues are more complicated today. The environment in which we live is one of a diverse and unplanned complex of laws, regulations, regulatory bodies, and private practices. All the more reason why libraries, and everyone who works in them, should be alert to the right to privacy and the policies that ensure that right is assured. Before digital and other technologies had the major impact on libraries that we see today, privacy and confidentiality of library records and personal data on library users were relatively simple affairs. We now live in a world in which many issues connected with cyberspace are "hot" and are affected by political and religious views. Our privacy codes need to be updated so that we can deal with modern circumstances without ever compromising our core commitment to privacy as an important part of the bond of trust between libraries and library users. That bond of trust is a precious thing and one that we should do our best to preserve. In the face of the technological change, it is more than ever important to preserve human values and human trust so that we can demonstrate that we are, above all, on the side of the library user and that user's right to live a private life.

NOTES

1. Preston, Alex. "The death of privacy." *The observer* [London] (August 3, 2014). www.theguardian.com/world/2014/aug/03/internet-death-privacy-google-facebook -alex-preston (consulted November 11, 2014).

2. See, among many others: McGee, Ellen M. and Maguire, G. Q. Jr. "Ethical assessment of implantable brain chips." *Paideia archive.* www.bu.edu/wcp/Papers/ Bioe/BioeMcGe.htm (consulted August 5, 2014). Scott-Curran, Stewart and Lampe, Tim. "Smartphone of the future will be in your brain." CNN Reports (October 12, 2012). http://edition.cnn.com/2012/10/05/opinion/curran-lampe-mobile-phones/ index.html (consulted August 5, 2014).

3. *Webster's Collegiate dictionary.*

4. McGrath, Peter. "Info 'snooper highway.'" *Newsweek*, volume 125, number 9 (February 27, 1995) pages 60—61.

5. Department of Health, Education, and Welfare. Secretary's Advisory Committee on Automated Personal Data Systems. *Records, computers, and the rights of citizens.* Washington, DC: GPO, 1973.

6. US Public Law 104-191. August 1996.

7. US Department of Health and Human Services. "Summary of the HIPPA privacy rule." www.hhs.gov/ocr/privacy/hipaa/understanding/summary/index.html (consulted August 11, 2014).

8. Brandeis, Louis and Warren, Samuel. "The right to privacy." *Harvard law review* (1890).

9. Cited in: Tuerkheimer, Frank M. "The underpinnings of privacy protection." *Communications of the ACM*, volume 36, number 8 (August 1993) pages 69–73.

10. Griswold v. Connecticut, 381 U.S. 479 (1965).

11. See, for example: Clinton, R. L. *God and man in the law: the foundations of Anglo-American constitutionalism.* Lawrence, Kansas: University Press of Kansas, 1997.

12. Abstracted in Schroeder, Deborah. "A private future." *American demographics*, volume 14, number 8 (August 1992) page 19; Privacy Exchange. "National Sector Laws." www.privacyexchange.org/legal/nat/sect/natsector.html (last updated March 27, 2003; consulted August 11, 2014).

13. University of Miami Miller School of Medicine. "Privacy/data protection project: US federal privacy laws." http://privacy.med.miami.edu/glossary/xd_us_privacy_law.htm (last updated May 11, 2005; consulted August 11, 2014).

14. European Commission. "Commission proposes a comprehensive reform of the data protection rules" (January 25, 2012). http://ec.europa.eu/justice/newsroom/data-protection/news/120125_en.htm (consulted August 13, 2014).

15. US Department of Commerce. "Safe Harbor." www.export.gov/safeharbor/ (consulted August 12, 2014).

16. US Department of Commerce. "Safe Harbor privacy principles" (July 21, 2000). http://export.gov/safeharbor/eu/eg_main_018475.asp (consulted August 12, 2014)

17. American Library Association. "An interpretation of the Library Bill of Rights." www.ala.org/advocacy/intfreedom/librarybill/interpretations/privacy (consulted August 12, 2014).

18. Hamilton, Anita. "The public library wants to be your office." *Fast company* (August 8, 2014). www.fastcompany.com/3034143/the-public-library-wants-to-be-your-office (consulted August 13, 2014).

CHAPTER 12

DEMOCRACY

Libraries are directly and immediately involved in the conflict which divides the world, and for two reasons; first, because they are essential to the functioning of a democratic society; second, because the contemporary conflict touches the integrity of scholarship, the freedom of the mind, and even the survival of culture, and libraries are the great symbols of the freedom of the mind.

—Franklin Delano Roosevelt

WHAT IS DEMOCRACY?

Democracy is, in essence, the concept of social fairness and justice. The word itself derives from two classical Greek words meaning "the people" and "to rule." "Democracy" is such a familiar word that we rarely think about it analytically. It is, at once, simple and devilishly difficult. "The people rule" could be as much a slogan for mob rule and the tyranny of the majority as it is for equity and justice. In addition, as anyone with eyes can see, even advanced democracies can be subverted by profoundly undemocratic forces (e.g., wealthy interests, supranational economic concerns, ethnic biases, mendacious advertising). Despite all those, the idea of democracy still shines, especially when contrasted with autocracy, plutocracy, and the various other tyrannous systems (historical and current) that are there to be studied.

Democracy is also an idea that is so deeply engrained in the minds of almost everyone on earth that it is almost heretical to question its universal applicability. The idea that the people rule is so instantly attractive that even undemocratic regimes frequently appropriate the word. Not for nothing do tyrannies call themselves "The People's Democracy of X" and, thus, pay lip service to the idea that the people are their own rulers.

Once one has accepted the idea of democracy, the questions are: Who are the *people* that rule? and *How* do the people rule? The answer to the first question is by no means as simple as it might appear. We should recall that it is only in quite recent times that the "people" who rule in a democracy are defined as all the people, and not just a group set apart by reason of their gender, ethnic origins, religion, and so on. The Greeks invented the word and the idea of democracy, but their "people" (*demos*) were a small minority of property-owning males. Any appeal to Greek ideals of democracy should also call to mind that they were built on the backs of unfranchised slaves, women, and oppressed "others."

As to how the people rule, in the political context that rule can be direct (absolute plebiscitary democracy, in which all vote on every public policy issue—which amounts to philosophical anarchism) or indirect (representative, in which the people rule through their elected representatives). Indirect democracy is much more practical in a complex world than direct democracy, but it requires a steady flow of information to citizens and for the citizenry to be knowledgeable about social and political issues. Beyond politics, democracy expresses a wide range of values concerned with social justice, the dignity and value of each human being, egalitarianism, and respect for differing ideas. For libraries, democracy is both a context and the keystone of a set of values that should pervade our activities and programs. Libraries serve democracy, not least when they are living examples of democracy in action.

THE AMERICAN IDEA

The Unitarian minister and prominent abolitionist Theodore Parker called democracy "the American idea."[1] There are those who would say that he discounted the claim of the French and British, the first of which took the revolutionary path, the other the evolutionary path. It is also possible to argue that some other countries have more-developed democracies than does the United States in the early twenty-first century. Be all that as it may, even its critics will concede that the United States has been working on the democratic challenge for longer than most others, and in the face of unique difficulties that are themselves eloquent tribute to the durability of democratic ideals.

DEMOCRACY'S CONTRADICTIONS

Philosophers know that democracy is an ideal—an ideal that contains internal contradictions.[2] Those contradictions must be understood and taken into account if such statements as "libraries are key to democracy" are to have any meaning. An ideal cannot be achieved without thoughtful, critical understanding of its underlying premises. One contradiction within democracy, noted by mathematicians and economists, is the fact that a collective preference may or may not be the sum of individual preferences. In other words, a majority of any group may have one preference but the group as a whole may have another.[3] Another contradiction is that the self-interest of individuals may make them incapable of wishing the greater good of society or even of understanding what that greater good may be. Despite these problems, even the most rigorous analysis of the idea of democracy leaves us with this (often misquoted) observation:

> No one pretends that democracy is perfect or all wise. Indeed, it has been said that democracy is the worst form of government except all those other forms that have been tried from time to time.[4]

If we consider the alternatives—all of which essentially amount to variously tyrannous rule by elites—most of us will settle for an imperfectly achieved ideal—democracy—over any form of domination of the many by the few. On the other end of the spectrum lie anarchy (impractical even in its philosophical form) and nihilism (the negation of humanity), neither of which is a model suited to a modern society.

WHAT IS THE RELATION BETWEEN DEMOCRACY AND LIBRARIES?

A developed democracy, in any country, is an idea that depends on knowledge and education for all. The ideal modern society is one in which mass literacy and mass education combine with accessible sources of information and knowledge to produce wide participation in all public policy decisions. The United States and all other developed countries possess the mechanisms of such a democratic ideal: high literacy rates, diverse information channels, and comprehensive public education. Evidently, these mechanisms have produced a far from ideal result. It is a sad irony that, as American democracy has reached its theoretical ideal (the enfranchisement of all adults, irrespective of gender and race), it is in danger because of an increasingly ill-informed, easily manipulated, and apathetic electorate. A culture of sound bites, political ignorance, vacuous infotainment, Ayn Rand–ian selfish individualism, and unreasoning dislike of government are vitiating the rights for which, at different times, revolutionaries, women, and ethnic minorities fought. Libraries are part of the solution to this modern ill. As an integral part of the educational process and as a repository of the records of humankind, the library stands for the means to achieve a better democracy. The best antidote to being conned politically is a well-reasoned book, article, or other text. All values and ideas that dominate library discourse and practice are democratic values and ideas: intellectual freedom, the common good, service to all, the transmission of the human record to future generations, free access to knowledge and information, nondiscrimination, and so on. A librarian who is not a (small-"d") democrat is almost unthinkable. Libraries have grown and flourished in the soil of democracy, and our fate is inextricably intertwined with the fate of democracy.

The Democratic Library

Not only is democracy the environment we need to succeed, but we should also commit ourselves to democracy within the library. That is, all libraries should be organized and managed in a democratic manner and with respect for the rights and dignity of all who work there. The "literature" of management is as extensive as it is stodgy, and the theories of management are as numerous as they are evanescent. I am as heartily sick as the next person of the annual management fad to which American universities seem to be fleetingly addicted. What is striking about all the alphabet soup of management fads—apart from their barbarous management-speak and their essential similarity each to the other—is the fact that they all embody values and ideas that have been commonplace in many libraries for decades. It is always galling when it dawns on one that the jargon of this year's management fad may be different but, essentially, is preaching the same old cooperation, tolerance, participation, mutual respect, encouragement of innovation and diversity, and so on. They always add up to what a former colleague of mine called "applied feminism"—virtues that are manifest in the democratic nature of well-run libraries.

The Library as an Integral Part of Democracy

The collective resources held and given access to by all our libraries constitute the memory of humankind. Just as a human being without memory is incapable of dealing with life, a society without memory cannot function. If an informed and educated citizenry is essential to democracy, it is obvious that the collective memory provided by libraries is as essential to democracy as classroom instruction, one-on-one teaching, and any of the other components of effective education. Moreover, because libraries are an important part of lifelong learning, they play an educational role for citizens throughout their lives and not just for those in formal educational programs. There is a reason why antidemocratic individuals and groups seek to censor publications and to control what is or is not held by libraries. That reason is called the power of ideas. A single thread runs from *1984* through *Fahrenheit 451* to today's books and movies about totalitarian futures—censorship as an important part of mind control. The case of Russia today is illuminating on this point. Freedom of the press and freedom of expression characterized modern Russia's faltering steps toward democracy, after centuries of repression by tsars and commissars. They were among the few bright features of a darkling picture, but they are lights that have faded in that tragic country as it stumbles toward an uncertain future. In that respect and at least for now, democracy has faltered, if not yet failed entirely. Consider too the case of China, an economic giant and a democratic pygmy in which censorship of all kinds is rampant. Literacy is important, but it is a tool that can be used effectively only in an environment of free expression and the widespread dissemination, availability, and preservation of that free expression. Russia and China, more recently, have had high levels of literacy and education for many decades, but what does that profit them if the lifeblood of democracy—free access to all knowledge and information—is denied their citizens?

Knowledgeable Citizens

The nature of modern politics and political contests in the West has made it difficult for the citizenry to come to informed and knowledgeable conclusions. Political advertising and campaigning—which, in most states, means television and online advertising and campaigning—is the antithesis of unbiased and straightforward information. In fact, campaigns for election and about public policy issues that are built on images and spin are explicitly and intentionally deceptive. They seek to present things and people as they are not and substitute emotion for reason and feelings for thought. It is easy to blame this style of campaigning and presentation of issues as the sole or most important affliction of modern American democracy. It is easy, but it is wrong. Any truthful campaign adviser or advertiser will tell you that there has to be something that is real at the kernel of what they are selling. They will also tell you that the most vigorously pushed person or issue cannot succeed unless there is some degree of consonance between the image and reality. The real danger lies in the context in which those images and ideas are absorbed. They dominate because so many live in an environment of ignorance. Citizens who lack understanding of political issues or who cannot relate those issues to a wider societal understanding are as easy prey to political advertising as they are to commercial advertising.

Libraries as Foes of Ignorance

Libraries offer good information and authentic recorded knowledge as well as assistance in locating and assessing that information and recorded knowledge to all, from the earliest days of childhood to the later days of life. Put simply, there is no reason for any citizen of the United States to remain ignorant of any public policy issues as long as she has access to a library and its services. The problem arises when libraries are underused or not used at all. It also arises when seekers of knowledge and truth substitute online use for use of the whole range of library materials. Almost all people now have the ability to survey a number of newspapers and journals online and, thereby, to read about public policy issues from a variety of perspectives. Because those newspapers and most journals are electronic versions of their print publications, the authenticity of their content is not usually in doubt. Once the reader leaves the newspaper and journal island for the rest of the online swamp, the picture changes. If one were to rely entirely on one's ability to locate quality online resources other than newspapers and journals, one's understanding would be little better than that of someone who watched only television advertisements.

Promoting Democracy

If libraries are to combat ignorance, they must ensure that citizens use libraries and see them as repositories of democratic ideas and as central to the functioning of democracy. Perhaps the time has come for more libraries to move from passivity to intervention in politics—not in the sense of taking political sides but in supplying the information and recorded knowledge citizens need and encouraging informed and knowledgeable discussion of public policy. The library that is "the one good place in the city" (see chapter 4) can be a forum of ideas exchanged in spoken as well as written form. Such activity can take many shapes: town hall–type meetings, educational programs, outreach services to linguistic minorities, and all manner of forums and clubs.

The library can provide not only space for citizens to gather but also the recorded knowledge and information necessary to fuel the discussion. As a variation on the theme, some libraries have sponsored groups that meet on a regular basis—a kind of public policy book club.

Libraries of all kinds can encourage democracy using many different approaches: exhibits, lectures, teleconferences, reading lists, websites, and every other way in which we can help people to become more aware and informed. The Library of Congress has always seen itself as a leader in promoting education in democratic values.[5] Those of us in less splendid libraries with fewer resources can, nevertheless, play our part in giving access to and disseminating the knowledge and information on public issues that the public needs.

Information Policy

There have been calls for an "information policy" ever since electronic resources began to play a major part in modern life. The idea is that the government, in order to ensure that democratic values endure, should set out policies that govern the flow and use of information, particularly digital information. The fixity and authenticity of print publications have enabled us not only to live without any such policy but also to recoil in horror from the very idea of government interference in, and control of, the flow and use of recorded knowledge and information. The late Hugh Atkinson often observed, acerbically, that the United States once had an "information policy"; it was called the Sedition Act.[6] His point was that any mechanism that allowed government to control what is written and disseminated to good ends could equally easily be used for bad antidemocratic ends, including censorship. Despite this clear and present danger, people of goodwill have continued to call for national policies that guarantee such good things as privacy, universal access, security, and intellectual property rights. These are good things (as noted elsewhere in this text), and the ubiquity of digital technology has changed the environment without doubt; but do we really want the government to create and enforce the rules governing what we write and read (in digital or any other form)? There is a need for librarians, their professional associations, and researchers in the field to engage with public policy. As stated in one paper:

> The library community's insufficient understanding of policy and politics is evident in both the practical and philosophical ways in which libraries engage within these arenas. The ill-fated legal challenge to CIPA provides a practical example. The intent of the law—to protect children from harmful materials online—was very popular. Yet, by requiring the placement of filters on all computers, not just those accessible to children, the law is clearly unnecessarily broad. The library community's decision to challenge the law on its face and in absolute terms, rather than waiting for it to be implemented, was ill-advised. By challenging the law in this way, libraries relinquished the opportunity to make their case based upon actual incidents in which people were unable to reach information due to the expansiveness of the law or cases of problems with filters under the law to demonstrate its overreach. Instead, the Supreme Court was able to rule entirely in the abstract and produce an opinion

that evidenced a lack of comprehension of both technology itself and of the operations of libraries.[7]

Beyond library concerns, there have been calls for a radical restructuring that would change everything about the online ecosystem; for example:

> the nationalization of the ISP/cellphone industry and its conversion to a public utility; the nationalization of huge Internet monopolies that are impervious to antitrust; the adoption of a massive public subsidy to pay for independent, competitive, uncensored, noncommercial news media.[8]

Others think that there should be rules but that those rules should evolve from online users themselves, without any legal intervention or government role in their formulation (a view that strikes me as touchingly utopian). Yet another school thinks that cyberspace is inherently anarchic and uncontrollable and any attempt to write and enforce rules for it is to try to catch lightning in a bottle. One salutary note: the country that has the most effective information policy in the world today is the People's Republic of China, having had great success in suppressing Internet access to most of its citizens and effectively controlling much of the external broadcasting to that nation.

The most likely outcome of all the changes that we are experiencing is that we will stumble into a variety of solutions and apply common sense, consensus, existing laws, and constitutional principles to individual cases in the electronic environment with greater and lesser success. Then, at some distant date, we will see that a set of policies has emerged without a grand plan or centralized control. My belief is that democracy is strong enough to survive the changes wrought by the proliferation of online and digital communication and to absorb those changes into the warp and woof of an enduring democratic society.

DEMOCRACY AND THE NET

Extravagant claims were made in the early days of the Internet as to its potential as a force for good in the world. In particular, many believed that online access would empower the individual in a corporate age, liberate the powerless living in undemocratic societies, and create a flowering of individual expression that would dwarf anything we have ever seen. There is no doubt that online communication—together with other aspects of modern technology—has made it more difficult for repressive regimes to keep their citizens in the dark. There is no doubt that those with online access are able to express themselves to a potentially worldwide audience. Online political activity is increasing at a great rate, and any voter or potential voter with online access at home or in a library can find information about candidates with great ease. Those who think that the Internet is a democratizing force have to deal with the fact that online political information (and disinformation) is no better and no worse than that found in TV and other media political advertising. Unfortunately, propaganda is propaganda no matter where it is found. As for the ability of everyone to publish her own thoughts and ideas online, that runs full tilt into the problem of everyone talking and few listening. The natural human response to a tsunami of bloggery, opinion, assertion, propaganda, comment, trolling, and the rest is to retreat into a safe and limited set of trusted resources—a kind of gated community of the mind.

The logical and inevitable result of unfiltered online dissemination is "publications" such as the *Drudge report* and *BuzzFeed*, online garbage cans of gossip, innuendo, and unsubstantiated stories that have explicitly abandoned any remaining journalistic standards. Libraries must work with online advantages and disadvantages by helping our users benefit from valuable sources while being able to discriminate between valuable and meretricious sources. Democracy benefits from an informed citizenry and is imperiled by a misinformed and disinformed citizenry. We should dedicate ourselves to understanding the changes wrought by the digital revolution and to imparting that understanding to the users of our libraries by all the means at our disposal.

INSIDE THE LIBRARY

As a matter of principle, libraries should be run on democratic, consultative lines. It is a fact that all libraries of any size have a more or less hierarchical structure within which managers, librarians, staff, and other library workers operate. Full democracy and hierarchy are inimical. The question, then, is, how can we balance our desire for democratic values and the imbalance of power and influence between the constituent groups of the library workforce? Though difficult to achieve, that balance should always be sought and should be a consideration in all policy decisions.

A library, if well managed, is run on a combination of idealism and the quest for efficiency. Unlike private business—which can and does concentrate on profits (good) and losses (bad), and which can and does direct all its effort to maximizing the former and minimizing the possibility of the latter—libraries and other public service enterprises have more complex and sometimes contradictory aims. The desired balance can be summed up this way: "as much democratic participation as is consistent with the delivery of library service and the preservation of all our other values." Therefore, democracy as a library value can be a practical tool in, among other things:

- deciding to consult as widely as possible (not as widely as is convenient for management)
- creating an organizational structure that is as simple as possible
- letting decision making reside at the lowest point in the organizational structure that makes sense
- empowering library workers by giving them as much control over their working lives as is consistent with good library service
- making sure that there is constant communication that goes all ways in the library's organization—up, down, and sideways
- creating and maintaining many different avenues of communication
- working hard on the complicated demarcations between consultation, information, and participation
- being flexible in adapting plans, policies, and procedures as change demands
- never planning for planning's sake and making plans simple, briefly expressed, and widely understood

All these add up to a library version of what was commonly referred to as "participatory management"—a term that appears to have fallen out of favor, though its concepts of communication, participation, consultation, and the like are widely recognized parts of effective administration. It is, of course, a collection of concepts that are often honored more in words than in application.[9] The typical scholar-librarian library director of the period up to the 1960s rarely consulted the majority of his staff, still less regarded them as part of the management of the library. That has changed, more quickly in theory than in fact; but it could be that even lip service or partial participation is better than no participation at all.

Participatory management evolved in the business and industrial worlds as part of the move toward social responsibility and the desire of workers to be treated with dignity and respect. The commitment to participation was an expression of the moral corporate culture of the company or institution and of the moral autonomy of its workers.[10] The central idea was that participation not only makes an entity more efficient and productive but also empowers all its workers and raises the level of work satisfaction.

To apply participatory management in any corporate entity (including a library), one must overcome a number of obstacles, not the least of which is accepting that its full realization is next to impossible. The anarchist communes of the Swiss watchmakers in the Jura Federation in the nineteenth century may be the nearest to a totally democratic workplace and society that we are likely to achieve in this vale of tears.[11] It is not a model that we can even approach in modern society and modern institutions of any kind.

Let us see what participatory/consultative management comprises:

- collegial consultation on a broad range of topics, including all important policy directions
- broad mutual understanding of policies and issues throughout the library, from the top to the bottom of the organization
- good communication channels and diverse means of expression
- open, transparent mechanisms for the free flow of information and input
- willingness to participate and contribute on the part of everyone
- willingness to surrender authority and control
- willingness to be accountable and accept responsibility
- planning with effective input from all

None of these is easy to achieve, and the hurdles of control and complacency are difficult to overcome. Even more of an obstacle is the fact that we all work in a hierarchy that operates by equating power and pay, and by association, powerlessness and less pay. There are two things that libraries can use to achieve the participatory democracy they want. The first is to study and learn from the extensive history of participatory management in business, here and abroad. We can learn from the mistakes in that history, and we can learn about the limits that hierarchical structures impose on democratic ideas. Second, we can use the many positive virtues of librarians as a class—tolerance, education, openness to ideas—as tools in the participatory process.

What can libraries learn from the experience of business? A discussion of empowerment of workers in business organizations states:

> Managers love empowerment in theory, but the command and control model is what they trust and know best. For their part, employees are often ambivalent about empowerment—it's great as long as they are not held personally accountable.[12]

The article goes on to discuss the two types of commitment exhibited by employees. The author calls the typical state of affairs "external commitment," in which employees' working conditions, performance goals, and priorities are defined by others. Its opposite—internal commitment—applies to those who define their own tasks, work routines, and priorities, and who also define their goals in consultation with management. He points out that the inevitable inconsistencies between participation and lines of authority have produced contradictory programs that have disillusioned many employees who were told, in essence, "Do your own thing—the way we tell you." The ultimate aim of any organization is effectiveness and performance, not morale, work satisfaction, or commitment. As the article points out, when those personal goals take precedence, they "cover up many of the problems that organizations must overcome in the twenty-first century."

The best thing we can learn is that we have to deal with balancing opposites, managing within limits, and reconciling group and personal aims. In short, we need to approach democratization of the library workplace with common sense and maturity. The first step is to come to terms with the management structure. Even after you have made such a structure as simple as possible, given the nature of the library and the limitations on the power of the management to reorganize, there will still be a hierarchy, and there will still be groups in the library (management, librarians, staff) with different responsibilities and rewards. If your library is to achieve an appropriate level of democracy, those issues will need to be discussed and, when possible, resolved. There are limits on participation; it is important that they be clearly understood and delineated. The second step is to ensure that management is committed to consultation and communication and that librarians and other nonadministrative employees are committed to participation and to collective and individual accountability. The third step is to institutionalize participation and communication so that they become the environment in which the library operates, rather than an add-on in special circumstances. Last (and first), everyone who works in the library should respect and value the talents and aptitudes of everyone with whom she works, and respect and value their humanity, individuality, and dignity. That is the least that democracy and good librarianship demand.

DEMOCRACY WITHIN AND WITHOUT

Librarians have always, knowingly or otherwise, been small-"d" democrats. The idea of democracy is so entwined with all our beliefs that many of us hardly think of it and the consequences of the democratic idea. Be that as it may, our libraries are bastions of democracy in society, and democracy is an important value within our libraries. Democracy needs knowledgeable citizens; libraries are prime movers in providing knowledge and information to the citizenry. We instinctively turn to democratic ideas in how we run our libraries and cooperative library programs. Those ideas enable our libraries and programs to survive and flourish. Whenever we are faced with a dilemma in running libraries or providing library service, we could do a lot worse than ask the question, What is the democratic thing to do?

NOTES

1. Speech at an antislavery convention, Boston, 1850.
2. "Democracy." In *The Oxford companion to philosophy*, edited by Ted Honderich. Oxford; New York: Oxford University Press, 1995.
3. For example, majorities may and do vote for tax cuts and then lament the loss of services caused by those tax cuts.
4. Churchill, Winston. "Speech in the House of Commons," November 11, 1947.

5. Cole, John Y. "Books, reading, and the Library of Congress in a changing America." *Libraries and culture*, volume 33, issue 1 (Winter 1998) pages 34–40.

6. The reference is to the Alien and Sedition Acts passed by Congress in 1798, which, among other things, were used to suppress writings and newspapers that were hostile to President Adams and his administration.

7. Jaeger, Paul T., Bertot, John Carlo, and Gorham, Ursula. "Wake up the nation: public libraries, policy making, and political discourse." *Library quarterly*, volume 83, issue 1 (January 2013) pages 61–72.

8. McChesney, Robert. "Be realistic, demand the impossible: three radically democratic Internet policies." *Critical studies in media communication*, volume 31, issue 2 (June 2014) pages 92–99.

9   See, for example: Fast, Nathanael J., Burris, Ethan R., and Bartel, Caroline A. "Managing to stay in the dark: managerial self-efficacy, ego defensiveness, and the aversion to employee voice." *Academy of management journal*, volume 57, issue 4 (2014) pages 1013–1034.

10. Collins, Colin. "How and why participatory management improves a company's social performance." *Business and society*, volume 35, issue 2 (June 1996) pages 176–210.

11. Woodcock, George. *Anarchism*. New York: World Publishing, 1962.

12. Argyris, Chris. "Empowerment: the emperor's new clothes." *Harvard business review*, volume 76, number 3 (May–June 1998) pages 98–105.

CHAPTER 13

THE GREATER GOOD

People are autonomous individuals who may rightfully strive to achieve outcomes and goals that will personally benefit them, but as members of a human community are they not obligated to consider others' outcomes, variously termed the public interest, the greater good, or the common good? Society is no mere aggregation of independent individuals, but a complex set of interdependent actors who must constantly adjust to the actions and reactions of others around them, and such a social existence creates obligations based on respect, trust, and a sense of community.[1]

I have given a number of talks on values and libraries in the years since *Our enduring values* was published. In the course of thinking about values, preparing for those talks, and discussing the topic with many people, it has become clear to me that the values system that I have described and advocated has an overarching principle that underlies and pervades everything that I believe about librarianship—the greater good. This principle differs from utilitarianism—the greatest happiness of the greatest number—in that the greater good is not majoritarian. Utilitarianism seeks a benefit (happiness) for as many people as possible in the belief that widespread benefit will be positive for society as a whole. The "greater" of "the greater good" is not meant to be quantitative, but embraces the good of each individual.

The good of each individual is particularly important for libraries. It can be argued plausibly that libraries exist primarily to provide resources and services to minorities, often very small minorities. They should be guided not primarily by what the majority in their communities wants but what benefits every member of that community individually, now and in the future. In short, the greater good is a communitarian principle that is the antithesis of the individualism, materialism, and selfishness that dominate early twenty-first-century Western societies. As such, it is a radical principle (in fact, if not always rhetorically). In a political environment in which the leaders of a major party say they take their economic and social ideas from Ayn Rand novels, the idea of working together with the interests of minorities and the least powerful in the forefront is positively explosive.

That brings me to the point that we must confront: the accusation that librarians as a class and our professional associations are . . . [insert your favorite term of abuse] . . . "liberal," "left wing," and so on. Since the vast majority of librarians and library workers are animated by ideas of service to the community, freedom of speech, civil and political rights, and the like; and since such ideas are inimical to the economic and social interests of most of the wealthy and powerful, the "accusation" is spot on (in the accusers' terms, at least). It is a waste of time to try to counter having one label or another slapped on you. It is far more productive to identify the things in which you believe and to fit them into a coherent structure of belief and values.

I believe that the greater good provides such a structure. To put it briefly, our work in libraries must be directed to benefit not only the communities we serve and the wider society, but also every single member of that community and the wider society; that is, the direction that should underlie all our activities and should be the principle—animated by our values—that guides everything we do in libraries.

THE GREATER GOOD AND LIBRARIES

An article in *Issues in ethics* states:

> The common good, then, consists primarily of having the social systems, institutions, and environments on which we all depend work in a manner that benefits all people. Examples of particular common goods or parts of the common good include an accessible and affordable public health care system, and effective system of public safety and security, peace among the nations of the world, a just legal and political system, and unpolluted natural environment, and a flourishing economic system.[2]

I would argue that access to the full range of library services for all should be a component of the ecology of the greater good, what the authors call the social systems, institutions, and environment in which the common good depends. Most important, if we see libraries collectively as a common good, we will focus on what truly matters: the benefit for society and for all individuals of unfettered access to and use of the human record. That is what libraries are about—they are not businesses with "customers" to be exploited but vital services to members of communities; library technology is not an end in itself but a tool to be used to facilitate that unfettered access; and the right to that common good should not be dependent on money, social standing, or any of the many ways in which humans divide and discriminate.

THE GREATER GOOD AND STEWARDSHIP

As far as libraries are concerned, stewardship has two parts: the need to preserve the human record and transmit it to all future generations, and the need to be good stewards of library education. We do the first to benefit every person in the future—people that we do not and cannot know living in societies that we can only speculate about. What better illustration of the concept of the greater good could there be? Every act of acquisition, identification, cataloguing, conservation, preservation, maintenance of digital and digitized resources, storage in optimal conditions, and the like, is the epitome of selflessness dedicated to the many or few yet unborn who will benefit from that act in some unknown future. As for being good stewards of library education and defending it from the I-vandals, those too are selfless endeavors dedicated to the librarians of the future, who we hope and trust will play their part in the unending effort to make the human record accessible and preserve it for their posterity.

THE GREATER GOOD AND SERVICE

Few librarians are motivated by gain, prestige, or the acquisition of power (though I have met a scant, unhappy, and disappointed few over the years). It would be a grievous mistake to enter the profession seeing it as a gateway to glory. Thomas Gray told us that full many a flower is born to blush unseen and waste its sweetness on the desert air. Many librarians do their work unseen (blushing or otherwise), but their work is not wasted on the desert air. Far from it; that work is in service of communities, societies, and individuals, the majority unknown to them. In other words, our work is altruistic, motivated and informed by values, beliefs, and dedication to the ideal of service. Many (most?) librarians exist in environments that impose stress on their working lives—bureaucracies, underfunding, being asked to more with less, backlogs, antisocial hours, administrative incomprehension, and on and on. We cannot console ourselves with fat paychecks or the acclaim of multitudes, but we can console ourselves with the idea that what we do is important to all and, to risk being pious, service to humanity. Those intangible rewards are important to our psychological health.

This is not to argue—not at all—that our intangible rewards should be an excuse to pay us pittances. I am a strong believer in a fair day's pay for a fair day's work and of collective action to secure that fair pay. Further, I believe that librarians, along with teachers, social workers, and all the other professionals in work that serves communities, are paid far less than they are worth for complex reasons, not least because their work forces are predominantly female. Yet another reason for us all, female and male, to support gender equity in pay and in all of life. Librarians are not angels in the house; they are dedicated and educated professionals and should be paid accordingly.

THE GREATER GOOD
AND INTELLECTUAL FREEDOM

When librarians and professional associations defend intellectual freedom, they are, almost by definition, defending the rights of minorities—sometimes a minority of one. This is a classic case of the rights of individuals and of small groups being oppressed by majorities. The classic bases for censorship are sedition (a charge leveled at political minorities), blasphemy (a charge leveled at religious minorities), and transgressive sexual expression (a charge levelled at sexual minorities—sometimes the visible part of a hypocritical majority). Librarians believe that the best societies are those in which individuals have the right to read and view what they wish, the right to believe and say what they wish, and the right to their own opinions and thoughts. Any other society is a tyranny of one kind or another. Thus we see that the defense of the individual is the defense of society as a whole, because that society is better off when individual rights to read, view, write, and say are safeguarded.

THE GREATER GOOD AND RATIONALISM

A society that lacks dedication to the greater good can scarcely be said to be rational in its organization or policies. It makes no sense for a modern society to have a substantial uneducated or undereducated underclass. It makes no sense for a modern society to have substantial minorities who are permanently unemployed, homeless, ill, and/or hungry. It makes no sense for a modern society to spend more money on prisons than it does on schools. It makes no sense for a modern society to have to give benefits to the working poor because their employers do not give them a living wage. It also makes no sense for a modern society to have people in it who are denied library resources and services. Such a society may be acceptable to radical individualists, but radical individualism is not a rational philosophy. Reason tells us that the individual benefits when societies are whole, nurturing, and sanely organized. When we see universal library services as part of that greater good infrastructure, we can also see that libraries are part—an important part—of creating rational societies and that, in advocating for libraries, we are playing a part in creating a better world. Those who say that librarians and library associations should "stay out of politics" are both ignoring the realities of life and diminishing the role that library services play in the human quest for fairness, justice, and decent treatment for all.

THE GREATER GOOD AND LEARNING AND LITERACY

Learning and scholarship are the fruits of library use and the intellectual engines that drive societal development, including material and economic development. Literacy is the basic skill of both learning and scholarship. Learned people and great scholars may see further because they stand on the shoulders of giants, but the only reason why they know what those giants knew is because of the knowledge contained in the human record. We depend on scholarship and learning for societal progress, and it follows that learning is a major contributor to the greater good. In other words, it is in all our interests that we strive for universal literacy and work for a world in which literacy and scholarship are fostered, honored, and rewarded. That world is, by definition, a world of flourishing library services and resources. We know—because study after study has proven it—the economic value of libraries;[3] but we should also recognize the ways in which strong libraries contribute to strong societies in less quantifiable ways.[4]

THE GREATER GOOD AND EQUITY OF ACCESS

We start with the premise that everyone, regardless of any obstacle, is entitled to full access to library resources and services and that we should work in every way we can to remove all obstacles to that equity of access. That premise is, in turn, based on two beliefs: that all individuals benefit from full access to library resources and services, and that such individuals benefit the wider society by being so empowered. In other words, the social justice of equity of access is not only right in itself but of benefit to the individual and to society—the greater good.

THE GREATER GOOD AND PRIVACY

A just society is one in which freedom of thought and freedom of expression are protected. Thought and expression cannot be truly free if those thoughts and that expression are monitored by governments, commercial concerns, or any other bodies. A good society is one in which people feel secure in expressing their thoughts and opinions without fear of suspicion or sanction. The greater good is enhanced when all have that psychological security and can be free beings in a free society. Specifically, libraries contribute to that security and well-being by protecting the rights of their users to read, view, and use the human record free from prying eyes and the consequences of having their privacy invaded.

THE GREATER GOOD AND DEMOCRACY

I know no safe depository of the ultimate powers of the society, but the people themselves: and if we think them not enlightened enough to exercise their controul with a wholesome discretion, the remedy is, not to take it from them, but to inform their discretion by education.[5]

Democracy is a belief that the people—all the people—are the only "safe depository of the ultimate powers of society." Those ultimate powers must, of course, be exercised wisely and wisdom comes from and only from the acquisition of knowledge—education in its broadest sense. It is a pillar of librarianship that fruitful interaction with the human record is an essential (perhaps *the* essential) part of education. The greater good demands that libraries seek to provide that interaction so as to fulfill the democratic mandate. We see again the need for librarians to be aggressive advocates for their profession—one dedicated to democratic ideals and the empowering of an educated electorate.

NOTES

1. Announcement of the symposium "For the greater good of all: perspectives on individualism, society, and leadership." Jepson School of Leadership Studies, University of Richmond, Richmond, Virginia (January 2010).

2. Velasquez, Manuel, et al. "The common good." *Issues in ethics*, volume 5, number 1 (Spring 1992). www.scu.edu/ethics/practicing/decision/commongood.html (consulted September 9, 2014).

3. See, for example: Hawkins, Margaret, et al. "The economic value of public libraries." *APLIS*, volume 14, issue 3 (September 2001); and Chung, Hye-Kyung. "Measuring the economic value of special libraries." *Bottom line: managing library finances*, volume 20, issue 1 (2007) pages 30–34.

4. See, for example: Foster, Vonita White. "The price of not supporting school libraries." *Library media connection*, volume 32, issue 5 (March/April 2014) pages 30–31.

5. Letter from Thomas Jefferson to William C. Jarvis, September 28, 1820.

CHAPTER 14

KEEPING FAITH

The work goes on, the cause endures, the hope still lives.
—Edward Moore Kennedy[1]

Themes following words were written to me by one of the most thoughtful and intelligent library administrators I have ever known, more than fifteen years ago:

> On a personal and private note, I am glad that I am most of the way through my career. What I know and love about libraries probably will not exist in 20 years. I doubt that I would have been a librarian in the world that seems to be coming.

Can it be that her vision is correct? That what is true and valuable about libraries will cease to exist in the near future? With respect—and bearing in mind that her statement was made in the aftermath of a peculiarly trying time—I would say no. Further, I would say that the bleak vision of libraries ceasing to exist or losing all that makes them worthwhile will only be realized if we librarians let it happen. We can use the positive aspects of technology while resisting the negative aspects of some implementations of technology. We can hold fast to our values and proclaim our value. We can understand the complexity and diversity of libraries and the ways in which they evolve as their users and the communities they serve shape them. As Walt Crawford has written:

> We do ourselves a disservice when we speak of "the library." There's no such thing as "the library"—there are tens of thousands of individual libraries, each serving a unique community with a unique combination of collections, resources, and services. One strength of libraries is their sheer diversity particularly as libraries work together to meet future needs.[2]

One of the principal purposes of the examination of core values attempted in this book is to assist us, individually and collectively, to focus on the attributes and purposes of libraries that make them unique and valuable. I am convinced that such an examination of our values and purposes points to one inescapable conclusion: that libraries will continue indefinitely with their functions unchanged in essence. More, I am convinced that, if our society is to prosper spiritually, intellectually, and materially, libraries must continue to acquire and give access to, arrange, make accessible, and preserve the human record in all its manifestations and formats, and provide assistance and instruction in its use.

Librarianship is generally viewed as a staid profession resistant to change. Contrary to that image, we are gripped periodically by fads and manias, of which the obsession of some with the immanence of the all-digital future is merely the latest and most blatant (currently manifested in "gaming" and the inanities of social media). In such times, it is more than ever important to keep our eyes on the prize and to keep faith with our predecessors and successors. This is by no means an easy task in an atmosphere of hype and fantasy; however, pride in our achievements and value—and clear-eyed assessment of where we are and where we are going—will prevail. Beliefs rooted in reality and understanding always prevail over shallowness and anti-intellectualism. If we understand our beliefs and values truly, the profession my friend believed to be fatally weakened will become ever stronger. Our progress may be slow, but if we are valiant for truth, all the trumpets will sound for us.

OUR SINGULAR VALUE

Service is a key value of librarianship, but it is a value that we share with many other entities. *Equity of access* to recorded knowledge and information is a societal goal that we must lead in achieving, but librarians are not the only people in pursuit of that goal. *Privacy* is a universal concern, made even more urgent by technological advance. *Democracy* in library management and the struggle for democracy in the wider world are very important to us, but the whole world believes—or feigns to believe—in democracy, so we are by no means alone. Librarianship is, in my view, a supremely rational profession, but all professions aspire to rationalism. Librarians lead the fight for *intellectual freedom*, but we have many allies (as well as more enemies) in that struggle. *Literacy* is a value of all in most societies, but it has a special meaning for us, because it is the key to the one value that is unique to librarianship. That value is *stewardship*.

STEWARDSHIP

As I have written in chapter 5, our role as preservers and transmitters of the human record is the one unique value of the eight I have discussed. This is not to say that it is the most important of the eight. Indeed, I would say that each of the values covered by this book is equally important—no facet of a gem is more important than other facets. It is difficult to imagine an effective library or a productive career in librarianship that lacks any of the eight values to a significant degree. Be that as it may, stewardship of the records of humankind is the one task that falls to us and that we do not and cannot share with others.

The written, visual, and aural records of civilization come from all eras since the dawn of history; from all continents, countries, and communities; and in all formats, from medieval manuscripts to books, films, and digital resources. We have a duty to preserve and transmit all these records—a duty that, obviously, must depend on a pooling of work in local, regional, national, and international efforts of all kinds. All these collaborations are founded on a multitude of individual efforts and commitments and individual willingness to contribute to that grand and continuing task. The ultimate reason for preserving all these texts, images, and recorded sounds is to ensure that future generations can read, see, hear, and study them and, in so doing, acquire knowledge so that they can generate new knowledge. That new knowledge will be, in turn, contained in records consisting of texts, images, and sounds that themselves augment the human record. Thus the unending cycle of acquiring, creating, recording, preserving, and transmitting knowledge goes on to enhance society and advance civilization. None of this would be possible without the work we do. All the work of the creators of knowledge and the preservers of recorded knowledge and information would be for naught if future generations could not decode the texts, images, and sounds that transmit knowledge. There are messages from the past (such as the Azilian pebbles[3]) that remain inscrutable— marks that we cannot read, images that we cannot interpret—but they are few, and almost all the messages from the past that we still possess can be decoded. If our stewardship is to be effective, the ability of future humans to read and understand the texts and images of today and yesterday is vital. This is why true literacy and the ability to do sustained reading are central to our mission. Textual records are different in kind from images and recorded sound. It takes no skill to look at an image (though it takes great skill to comprehend all the content or artistic value of an image). Sound recordings are comprehensible—if the auditor understands the language or musical conventions—to anyone who has access to the machines that play that recording (the last is the rub for generations yet to come). Sustained reading, on the other hand, demands a range of complex and not easily acquired skills and a cultural and educational frame of reference that may not be readily available in the years to come. The question of preservation and onward transmittal of the human record (the most important aspect of stewardship) depends on our ability to be good stewards, but it also depends on the skills of the people of the future and the machines they use. Most important, it depends on the ability to read, to decode texts, and to understand the recorded knowledge of the past.

READING—THE VITAL SKILL

The importance of reading to personal development, education, and society cannot be underestimated. Apart from the odd preacher of postliterate societies, most people accept that sustained reading is an important part of human and societal development. One hundred years ago, people in hundreds of thousands read books by then popular authors loved by all classes (the beau ideal being Dickens).[4] Does this mean that the crowds that waited on the wharves of New York City for shipments of *The Old Curiosity Shop* and then wept in the streets on reading the latest installment were simply the equivalent of the massed millions who watch reality TV or follow the witless Kardashians online? Michael Kammen draws an interesting distinction between popular culture and mass culture:

> I regard popular culture—not always but more often than not—as participatory and interactive, whereas mass culture . . . more often than not induced passivity and the privatization of culture.[5]

Dickens (a great writer by any standard) was a popular culture figure of the first order in the nineteenth century, but his books required levels of literacy, general cultural knowledge, and involvement that are higher by many magnitudes than the minimal skills and involvement demanded by today's mass culture. Irrespective of whether one is reading print on a page or words on a screen, reading is not a passive activity. It requires an investment of one's knowledge and understanding in order to be productive. One interacts with a complex text in a manner that is qualitatively different from, for example, mass-culture television viewing or watching videos online. That is why reading and an enthusiasm for reading are among the most important gifts that we can give to children. The following is from an interview of the English humor writer Sue Townsend by Lynn Barber:

> I said something about [Townsend's] "deprived childhood," but she said no, in one crucial respect it was not deprived: "My parents were bus conductors, but they were readers, and that's what makes the difference. Reading gives you choices, you don't feel constricted by your class."[6]

Reading gives you choices. It can be that the world of the future will be dominated quantitatively, as it is today, by mass culture; but the alternatives, represented by popular and high culture, will endure and dominate qualitatively.

Libraries Have a Future

Dear Reader,

I believe with all my heart that we librarians and our libraries will continue to carry out our historic mission, not least because that is what society and individuals in society demand. We will profit from existential debates about the future of libraries and the meaning of librarianship because introspection—if positive in attitude—brings strength. I hope this discussion of our core values contributes to that self-examination and to the resultant strengthening of our resolve and value. I also hope that we will work together to create a new golden age of libraries in which we will come to understand and to actualize our commonality of purpose in the midst of the diversity of our missions.

Keep faith!

Michael Gorman
Chicago, Illinois
September 2014

NOTES

1. Speech at the Democratic National Convention, 1980.
2. Crawford, Walt. *Being analog.* Chicago: ALA, 1999. page 90.
3. Mussi, Margherita, and Peresani, Marco. "Human settlement of Italy during the Younger Dryas." *Quaternary international,* volume 242, issue 2 (October 2011) pages 360–370.
4. See, for example: Mitch, David Franklin. *The rise of popular literacy in Victorian England.* Philadelphia: University of Pennsylvania Press, 1992.
5. Kammen, Michael. *American culture, American tastes: social change and the 20th century.* New York: Knopf, 1999. page 22.
6. "Double Vision" *The observer [London]* (October 10, 1998) pages 25–28.

INDEX

bibliographic control standards, 137–138
of electronic resources, 138–140
as processing service, 95
cell phones, 177–178
censorship
greater good and, 215
Internet filtering, 119–122
library as integral part of democracy and, 199
library opposition to, 110–112
of online resources, 114–118
change
uncertainty with, 6–7
in wider world, 2–3
chat, 99
children
censorship of online resources, 111, 114–118
equity of access for, 161
intellectual freedom and, 118–119
Internet filtering, 119–122, 188
learning to be literate, 144–145
library privacy policy and, 189–190
literacy and learning in school/children's libraries, 152–153
school libraries, service community, 103–104
Children's Internet Protection Act (CIPA)
Internet filtering mandated by, 116
legal challenge to, 202–203
children's libraries
literacy and learning, 152–153
prized by community, 101
suggestions for, 71–72
China
censorship in, 199, 200
suppression of Internet access in, 203
Churchill, Winston, 197
CIPA
See Children's Internet Protection Act
Code of Ethics for Librarians (ALA), 29
collaboration
for equity of access, 171–172
for stewardship of human record, 221
collections, housing in ideal library, 72
collective learning, 9

collective memory, 199
colleges
See universities
Committee on Accreditation (COA), 87, 89
communication
comprehensibility of librarian, 98–99
for democracy in libraries, 205
digital, proponents of, 47
in participatory management, 206, 208
community
bond of trust with library, 84–85
equity of access and, 171
knowledge of community served by library, 100
of learning, 18
community college transfers, 103
companies/institutions, service community of, 104–105
comprehensibility, 98–99
Connecticut, Griswold v., 180
conservative values, 34
Consumer Reports, 121
Convention on Equity of Access, 172
Copenhagen Nordvest Culture House and Library, 68
Crawford, Walt, 13, 220
"The Crisis in Cataloging" (Osborn), 24–25
critical thinking, 64, 136
cult of information, 13–16
cultural heritage
human record and, 10–13
libraries and wider cultural context, 18–21
"culture houses," 68

D

data, 14
David, Christian, 8–9
decoding
of human record, 222
learning to be literate, 144
Deekle, Peter, 157
democracy
as American idea, 196–197
as central value of librarianship, 37

greater good (cont.)
  equity of access and, 216
  intellectual freedom and, 215
  learning and literacy and, 216
  libraries and, 213
  meaning of, 211–212
  privacy and, 217
  rationalism and, 215–216
  self-interest of individuals and, 197
  service and, 214
  stewardship and, 213–214
Greece, ancient
  democracy in, 196
  literacy in, 149
Griswold v. Connecticut, 180
Guédon, Jean-Claude, 45, 46

H

Hahn, Trudi Bellardo, 60–61
handicapped people
  See disabilities, persons with
Hanson, Massachusetts, 67
hardware, 82
Harris, Roma, 133
health information, privacy of, 179
Health Insurance Portability &
  Accountability Act (HIPAA), 179
Herman, Peter, 17
high school graduates, 103
high school students, 102–103
HIPAA Privacy Rules, 179
history, of privacy, 180–181
history/philosophy
  central values of librarianship, 35–37
  Fink's taxonomy of values, 33–35
  librarianship as practical not
    philosophical, 23–25
  pragmatism and idealism, 25–26
  Ranganathan's Five Laws, 26–27
  Rothstein's ethos, 29–32
  Shera's social epistemology, 27–29
Horace, 75
hospices, 105
hospitals, 105, 155

Hough, Kirsten J., 118
human contact
  library as place and, 60–62
  service encounter, 95–99
  for service improvements, 93
human record
  all-digital library, requirements for, 58
  book as effective means for, 17–18
  cultural heritage and, 10–13
  description of, 8–9
  digitization and, 43
  equity of access library resources/services,
    161–163
  greater good and, 213–214, 217
  learning, ways of, 9–10
  learning by interacting with, 146
  libraries and wider cultural context,
    18–21
  library's role regarding, 15–16, 220
  preservation of, 76–84
  stewardship of, 221–222
  symbolic language/collective learning,
    8–9
  "traditional" library and, 44
humanistic values, 34
humans
  altruistic service for, 92
  library as place, need for, 59, 60–62
  symbolic language/collective learning,
    8–9
  ways of learning, 9–10

I

idealism
  conflict with pragmatism, 25–26
  idealistic values, 34
ideals, for library as place, 72–73
illiteracy, 154–155
imaginative/aesthetic creations, 14
individualism
  cult of information and, 15
  greater good and, 212, 215
industrial economy, 92–93
inequity, 166

information
- clash of culture/values, 14–15
- competence, 134
- definition of, 14
- preservation of human record, 76–77
- "traditional" library and, 44
- use of word, 13

information policy, 202–203

information science, 86–87

information technology
- cultural institutions and, 20
- libraries' embrace of, 15–16
- *See also* digital technology; technology

informational privacy, 177

inquiry, patterns in, 97–98

institutional barriers, 164

institutions, library services of, 104–105

instruction, 59
- *See also* education; library instruction

intangible cultural heritage, 11–12

integrated library
- arguments for/steps for, 63–64
- need for physical library, 59

intellectual freedom
- as central value of librarianship, 36
- children/adolescents and, 118–119
- equity of access and, 162
- greater good and, 215
- imposition of beliefs on others and, 5
- Internet filtering, 119–122
- librarians in fight for, 221
- meaning of, 109–110
- online evils, fighting, 114–118
- real-life examples, 113–114
- relationship between libraries and, 110–112
- statement on, 112–113
- as value of Rothstein, 29, 31

Intellectual Freedom Manual (ALA), 110

intellectual theory, 25

International standard bibliographic description (ISBD) standards, 137

Internet
- all-digital library, requirements for, 58–59
- comparison to libraries, 8
- democracy and, 203–204
- digital divide as barrier to all-digital library, 62–63
- filtering, 119–122, 188, 202–203
- intellectual freedom and, 114–118
- library equity of access, 166–169
- loss of privacy and, 175–177
- privacy laws, U.S./EU, 181–184
- "protection of children" as excuse for censorship, 111
- as threat to literacy, 157
- *See also* digital resources; online resources

Issues in ethics (journal), 213

J

Jackson, Heather Lee, 60–61

Jaeger, Paul T., 202–203

Japanese popular culture, 117–118

Jefferson, Thomas, 77, 217

Jepson School of Leadership Studies, University of Richmond, Richmond, Virginia, 211

Johns, Adrian, 78

Johnson, Debra Wilcox, 153

journals
- *See* scholarly journals

Jura Federation, 206

justice, 195

K

Kammen, Michael, 223

Kaplan, Abraham, 25

Kehr, Dave, 80–81

Kelley, Walt, 143

Kennedy, Edward Moore, 219

keyword searching, 119–121

knowledge
- definition of, 14
- democracy and, 198
- human record and, 9–10
- knowledgeable citizens for democracy, 200
- of librarian for service encounter, 97–98
- libraries as foes of ignorance, 200–201
- preservation of human record, 76–77

knowledge (cont.)
reading and, 147
social epistemology, 27–29
stewardship of human record for, 222
"traditional" library and, 44
Kroski, Ellyssa, 7–8

L

"the 'L' word" wars, 85–86
Lanier, Jaron, xii
Lankes, R. David, 50
Law of Unintended Consequences, 48
laws
federal privacy laws, 182–183
intellectual freedom constrained by, 109–110
LC *List of subject headings* (LCSH), 137, 139
learned societies, 20
learning
to be literate, 144–-147
collective learning, 9
lifelong learning through literacy, 147
ways of learning, 9–10
See also library education; library
instruction; literacy and learning
Lewis, Andrew, 176
LI
See library instruction
librarian
in all-digital future, 52–53
democracy in library and, 198, 204–208
equity of access campaign, 171–173
equity of access steps, 165–173
faith, keeping, 219–224
greater good and, 212–217
intellectual freedom, duties regarding,
110–112
library education, 85–89
library organization with rationalism,
128–130
literacy and learning, actions for, 152
literacy and learning, promotion of,
152–155
literacy and learning, relationship with, 151
Rothstein's list of librarian skills, 32

service encounter, 95–99
staffing of integrated library, 64
things librarians are tired of hearing, 7–8
librarianship
central values of, 35–37
Fink's taxonomy of values, 33–35
as practical, not philosophical, 23–25
pragmatism and idealism, 25–26
preservation of, 84
Ranganathan's Five Laws, 26–27
rationalism and, 127–128
Rothstein's ethos, 29–32
service, importance of, 105–106
service value of, 92
Shera's social epistemology, 27–29
stewardship as singular value of, 221–222
libraries
changes in wider world and, 2–3
cult of information and, 13–16
cultural heritage, role in preservation of, 13
democracy, relationship with, 198–203
democracy inside, 204–208
digital revolution and, xi–xiv
Enlightenment principles and, 126–127
equity of access campaign, 171–173
equity of access in action, 163–165
equity of access, relationship to, 161–163
equity of access, steps to, 165–173
faith, keeping, 219–224
future of, 224
greater good and, 212–217
importance of collections, librarians,
organization/retrieval system, 8
intellectual freedom and, 110–112
literacy and learning, relationship with, 151
misunderstandings about, 7–8
organizing, 128–130
preservation of, 84–85
privacy, relationship with, 185–188
privacy in action, 188–192
rationalism, relationship with, 127–128
service, relationship with, 92
service in, test of, 93–95
survival of, reasons for, 53–54

literacy divide

    consequences of, 150–151

    description of, 148–150

literate, definition of, 144

Living Human Treasures, 12

Los Angeles, California, public school system, 104

Lubetzky, Seymour, 24

M

MacLeish, Archibald, 25, 28

management

    democracy and, 198–199

    democracy in libraries and, 205–208

    scientific management, 15–16, 20

    See also organization

Mann, Thomas, 97–98

manuscripts

    attributes of, 77–78

    preservation of, 80

maps, preservation of, 80

MARC standard

    for bibliographic records, 137

    cataloguing of electronic resources, 139

Márquez, Gabriel García, 176

Martell, Charles, 46

mass culture, 223

Mays, Vernon, 69

McChesney, Robert, 203

McCorduck, Pamela, 156

McCormack, John, 80

McGrath, Peter, 178

McNealy, Scott, 176

McNulty, Robert, 61

meaning, search for, 4

metadata, 139

microforms, preservation of, 81–82

Miller Art Gallery, Sturgeon Bay, Wisconsin, 68

minorities

    equity of access and, 162

    greater good and, 212

    greater good and intellectual freedom for, 215

    literacy divide and, 150

minors

    See adolescents; children

Miodownik, Mark, xi, xiii–xiv

MLS degree, 88, 89

mobile libraries, 101

mobile phones, 177–178

Modern Language Association, 84

money

    See funding

morality

    censorship of online resources for children/adolescents, 119

    Internet filtering and, 117

    values and, 2

"Morning edition" (NPR), 7

Morris, William, xiv

multiuse buildings, 67–68

museums, library alliance with, 19

music scores, preservation of, 80

N

National Assessment of Adult Literacy, 148

natural heritage, 11

natural rights, 181

Neighborhood Children's Internet Protection Act (NCIPA), 116

Netherlands, 68, 118

neuroplasticity, 147

New York Public Library, 70

New York Times, 80–81

nihilism, 35, 197

O

obscenity

    censorship of online resources, 115, 116

    government restriction of, 110

Occam's Razor, 129

The Old Curiosity Shop (Dickens), 223

Old-Shoe Syndrome, 128

Olson, Hope, 91

online access

    democracy and, 203–204

    digital divide as barrier to all-digital library, 62–63

literacy of nation, assessment of, 147–150
  sustained reading for literacy, 157
  in virtual library future, 49
  as vital skill, 222–223
reason, 125–126
recall, 135
records
  See human record
"re-entry" students, 103
reference desk, 95–99
relevance, of documents, 135
religion, 60
research institutes, library alliance with, 20
Resource description & access (RDA), 137
resources
  See digital resources; online resources
retirement homes, library services in, 105
Richardson, William J., Sr., 23
rival values, 35
Roe v. Wade, 180
Roosevelt, Franklin Delano, 195
Rotenberg, Marc, 178
Rothstein, Samuel, 29–32
Russia, 199, 200

S

sacred places, need for, 60
Safe Harbor program, U.S.-EU, 184
safeguarding, 12
San Francisco Public Library, 72
San Jose Public Library, 67
San Jose State University, 17, 67
satisfaction values, 34
Scandinavia, 68
Schlessinger, Laura, 120
scholarly journals
  article as desired object of, 43
  digital form, availability in, 58–59
  digital journals in all-digital future, 51–52
  preservation of, 79
  in virtual library future, 49
school librarians
  role of, 103–104
  as teachers, 130–131

school libraries
  equity of access, ways to increase, 164–165
  literacy and learning, 152–153, 154
  service community of, 103–104
Scientific American, 17
scientific management, 15–16, 20
search engines, 58
secret life, 176
selection, library collection, 83–84
self-check device, 186
senior citizens, 101
September 11, 2001 terrorist attacks, 176
serials
  See scholarly journals
service
  in academic libraries, 101–103
  bottom line, 105–106
  as central value of librarianship, 36
  comforting afflicted, 100
  in companies/institutions, 104–105
  in Fink's professional values, 33
  Five Laws of Library Science and, 27
  greater good and, 214
  as key value of librarianship, 221
  librarianship rooted in, 25
  library user, knowledge of, 100
  meaning of, 91–92
  in other kinds of library, 105
  processing services, 94–95
  in public libraries, 100–101
  relationship with libraries, 92
  in school libraries, 103–104
  service economy, switch to, 92–93
  service encounter, 95–99
  test of service in libraries, 94
service economy, 92–93
service encounter
  approachability of librarian, 96–97
  knowledge of librarian, 97–98
  librarian should be comprehensible, 98–99
  overview of, 95–96
sex
  censorship of online resources, 115, 116,
    117–118

sex (cont.)
  children/adolescents, First Amendment
    rights of, 118–119
  Internet filtering of, 121
Shera, Jesse
  as important library thinker, 24
  on philosophy of librarianship, 25
  on preservation, 76
  social epistemology, 27–29
significant documents
  determination of, 82–84
  value judgment about, 79
social justice, 159
social media
  growth of, 2
  library literature on, 16
  loss of privacy with, 176
  promotion of literacy with, 152
social values, 34
societal barriers, 164
sound recordings, 80
sources, 134
spaces
  See library spaces
spatial privacy, 177
special libraries
  literacy and learning, 154–155
  services of, 104–105
spirituality, 126
staff, library, 128–130
standardization
  digital resources lack, 79
  as print attribute, 77
State of America's Libraries (ALA), 65
Statement of core competences (ALA), 87
Stedman, Lawrence, 149
stewardship
  as central value of librarianship, 35
  in Fink's professional values, 33
  Five Laws of Library Science and, 27
  greater good and, 213–214
  in library context, 76
  library education, 85–89

meaning of, 75
preservation of human record, 76–84
as singular value of librarianship,
    221–222
survival of library/librarianship, 84–85
three things for good stewardship, 89–90
Stone, Karen, 66
Stonehouse, John, 159
sustained reading
  in all-digital future, 52
  bringing students back to, 156
  Internet filtering and, 122
  for lifelong learning, 147
  for literacy, 145, 146, 157
  as vital skill, 222–223
symbolic language, 8–9

T

Tarantino, Quentin, 115
Tax, Meredith, 126
taxonomy of values, 33–35
teachers, human learning from, 146
teaching, 130–136
  See also education; library education;
    library instruction
technology
  for alternatives to literacy, 155–157
  changes in wider world and, 2–3
  equity of access and, 166–169
  in integrated library, 63–64
  literacy and, 149
  privacy, impact on, 177–180
  privacy, loss of, 175–177
  privacy, present/future of, 181–184
  for service improvements, 93
television watching, 118
text
  ability to read, 156–157
  decoding human record, 222
Thompson, Sally, 153
"tiered" service, 99
Townsend, Sue, 223
"traditional" library, 44

trust
   between library patron and library, 185
   library privacy policy and, 191–192
Tyckoson, Dave, 99

U

ultrafiche, 82
uncertainty, 6–7
undergraduate libraries, 131–132
understanding, 144
Unesco
   aims of, human record and, 12–13
   definition of cultural heritage, 10–11
   definition of intangible cultural heritage,
      11–12
"unfettered access," 160
union catalogue, 137–138
United Nations, 12
Universal Bibliographic Control (UBC),
   137–138
universities
   academic libraries, service communities
      of, 101–103
   in all-digital future, 50
   literacy and learning, 154
   in virtual library future, 49
U.S. Constitution
   intellectual freedom protected by, 109,
      110–111
   privacy, protection of, 180–181
U.S. Department of Commerce
   on digital divide, 62
   involvement in privacy issues, 182
   privacy principles of, 184
U.S. Department of Health and Human
   Services
   involvement in privacy issues, 182
   privacy rules, 179
U.S. Department of Health, Education, and
   Welfare, 179
U.S. Supreme Court, 180
user
   See library user
U.S.-EU Safe Harbor program, 184

utilitarianism
   Five Laws of Library Science and, 27
   greater good principle *vs.*, 212
   as philosophy, 24

V

value, 6–7
value judgment, 79
value system, 1
values
   central values of librarianship, 35–37
   change, dealing with, 6
   changes in wider world, 2–3
   cult of information, 13–16
   definition of, 1
   of Enlightenment, 127
   Fink's taxonomy of values, 33–35
   Five Laws of Library Science and, 27
   human record, 8–10
   human record, cultural heritage and,
      10–13
   intellectual freedom and clash of values,
      113–114
   libraries' wider cultural context, 18–21
   library building should embody enduring
      values, 72–73
   misunderstandings about libraries, 7–8
   reading, importance of, 16–18
   reason for, 4–5
   Rothstein's values of librarianship,
      29–32
   from Shera's social epistemology, 29
   value and, 6–7
   when values are dangerous, 5
Van Slyke, Abigail A., 57
Velasquez, Manuel, 213
veracity, 78, 79
videos, preservation of, 80–81
violence
   censorship of online resources, 115, 116,
      117
   children/adolescents, First Amendment
      rights of, 119
virtual communities, 168–169

virtual library
   living with, 48–53
   meaning of, 45
   reasons for, 46–48
   See also all-digital library
virtual patron, 168–169
virtual reality, 156–157
visual literacy, 156

W

Wade, Roe v., 180
War on Terror, 176
Webster's Collegiate dictionary, 177
Webster's Third new international dictionary
   definitions of read, peruse, and literate,
      143–144
   ethics definition, 2
   service definition, 91–92
Weigand, Wayne, 15
Westin, Alan, 182
Why Johnny can't read (Flesch), 148
Wilde, Oscar, 149
wireless networks, 67
Wood, David, 145
work values, 34
World Catalogue, 137–138
World War I, 41
World War II, 41
Worstall, Tim, xi
writing, 145–146

X

"X Public Library and Information Center,"
   Illinois, 69

Y

"Year in Architecture" (*Library Journal*), 65
young people
      See adolescents; children

Z

Zeithaml, Valarie A., 96, 98

CPSIA information can be obtained
at www.ICGtesting.com
Printed in the USA
LVHW010959011118
595553LV00002B/2/P